Lost City of the Incas

BY HIRAM BINGHAM

LOST CITY

of the

INCAS

-

The Story of MACHU PICCHU *and Its Builders*

-

HIRAM BINGHAM

GREENWOOD PRESS, PUBLISHERS
WESTPORT, CONNECTICUT

Library of Congress Cataloging in Publication Data

Bingham, Hiram, 1875-1956.
    Lost city of the Incas.

    Reprint. Originally published: 1st ed. New York :
Duell, Sloan and Pearce, 1948.
    Bibliography: p.
    Includes index.
    1. Machu Picchu (Peru) 2. Incas.   I. Title.
F3429.1.M3B617   1981   985'.37   81-7196
ISBN 0-313-22950-3 (lib. bdg.)   AACR2

This is a reprint of the First Edition.

Reprinted with the permission of Elsevier/Nelson Books.

Reprinted in 1981 by Greenwood Press
A division of Congressional Information Service, Inc.
88 Post Road West, Westport, Connecticut 06881

Printed in the United States of America

P

In order to keep this title in print and available to the academic community, this edition
was produced using digital reprint technology in a relatively short print run. This would
not have been attainable using traditional methods. Although the cover has been changed
from its original appearance, the text remains the same and all materials and methods
used still conform to the highest book-making standards.

To

Suzanne Carroll Bingham

with
admiration and affection

Preface

FEW AMERICANS realize how much we owe to the ancient
Peruvians. Very few people appreciate that they gave us the white
potato, many varieties of Indian corn, and such useful drugs as
quinine and cocaine. Their civilization, which took thousands of
years to develop, was marked by inventive genius, artistic ability,
and a knowledge of agriculture which has never been surpassed. In
the making of beautiful pottery and the weaving of fine textiles
they equaled the best that Egypt or Greece could offer. Although
the Incas governed their millions of subjects with firmness and
justice under a benevolent despotism that allowed no one to be
hungry or cold, they had no written language, not even hieroglyphics. Accordingly our knowledge of them has had to depend
on what we can see of what they left, aided by the chroniclers of
the sixteenth century, contemporaries of Pizarro and the Conquistadors, most of whom looked upon their history and politics
through European eyes. Even the Inca Garcilasso de la Vega had
been in Spain forty years when he wrote his famous account of
his ancestors.

Some four hundred years ago, the last of the Incas were living
in one of the most inaccessible parts of the Andes, the region
lying between the Apurimac River and the Urubamba, two important affluents of the Amazon. Here they were shut off from
that part of Peru which was under the sway of Pizarro and the
Conquistadors by mighty precipices, passes three miles high,
granite canyons more than a mile in depth, glaciers and tropical

vii

jungles, as well as by dangerous rapids. For thirty-five years they enjoyed virtual independence as their ancestors had done for centuries. They had two capitals: Vitcos, a hastily constructed military headquarters where they occasionally received refugees, Spanish emissaries and Augustinian missionaries, and Vilcapampa, their principal residence, a magnificently built sanctuary to which no Spaniards ever penetrated.

With the death of the last Inca in 1571, Vitcos was abandoned. It was a fortress on top of a mountain and inconvenient as a dwelling place. Its name was forgotten and its location obscure until we found it. The royal city of Vilcapampa was completely lost. It was a sacred shrine hidden on top of great precipices in a stupendous canyon where the secret of its existence was safely buried for three centuries under the shadow of Machu Picchu mountain. Its ruins have taken the name of the mountain because when we found them no one knew what else to call them.

This marvelous Inca sanctuary, which was lost for three hundred years, has at last become a veritable Mecca for ambitious tourists. Everyone who goes to South America wants to see it. It used to be two or three hard days' journey from Cuzco, on mule-back and on foot, but now it can be reached by train and mule in one day. Possibly a motor road will be built there before long. Furthermore, Cuzco, which used to be a week away from Lima, can now be reached by airplane in a few hours! Pilgrims come from Buenos Aires and Santiago as well as from New York and Washington. They all agree with the late Frank Chapman of beloved memory that "in the sublimity of its surroundings, the marvel of its site, the character and the mystery of its construction, the Western Hemisphere holds nothing comparable."

After I found it in 1911, Yale University and the National Geographic Society made it possible for me to explore the region thoroughly and to publish the results of our studies. Those reports have long since been out of print. Meanwhile, various documents have come to light and professional archaeologists have advanced our knowledge of the Incas to the point where it has seemed

worth while to collect all that is known about Machu Picchu, its
origin, how it came to be lost and how it was finally discovered,
and present it here in popular form for the benefit of those who
may be curious about the Incas and the sacred city that they successfully hid from the Spanish conquerors.

In the heart of their country, about fifty miles away from their
capital city of Cuzco, is the Grand Canyon of the Urubamba, one
of the most wonderful places in the world. For centuries travelers
could not visit it because a sheer granite precipice, rising two
thousand feet from the banks of the river, defied all efforts to pass
it. The planters who raised coca and sugar in the lower valley
could only bring their produce to market over a snow-covered
pass as high as the top of Pike's Peak. Finally they persuaded the
Peruvian government to open a river road by blasting it across
the face of the great granite precipice. They had been using it
for several years without being aware that on top of a steep ridge
two thousand feet above them were the ruins of a great Inca
sanctuary. Raimondi, greatest of Peruvian explorers, was ignorant
of them. Paz Soldan's elaborate geographical dictionary of Peru
makes no mention of them although their existence had been
rumored in 1875. Charles Wiener, an energetic French explorer,
had looked for them then without success. They had been visited
by several energetic mestizos and a few modern Indians. Quite a
number of ambitious treasure hunters had tried to find the last
Inca capital. The new road made possible the discoveries of the
Peruvian Expeditions which are herein described.

Acknowledgments

SIR CLEMENTS MARKHAM was for many years the pioneer in Peruvian history. His translations of the Spanish chronicles have been freely used. Most of them were originally published by the Hakluyt Society. Even Sir Clements, however, never undertook to translate the longest of the old chronicles, Antonio de Calancha's *Coronica Moralizada* of the Augustinians in Peru. It is an awe-inspiring folio of a thousand pages and was published in 1638, an omnigatherum of fact and pious fancy. No one has dared attempt another edition since 1639. It gives such a full account of the efforts of those early missionaries to convert the Incas and their people in the province of Vilcabamba that I have tried to give a faithful version of the more interesting parts of the narrative, even though the style is cumbersome and the monastic vocabulary is redolent of the sixteenth century. In this I must acknowledge the help of Professor Osgood Hardy of Occidental College and of Miss Shelby of the Library of Congress.

Another translation which I have attempted is part of the story of Manco II which was written or dictated by his son Titu Cusi and has been published by H. H. Urteaga and Carlos A. Romero, to whom we are greatly indebted for their scholarly edition.

My ideas with regard to the age and accomplishments of the early Peruvians are based in large measure on the observations of O. F. Cook, our most distinguished authority on tropical and subtropical agriculture, who was with me in Peru. His article, "Staircase Farms of the Ancients," published in the National Geographic Magazine, was an epoch-making contribution to our knowledge of early American culture. Unfortunately his views and mine are not always accepted by other writers!

A very considerable part of the material in this book is of necessity based on my own books and articles including *Across South America, Vitcos, In the Wonderland of Peru, Inca Land*, and *Machu Picchu, a Citadel of the Incas*, which have all been out of print for some years. I have also included selections from the reports of various members of my Peruvian expeditions, some of which have been printed elsewhere, as set forth in the Bibliography at the end of *Inca Land*.

Philip Ainsworth Means was a member of the Peruvian Expedition of 1914. His *Ancient Civilizations of the Andes* and his *Fall of the Inca Empire*, besides many of his articles and translations of Spanish chronicles, are a treasure house for students of Peruvian antiquity.

Other members of my expeditions to whom I am indebted and whose reports have have been used freely are: Dr. George F. Eaton, whose "The Collection of Osteological Material from Machu Picchu" is particularly valuable; Elwood C. Erdis, who was in charge of excavations in the city; Edmund Heller, the distinguished naturalist who made a remarkable collection of the birds and mammals of the Cordillera Vilcabamba; Doctors William G. Erving, Luther T. Nelson, and David E. Ford who were our surgeons; Topographers Albert H. Bumstead, Clarence F. Maynard, H. L. Tucker, Robert Stevenson, E. L. Anderson, and J. J. Hasbrouck, who made the maps which enabled us to add to geographical and archeological knowledge; and Assistants Paul Lanius, Geoffrey W. Morkill, Osgood Hardy, Paul Bestor, and Joseph Little, who helped me in many different ways.

To Melville Bell Grosvenor of the National Geographic Society, whose father, Dr. Gilbert Grosvenor, was one of my most enthusiastic backers in the days of my explorations, I am indebted for generous assistance in helping me to prepare and select the illustrations used in this volume. Most of the photographs were taken by me but a few were taken by other members of the expeditions, as indicated in the table of illustrations. Complete sets of the twelve thousand photographs which we took in 1911, 1912, 1914, and 1915 are on file in the Hispanic Society of America, the National Geographic Society, and Yale University.

Contents

Illustrations

Lost City of the Incas

Part 1
The Builders

1.

The Incas and Their Civilization

I N THE BEGINNING THE word Inca, which means king or emperor, was the term applied only to the chief of that remarkable people whose courage and genius for organization had enabled them to conquer most of Peru, Ecuador, and Bolivia, as well as the northern parts of Chile and Argentina. Then came the Spanish conquistadors in the sixteenth century and applied the term to the ruling class, members of the Inca's family and the nobles and priests who governed the Inca Empire. Soon, however, they were all killed off and by the end of the century scarcely one was to be found anywhere. To-day we use the term Inca to cover the race who in the course of several thousand years built up a great civilization in the highlands of Peru and Bolivia. The builders of Machu Picchu were the descendants of generations of skilled artisans, but those who directed the workmen were the Incas whose capital for centuries was Cuzco.

Strictly speaking, the first Inca was a war-like chieftain of the Quichua tribe of Indians who ruled over Cuzco about 1200 A.D. and was worshipped as a demi-god, the son of the Sun. It was per-

3

haps only a hundred years before the arrival of Pizarro and the conquistadors that the ninth Inca, properly so called, extended the Empire as far north as Ecuador and as far south as Argentina. As a matter of fact the Inca Empire had just about reached its apogee and passed its prime when the Spaniards landed. Had they arrived in the days of the great Inca Pachacuti (ca. 1450) they would have received short shrift. As it happened they arrived when the empire was weakened by a long civil war.

As there are no written records and the interpretation of the *quipus* or knotted cords as well as the history of the past depended on the memory or the imagination of the persons who were interviewed by the first Spanish chroniclers, we cannot be certain of dates or events. It appears likely that the development of such arts and sciences as Agriculture, Metallurgy, Ceramics, Weaving and Engineering took place chiefly in the centuries which preceded the first Inca. Yet it has become convenient to use the term Inca to apply to the civilization and the people whom the Spaniards found in Peru, just as we use the term Aztec to apply to the civilization of Mexico and the term Maya to apply to the civilization found in Yucatan and Guatemala. Actually there were many Peruvian tribes that had been independent nations long enough, before they were conquered by the Incas, to develop remarkable artistic ability in ceramics and textiles.

One of the most interesting places in the world is Cuzco, the ancient capital of the Empire of the Incas. In the days of the Spanish Conquest of Peru it was the largest city in America. On a hill back of it is a very old fortress, a place of refuge for centuries. The northern wall of that fortress is perhaps the most extraordinary structure built by ancient man in the Western Hemisphere. In fact, as an achievement of engineering, it stands without parallel in American antiquity. The smaller blocks in the wall weigh ten or twenty tons. Larger blocks are estimated to weigh two hundred tons. A few of the largest weigh three hundred tons! And yet they are fitted accurately together. There are no clamps. There was no cement used in constructing the wall.

The gigantic polygonal blocks cling so closely together that it is impossible to insert the point of a knife between them. And they were brought from quarries more than a mile away where they were fashioned by people using stone tools. They were moved over an inclined plane by levers. The Incas had no iron or steel, but they had bronze crowbars of great strength. They had no derricks or pulleys or wheels but they had thousands of patient workers. The determination and the perseverance of the builders staggers the imagination. It makes one admire the Incas and wish to learn more about them.

ARCHITECTURE

As we study their architecture we see that it is marked by good proportions and symmetrical arrangement as well as by massiveness and solidity. Some of their temples and palaces were built of carefully selected ashlars of white granite. The lower tiers of a wall are made of larger blocks than the upper. This gives it a look of massive security. The upper courses, gradually decreasing in size, lend grace and dignity to the structure. Since instruments of precision were lacking, everything had to be done by the trained eye of the artistic architect. The result is softer and much more pleasing than that of the mathematically correct walls of our world. We must admit that they were superb stone masons. Everyone who visits Machu Picchu will agree to that.

In the city of Cuzco, as well as in other well-known Inca towns, the walls of temples and palaces are not perpendicular but slope slightly inward. They are of so-called Egyptian style, being narrower at the top than at the bottom.

If one visits outlying places one finds story-and-a-half houses with gable ends. They seem to be characteristic of structures which were built not very long before the Spanish Conquest. Usually on the outside of each gable end may be seen a row of roughly cylindrical blocks or stone pegs bonded into the wall and projecting a foot or so from its surface. At first sight one might suppose this characteristic feature of Inca architecture to be merely ornamental, since these stone pegs suggest the idea of being the petrified ends of wooden beams and purlins. This pleasant theory of wooden origin, reminiscent of Doric architecture, appears to be incorrect. In the gable ends of some modern Indian huts wooden pegs similarly placed are used as points to which the thatched roof is tied. It would appear, therefore, that the stone pegs bonded into the Inca gables were not merely ornamental but real pegs serving a useful purpose.

One day, in the process of carefully cleaning the gable ends of a very finely built Inca house at Machu Picchu, we made an interesting discovery of an architectural feature which had hitherto entirely escaped the notice of archaeologists or architects. Buried in the sloping edge of the gable wall was a thin slab of rough stone with a chamfered hole or eye about two inches from the outer end. We called this an eye-bonder. It was set into the gable wall at right angles to its slope in such a way as to be flush with the surface, a little space being left on each side so that the eye could easily be reached when it was desired to lash the purlins to the steep pitch of the gable. Investigation showed that there were usually eight or ten of these eye-bonders in every gable. These little stone slabs were about two feet long, six inches wide, and two inches thick. The chamfered hole apparently was bored by means of pieces of bamboo rapidly revolved between the palms of the hands, assisted by a liberal use of sand and water. Of course, such a method required time and patience, but produced results just as satisfactory as the use of mallet and chisel and was less likely to split the stone.

The Incas did not use tiles or shingles to cover their roofs, but had to depend on thatch made of grass or bushes. The thatch was tied to the purlins and was kept from blowing away by being tied to the ends of the projecting roof pegs while the purlins themselves were fastened to the gables by being tied to the eye-bonders.

So far as I have been able to learn, this method of supporting a thatched roof on a sloping gable was invented and perfected by the Incas and has never been used in any other part of the world. Possibly its invention was due to the fact that the plateau where Inca architecture flourished is treeless and wind-swept. Incidentally, the absence of trees in the temperate valleys of the Peruvian highlands was not due to the altitude because I found primeval forests growing at 15,000 feet in the more inaccessible parts of the Cordillera Vilcabamba. It undoubtedly was due, as in China, to the very long period of human occupation and the necessity for fuel. Had there been more forests and plenty of wood they would have not have had to build stone houses.

The doors of Inca houses were usually high enough so that the tallest Peruvian could enter comfortably without bumping his head. As in ancient Egypt, the bottom of the door is wider than the top. Lintels were sometimes of wood if the buildings were constructed near a forested region, but otherwise were composed of two or three long blocks of stone. In more important structures the Incas went to the trouble of using monolithic lintels even when they weighed one or two tons. Since they had no derricks or pulleys it is believed that they raised a monolithic lintel to its place by building a mound of earth and stone in front of the door. Then by using levers made of hard wood, possibly rollers of the same material, and the principle of the inclined plane, they brought the heavy lintel to the top of the door without serious rouble. When they had fitted the lintel securely in place, the mound was removed.

Their houses were frequently arranged around a courtyard so as to form a compound as in the Far East. To this compound there was usually but one entrance. Sometimes the facade of the gateway had a re-entrant angle as though the doorway had been let into the back of a large niche. Entrances to compounds were furnished with the means of fastening a bar across the inside of the door. Stone cylinders or pegs, which I have called bar-holds, were keyed into the gateposts during their construction. Sometimes the bar-holds were anchored into the wall by being set into a cavity cut out of one of the larger blocks of the gatepost. It was feasible to lash a bar to the bar-holds which were able to resist at least as much pressure as the cross-bar which was lashed to it.

It is possible, however, that these bar-locks supported nothing more formidable than a taboo stick which would prevent a super-stitious person from entering a compound where he was not wanted. There is a reference to this subject in the will of one of the Spanish conquistadors in which he declares that when an Indian left his home the doors were left open except that there was "a little stick across the door as the sign that the master was out and nobody went in." In a memorial addressed to his sovereign, Philip II, he added, "When they saw that we placed locks and keys on our doors they understood that it was from fear of thieves and when they saw that we had thieves amongst us they despised us."

The practice of placing only a little stick across the door was made possible in part by the fact that among the Incas private property of individuals was limited to a few personal possessions, dishes, shawl pins, cooking utensils, and clothing. Under a benevo-lent despotism like that of the Incas where no one was allowed to go hungry or naked, where everyone was told what to do and when to do it, and where everything of importance belonged to the ruler, there was no object in attempting to acquire the personal possessions of others, nor was there any incentive to accumulate anything which was not in daily use.

The use of bar-locks, eye-bonders, and roof-pegs by the Incas is an evidence of inventive genius which testifies to long occupancy in the highlands. Those devices are not found in Asia or Europe. They were not borrowed or imported. They were autocthonous.

So far as we know there was no furniture in the houses of the Incas. They used neither chairs nor tables but sat on the ground or on a pile of blankets made from the wool of the llama or alpaca. The place of furniture was taken by a series of niches ar-ranged symmetrically in the walls. These niches were usually about three feet in height, ten inches in depth, and two feet in width, narrower at the top than at the bottom and placed in the wall so as to be nearer the floor than the ceiling. They may have been designed originally for ceremonial purposes but they came eventually to be recognized as a great household convenience. Crudely made niches can be seen today in the huts of the mountain Indians where they take the place of shelves, cupboards, and bureaus. Stone pegs usually were placed between the niches and on a level with their lintels. They made handy hooks for all sorts of purposes. It is quite possible that from them were hung the characteristic water or chicha jars which had pointed bottoms. Their handles are so placed in the line of the center of gravity as to make it easy to suspend them and easy to pour out a drink by using a nubbin on the shoulder of the jar without having to take the jar down from the peg.

The pegs were also convenient for fastening one end of a hand loom, while the weaver sat on the ground with the other end of the loom tied to his or her waist. Sometimes a ring stone was bonded in the wall at a convenient height. Since the Peruvians were famous weavers, made warm clothing and blankets of both wool and cotton, these ring stones and pegs were undoubtedly in frequent use for that purpose.

Inca architects were careful about drainage and guarded against the accumulation of ground water wherever it was not wanted. Small channels or conduits were constructed under their storehouses and under the walls of courtyards wherever pools were likely to collect.

Civil Engineering

In the making of roads, bridges, aqueducts, and irrigation ditches they showed a remarkable knowledge of engineering. At the time of the Spanish Conquest the Incas' paved roads ran for thousands of miles through the Central Andes from Quito, the capital of Ecuador, all the way to Argentina and Chile, as well as from the Pacific Coast over the mountains to the warm valleys of the eastern Andes. Since they had no wheeled vehicles it was not necessary for the surface of their roads to be leveled. Where the road had to be taken over a steep hillside, stone stairways were constructed. Where the road had to pass a small precipice, tunnels large enough to permit the passage of a loaded beast of burden, whether man or llama, were cut out of the solid rock.

Over these roads trained runners, operating in relays, carried messages with extraordinary dispatch from the capital of the empire to distant magistrates. It is said that fresh fish caught in the Pacific Ocean were brought over the mountains by the special messengers of the Inca Emperor and reached his table in excellent condition. Post houses were provided at convenient intervals so that a runner would not have to exhaust his strength before his message could be picked up and carried forward with the least possible delay. Furthermore, the runners were permitted to chew coca leaves to deaden fatigue.

The Incas had never acquired the art of writing, but they had developed an elaborate system of knotted cords called *quipus*. These were made of the wool of the alpaca or the llama, dyed in various colors, the significance of which was known to the magistrates. The cords were knotted in such a way as to represent the decimal system and were fastened at close intervals along the principle strand of the *quipu*. Thus an important message relating to the progress of crops, the amount of taxes collected, or the advance of an enemy could be speedily sent by the trained runners along the post roads.

Caravans of llamas carrying supplies could proceed safely, if slowly, over the most mountainous country. *Tambos,* or rest houses, as well as storehouses, were built wherever it was likely that those who traveled on the Inca's business—and there were no other travelers—would need to find suitable accommodations and supplies. The storehouses were large enough to provide for companies of soldiers as well as llama drivers.

The roads were carried across rivers on suspension bridges made by braiding together countless strands of lianas, the ropelike vines found frequently in the jungles of the Amazon Basin. Using huge cables of remarkable thickness, the Inca engineers were able to construct bridges two or three hundred feet in length whenever it was necessary. These bridges, of course, sagged in the middle, swayed in the wind, and were not at all pleasant to use. Furthermore, they could be destroyed easily, but the death penalty awaited anyone found guilty of such an act. Had they not been so highly regarded, or had the Incas had the foresight to destroy them when Pizarro and his conquistadors started to enter the Central Andes, the conquest of Peru would have been extremely difficult, if not well-nigh impossible.

IRRIGATION

No less striking than the remarkable system of highways were the irrigation ditches which ran for scores of miles in the Central Andes. The height of the mountains, often rising to 18,000 or 20,000 feet, forces the moisture-laden winds coming from the east across the humid basin of the Amazon to deposit their burden in heavy rains on the eastern slopes of the great Andean chain. Little rain ever falls on the western slopes. In fact, one of the greatest deserts in the world is the two-thousand-mile coastal strip extending from central Chile to Ecuador.

The soil in the bottom of the valleys that cross this region is rich enough to grow luxuriant crops of sugar cane, cotton, and corn, but it needs to be regularly irrigated in order to do so. For this purpose the rivers, fed by melting snow in the high Andes, are deflected into irrigation ditches which follow the contours of the valleys for many miles. Inca engineers must have had good eyes and a fine sense of grading since they had none of the instruments on which our engineers depend to lay out similar projects. Imagine running a perfect contour for twenty miles!

Not only did the Incas provide their fields with necessary water, they also saw to it that their towns and cities had adequate supplies and for that purpose built fine aqueducts.

AGRICULTURE

To the Incas the art of agriculture was of supreme interest.
They carried it to a remarkable extreme, attaching more importance to it than we do to-day. They not only developed many
different plants for food and medicinal purposes, but they understood thoroughly the cultivation of the soil, the art of proper
drainage, correct methods of irrigation, and soil conservation by
means of terraces constructed at great expense. Most of the agricultural fields in the Peruvian Andes are not natural. The soil has
been assembled, put in place artificially, and still remains fertile
after centuries of use.

The Incas learned the importance of fertilizers to keep the soil
rich and fruitful. They had discovered the value of the guano
found on the bird-islands that lie off the coast of Peru, setting aside
various of these islands for the benefit of different provinces. No
one was allowed to visit the islands during the breeding season.
Although hundreds of thousands of fish-eating birds inhabit the
islands, the Incas punished by death anyone killing a single guano-
producing bird.

They depended on terrace agriculture. It is seen in its most
conspicuous form on steep slopes. Terraces are found in many
other countries, notably in east Asia and the Philippines, but it is
very doubtful whether any equal those constructed by the Incas.
In Peru the artificial reconstruction of the surface soil was not
limited to slopes, but was also undertaken in large areas of re-
claimed land in valley bottoms. They even narrowed and straightened the courses of the rivers, filled in the land behind strong
walls and topped off the work with a surface layer of fine soil.

The system of terrace agriculture which they developed consists roughly of three parts, the retaining wall and two distinct
layers of earth that fill the space behind the wall. The underlying
stratum, an artificial sub-soil, is composed of coarse stones and clay
to a thickness that depends upon the height of the retaining wall.

This stratum was covered by a layer of rich soil two or three feet deep.

Fortunately for the Incas the soils in the terraced districts are tenacious and not readily eroded. A few sods or a small ridge of earth will hold in check a stream of water, thus greatly facilitating the irrigation of the terraces. In places, large stones deeply grooved lengthwise served as spouts to carry the water out from a terrace wall thus avoiding the danger of erosion or undermining.

The height and width of the terraces depended entirely on the gradient of the slope. Terraces on very steep slopes were narrow shelves sometimes only three or four feet wide although the usual range is from six to fifteen feet. The height is usually from eight to fourteen feet. In parts of the Andes, hillsides containing one hundred terraces, one above the other, are not uncommon. In many places they are used by the modern Indians for raising crops of wheat and barley. Originally they were used chiefly for potatoes and maize.

Long banks of terraces are interrupted at regular intervals by passageways that serve the double purpose of roads for reaching the terraces, and drainage channels to permit surface water from the upper slopes to flow freely down without washing away any of the precious soil which had been brought to the terraces in baskets or mats carried on men's backs. It fairly staggers the imagination to realize how many millions of hours of labor were required to construct these great agricultural terraces. Since terraced agriculture is well known in the Philippines and in Asia, some writers are inclined to maintain that the Incas did not originate it but brought it with them when they migrated from Asia, if and when they did. If they came from Asia it is strange that they did not bring any Asiatic food plants or seeds with them.

Mr. O. F. Cook, the distinguished authority on tropical agriculture who was the botanist on one of my Peruvian expeditions, tells me that the Incas and their predecessors domesticated more kinds of food and medicinal plants than any other people in the world.

They found a small plant growing in the high Andes, with a tuberous root about the size of a small pea. It proved to be edible and from it, in the course of the centuries, they finally developed a dozen varieties of what we call the "Irish" or white potato, suitable for cultivation at elevations varying from sea level to fourteen thousand feet above it. After the Spanish Conquest of Peru, it took Europeans nearly three centuries to appreciate the staple food of the Incas. In fact, had it not been for famines in France and Ireland it is hard to say when the Peruvian potato would have been accepted as part of their daily ration.

The skill and ingenuity of the Inca agriculturists was shown not only in the breeding and raising of many kinds of potatoes, but also in the very many varieties of maize or Indian corn, suitable for cultivation at varying elevations, which they developed. No one knows exactly the plant from which maize was originally derived. Agricultural experts are divided in their opinion as to whether it was domesticated from an Andean plant which has long since disappeared or whether it was brought from Guatemala. Central American authorities, specialists in Maya civilization, are convinced that corn originated in Guatemala where there is a wild plant remotely resembling it. There is no doubt, however, that the Incas had more varieties of maize, a whole series that were unlike any that are known from Central America or Mexico, and had gone to a far greater extreme in developing them than did the Mayas.

We do not know, probably we shall never know, when corn was first cultivated in Peru. Mr. Cook believes that the cultivation of corn goes *very* far back in Peru, not only because of the abundance of specimens found in ancient graves but also because the types of maize which furnish the bulk of the Peruvian crop are peculiar to that region.

An Inca food plant almost unknown to Europeans is *canihua*, a kind of pig weed. It is harvested in April, the stalks are dried and placed on a large blanket laid on the ground as a threshing floor. The blanket serves to prevent the small greyish seeds from escaping when the flail is applied.

Another unfamiliar food plant, also a species of pig weed, is called *quinoa*. Growing readily on the slopes of the high Andes at an elevation as great as most of our Rocky Mountains it manages to attain a height of three or four feet and produces abundant crops. The seeds are cooked like a cereal and are very palatable.

At lower elevations in the Andes the Incas developed another series of root crops, most of which are still unfamiliar to us, but one, the sweet potato, has achieved world-wide popularity. First domesticated from a wild plant found in the eastern Andes, it is called *cumara* by the Quichuas in the Urubamba valley. All over Polynesia it bears virtually the same name, kumala or kumara. Evidently from Peru it seems to have spread over the Pacific Ocean. One of the greatest achievements of the extraordinary group of ancient navigators whom we call Polynesians was to plant it in Hawaii, Samoa, Tahiti, New Zealand, and everywhere they went with their great double canoes.

In addition to discovering and developing useful food plants, the Incas also were the first to learn the advantages of certain medicinal herbs, particularly quinine, long known as a specific in the cure of malaria. They also discovered the specific effects of cocaine, which is extracted from coca leaves, but only allowed it to be used by those engaged in such strenuous activities as the marathons of their post runners. Judging by the "medicines" sold by the Indian "druggists" who display their wares in the market places of the mountain towns, the ancient remedies included such minerals as sulphur, such vegetables as the seeds, roots, and dried leaves of tropical jungle plants, and such animals as star-fish!

Domestic Animals

Not only were the Incas remarkable for domesticating plants, they also showed great skill in domesticating animals. In the Andes is a little rodent, called a *cuy*. It is extremely timid and difficult to catch. We call it a guinea pig although it never came from Guinea and is not a pig. Discovering that it was very palatable when roasted over an open fire or boiled in a stew the Incas domesticated it and developed a dozen different varieties, all of which are so tame that they can be trusted to run about the floor of an Indian's cabin making no effort to escape and are ready to be caught, killed, cooked and served as a delicious morsel whenever company appears unexpectedly.

Father Cobo, a learned Jesuit, who traveled extensively in the Andes in 1600, tells how guinea pigs were cooked in his day. In preparing a stew, red pepper was added, also smooth little pebbles from the river! These were placed in the belly of the *cuy* after being thoroughly heated, so as to hasten the process of cooking. He states with praiseworthy candor, "this dish is more esteemed by the Indians than any of the more delicate ones which Spaniards make. The flesh of the domesticated kind is more delicate. The three wild kinds are somewhat smaller than the domesticated and are found in great numbers in the fields."

The Incas domesticated at least three varieties of dogs but there is no evidence that, like the Polynesians, they used any of them as an article of food.

Another interesting product of Inca skill at breeding animals has to do with the native American camel, known as the *guanaco*. Not so very long ago vast herds of guanaco were still to be found in Patagonia where they enjoy a climate very similar to the highlands of Peru. These little camels measure more than six feet and sometimes as much as seven feet to the top of the head. Guanaco hunting used to be regarded as the finest sport in South America. They are exceedingly shy and it requires no little patience to get within gun shot of them. Guanaco are very inquisitive and restless but keep a sharp look out for danger. Both their vision and power of scent are wonderfully good. The herds, composed principally of females, are presided over by vigorous old males who stand sentry on a bit of high ground and give timely notice of any strange object, then they all gallop off very fast, although their ordinary pace is a trot. Notwithstanding their extreme shyness they were caught and tamed by the early dwellers in the highlands.

Ability to catch such timid, fast animals was undoubtedly due to the use of the *bolas*, a remarkable weapon or missile consisting of two balls or stones connected with strong cord. The throwing of *bolas* so as to entangle the legs of birds and animals is an extremely difficult art. Had the ancient Peruvians not been familiar with this useful device, but depended entirely on sling-stones, arrows or clubs, it is doubtful whether they would have been so successful in securing and domesticating the little camels.

Although guanacos are all of one color, the llamas and alpacas that were developed from the little native camels are of many different colors. Furthermore, the Incas actually succeeded in the difficult and tedious process of breeding the little camels into two varieties for entirely different purposes. One, the llama, is streamlined and well adapted to act as a beast of burden even though it is neither large enough nor strong enough to carry more than ninety or a hundred pounds. It has legs fairly free from wool and its hair is coarse and able to stand the chafing caused by the loads they carry. On the other hand, the alpaca, descended from the same ancestor as the llama, is conspicuously wooly, both as to its legs and neck. Its hair is fine and soft and is welcomed in modern commerce as one of the most desirable materials obtainable for making luxurious woolen garments. Due to the fact that shrewd cloth merchants, many years ago, adopted the name "alpaca" for a rather coarse material made from sheep's wool and cotton and used extensively in the manufacture of thin black coats, the term "alpaca" is not used in commerce to designate the real article. Overcoats and shawls made of the beautiful soft wool of the Peruvian alpaca are usually said to be "camel's hair," "vicuña" or even "llama!" Few purchasers in the Northern Hemisphere know that llama wool is too coarse to be desirable for such purposes.

On the other hand, if the material were called "alpaca" the purchaser would not expect it to be any softer or more attractive than the ancient product of Yankee ingenuity.

It is interesting to note that the Incas and their influence throughout the Andes apparently did not extend any further north than the known limits of the llama. In fact, the development of their culture may be said to have depended in large measure on their success in domesticating this little American camel. Their ability to raise and train hundreds of thousands of llamas which could and would carry useful loads enabled the mountain people to carry out engineering and agricultural works far more extensive than could have been accomplished had they been obliged to depend entirely on human burden-bearers.

LANGUAGE

Some American archaelologists are prone to shorten the length of time during which the civilization of the Incas was developing. Because the Mayas of Central America used hieroglyphics and invented a calendar it is easy to grant them a couple of thousand years, while the Incas are limited to a few hundred. Technically they are right, if one chooses to restrict the use of the word Inca to the few centuries when the rulers were actually called Incas. But if one uses the term Inca to characterize that remarkable civilization discovered by the Spaniards in the sixteenth century, with its advanced agriculture, its magnificent engineering works and its success over centuries in producing from an exceedingly wild ancestor two such distinct domestic and pure-bred animals as the llama and alpaca, it becomes evident that the period covered by the growth of this ancient Peruvian civilization certainly must have lasted for several thousand years.

This theory is also confirmed by the many varieties of both potatoes and corn found in Inca land, and also by the fact that the guinea pigs, which they domesticated and bred are as widely different in color and in coat as are the cats of the Mediterranean region which are known to be of extremely ancient lineage.

Unfortunately the ancient Peruvians never developed any form of script or picture writing. It is indeed a great pity that the Incas never had the opportunity, as did the Greeks and Romans, to come in contact with a people like the Phoenicians who were clever enough to invent an alphabet.

The language of the Incas was the *Quichua* tongue. Originally it was used only in a small area around Cuzco where the Inca dynasty originated, possibly in the tenth or eleventh century. During the next five hundred years, when the Incas succeeded in subduing the native races as far north as Ecuador and as far south as Argentina, they carried the Quichua language with them and insisted on its being learned by the conquered peoples so that it had a wide distribution by the end of the Sixteenth Century.

Today the total population of Peru is about seven million. A recent census reports that two and one-half million speak Quichua and two-thirds of these speak no other language. Although there are many different languages spoken by small forest tribes in the Amazon basin, there are only two aboriginal languages numerically important in the Andes, Quichua and Aymara. In the region around Lake Titicaca and in northern Bolivia the Indians speak Aymara which has a phonetic system and grammar similar to Quichua. Neither of these languages are related in any way to those of eastern South America nor to any outside the continent. Philological experts are of the opinion that nearly five million people in South America still speak the language of the Incas. Obviously it is by far the most important native language in either north or South America. That this phonetic system is so widespread is in itself a remarkable tribute to the extraordinary people who were so successful in breeding animals and plants.

There are few words in Quichua to denote abstract qualities. On the other hand, the people obviously were not militaristic for the word meaning "soldier" also means "enemy." The extent of the empire is emphasized by the fact that the word for "foreigner" means "those belonging to a city a great distance off." The importance of agriculture is strikingly demonstrated by the fact that in Quichua there is but one word for "work" or "cultivate." Apparently cultivating the soil was the only thing which rated as work.

An interesting commentary on the habits of the ancient people and a sidelight on their manners and customs is the abundance of expressions in Quichua for all stages of drunkenness. One of their principle activities was the manufacture of beer or *chicha*. It was brewed from sprouted corn that had been boiled and crushed under the rocking stones which served the Andean people as an upper mill-stone or pestle. The Indians of Mexico and Central America in grinding their corn use a muller, pushed back and forth on a slab. This is more fatiguing and requires more effort than the rocking stone invented in the Andes. The fact that the most common necessity of the household, a means of grinding corn, was not the same with the Incas as with the Mayas, points to the long period of separate evolution.

Pottery

In addition to agriculture and the breeding of useful plants and animals, the Incas carried to a remarkable extreme the manufacture of graceful, symmetrical pottery. They learned to recognize different kinds and qualities of potter's clay. They selected localities marked by the finest type of clay for the worship of favorable divinities and the manufacture of the most delicate dishes. It seems likely that a form of potter's wheel must have been used in the manufacture of their jars.

There was nothing crude or uncouth about their pottery. Most of it was made with the utmost skill, hard finished with polished and painted surfaces from which every trace of the process of manufacture had been removed. Unlike the primitive pottery of the Indian tribes in the Amazonian Basin, and in many parts of America, Inca pottery gives abundant evidence, in its symmetry and fine proportions, as well as in its finish, that the makers were the inheritors of a thousand years of culture and love of beauty. Their pieces were admirably designed for the uses to which they were put and had just enough decoration to please and satisfy the most fastidious owner.

On the Peruvian coast, the ancient peoples who were conquered by the Incas carried their pottery making to a much more elaborate degree than did the Incas. Inca designs were nearly always geometrical and conventional. They included squares repeated one within the other, cross-hatching, rows of triangles, parallel lines, rows of lozenges, elaborate scrolls, a conventionalized necklace design consisting of a large number of disks each suspended by separate strings from the principal cord. This necklace design may possibly have been a representation of the royal fringe of sovereignty, the crown of the Incas.

The bar and double-cross pattern which occurs frequently on the handles of Inca pottery is clearly imitative of ancient basketry and derives from the easiest form of making handles. This pattern took the fancies of the ancient potters and consequently reappears in various panels and frequently constitutes the central portion of a geometrical design.

In many museums little attention is paid to Inca pottery partly because it is rare and partly because its graceful, symmetrical shape is not unique but is even reminiscent of the classical forms found in the Mediterranean. Some of the two-handled jars are almost identical with one found in ancient Troy. Others resemble Greek forms.

The most striking Peruvian pottery exhibited in collections comes from the sea-coast of northern Peru, where, before the days of the Inca Empire, native potters excelled in producing realistic human groups and even vivid portraits. Some of the Peruvian coastal pottery still stands unequaled in the life-like portrayal of human action and emotion. One finds the naked body depicted in many attitudes, some of them so degenerate as to be excluded from public exhibits. Mannequins in every conceivable posture, tragic groups representing human sacrifices, humorous caricatures of intoxication, persons afflicted with terrible diseases, comedy and tragedy, all are found represented in coastal ceramic art. The striking lack of any such tendencies in the pottery of the Incas leads to the conclusion that they must have had a strong prejudice against the use of the human form in decoration. This may have been due to the custom among the Peruvian highlanders of protecting themselves against the bitter cold of the high plateau by always having their bodies clothed. Thousands of years ago this custom may not have prevailed, since the Indians of the southernmost part of South America, who live amidst the snow and ice of Tierra del Fuego, are scarcely clothed at all. Once clothing had been invented, however, and its use furthered by the domestication of the wool-bearing alpaca and llama, comfort would dictate that it be continually used. As a result, custom would, in the course of time, decree that any exposure of the body was indecent. The growth of such strict ideas of decency would naturally promote a sense of shame which would lead to the practice of using geometric patterns or conventionalized birds and animals rather than the human form. Consequently it is not surprising that Inca pottery does not represent the human form even though their highly developed sense of the beautiful induced them to make jars and dishes as graceful as those of ancient Greece. Practically all the pottery found in our excavations at Machu Picchu was pure Inca.

The most characteristic Inca pattern and the most common of the vessels intended for holding liquids was a bottle-shaped vase with a pointed bottom, frequently two and two-and-a-half feet in height and capable of holding six or seven gallons of *chicha*, with two band-shaped handles attached vertically to the lower body, and a strikingly long neck. Each jar as a rule has two pierced, ear-like nubbins attached to its rim. The front of each bottle-shaped vase has on its shoulder a stout nubbin decorated to represent the conventionalized head of a fierce beast, usually with two eyes and a crudely incised mouth, and sometimes ears, lips, teeth and even nostrils. It has been suggested that the makers believed that the ill-natured demon who caused good *chicha* to be spilt might be frightened away by this uncouth animal. These nubbins could have been used to tie on a cover to keep the precious *chicha* from spilling, or for decorative tassels which would indicate the quality of the maker of the beverage. Since these jars were intended to be carried on the back and shoulders by means of a rope passed through the handles and around the big nubbin, they were nearly always decorated on only one side, and the side which rubbed against the back of the carrier was left undecorated. Although not at all like a Greek aryballus, that name has been applied to it by Peruvian writers for many years. So far as I know it is not found in any part of the world except where Inca civilization prevailed. Many examples of it were found at Machu Picchu.

A shallow dish or saucer used for drinking has a handle on one side, sometimes a broad loop but more often the conventionalized head of a friendly bird or animal, which sets comfortably under the thumb, and a small raised decoration on the opposite rim. These dishes are always carefully made, attractively painted only on the inside with elaborate geometric patterns. These saucers somewhat resemble in form the classic patera, which was used in pouring out libations at sacrifices. It is amusing to note that the Incas made the handle of these drinking ladles just as pleasing as they made the nubbins of the great jars fierce and revolting, no doubt to encourage drinkers to enjoy themselves.

In a mountain region where there is little fuel for open fires and where the drinking of cold water frequently brings on mountain sickness which is often disastrous, it is natural that the craving of the body for additional heat and liquid should be gratified by soup and beer. The utensils used for *chicha* are carefully painted and polished. In this they differed markedly from the fire-blackened cooking pots, or *ollas*, in which the Incas made their soups and stews.

A common form of *olla* has a handle on one side and a single foot or base. The side opposite the loop handle is usually decorated in low relief, possibly the echo of the base of a second handle. These beaker-shaped *ollas* were usually nine or ten inches high. The form undoubtedly was the result of a long process of evolution beginning with the introduction into the fire of a simple two handled pot. Then somebody discovered that by adding a base or a foot to it the pot could stand better in the embers of a small fire. Later the discovery was made that only the handle nearest the cook was really necessary since the other handle got too hot to be of much use and it was finally abandoned, its place being taken by a little ornament in low relief that was attached to the pot just before it was baked.

Another common design was a two-handled food dish with band-shaped handles ordinarily attached horizontally below the rim, wider than it is high and broad enough so that the hands of the diners might readily extract the delicacies therein, undoubtedly stews, which were an essential part of the ancient fare. These dishes were not used in the fire, but were of fine clay, carefully polished and soberly decorated on both sides with conventional geometric patterns.

Loving cups and dishes connected with drinking *chicha* were frequently amusingly decorated with fierce looking jaguars or pumas glaring at each other with open mouths and bared teeth. Or the handle might consist of the head of a laughing fox or coyote, exquisitely modeled. The spirit in which the modelling of these Inca dishes was worked out shows great artistic ability and frequently a nice sense of humor. Sometimes a drinking jug would be made in the form of a fat man with his hands comfortably supporting his stomach.

One-handled jugs were sometimes decorated with a human face in low relief, sometimes partly in relief and partly painted. Or a jug might have a handle decorated with a head of a fierce jaguar partly hollow so that a string could be passed through the teeth in such a manner as to support the jug from a peg.

Perhaps one of the most interesting and rarest forms of Inca pottery was a three-legged brazier with a band-shaped handle attached to its top, its mouth irregular in form, placed on one side. In the top are three openings or vent holes, the legs are solid and cylindrical and long enough to permit of a small fire being built underneath. Consequently the braziers were fire-blackened within and without. The Inca metallurgists gave them such hard usage that the frail little braziers did not last long and no perfect specimens have been found.

The usual size of the three-legged brazier was about seven inches high, six inches wide and seven inches long. They appear to have been intended for a charcoal fire in which metal could be kept hot while being worked. The vent holes on top would have admitted the insertion of blow pipes, a practice referred to in several of the early Spanish chronicles, and they were made thin enough to enable them to be rapidly heated. They were undoubtedly used in the manufacture of bronze knives, axes, chisels, and shawl-pins in which repeated heated and annealing were necessary.

METALLURGY

Inca bronze has been found to be remarkably pure, aside from very small quantities of sulphur. The proportion of copper in Inca bronze varies from 86% in some articles to 97% in others. Some archaeologists have taken the position that since the greatest quantity of tin is usually found in those bronzes that would seem to require it least, the presence of tin in Inca bronzes should be regarded as accidental. This hypothesis has been carefully considered by the experts of the largest copper companies now operating in the Andes. They all agree that so far as known ores of copper and tin occur in South America this is an untenable thesis for such ores are not found in combination. It is well known that during World War II enormous quantities of tin were recovered from Bolivian mines where our manufacturers were delighted to secure supplies to take the place of those that came from the Straits Settlements before the Japanese occupation. It is also well known that enormous deposits of copper are found in Peru and in Chile but not in combination with tin.

My friend Professor Charles H. Matthewson of Yale University, was the first modern metallurgist to make an exhaustive study of

Inca bronzes. He discovered that the percentage of tin contained in Inca bronzes was not governed by the uses for which they were intended, but by the requirements of the ancient methods of manufacture. Everything that we know about Inca metallurgy is based on Professor Matthewson's report.

The Incas learned the interesting fact that bronze containing a high percentage of tin yields the best impression in casting because during the process of solidifying it expands more than bronze having a low tin content. Hence the more delicate or ornamental pieces contain the highest percentage of tin. Artistic details were thus more strikingly brought out in the finished product. Of course, had the Incas possessed steel graving tools the case would have been different. However, the Inca metallurgists learned that the operation of casting small delicate objects is facilitated when there is about ten percent of tin in the mixture. Such alloys retain their initial heat longer and so remain longer in a fluid condition. Since small objects tend to cool rapidly this knowledge was particularly useful in the manufacture of ornamental shawl-pins and ear spoons and accounts for the higher percentage of tin the Incas used in making them.

Since these early metallurgists were unfamiliar with modern methods of heat treatment they were compelled to sacrifice the extra hardness and strength obtainable in casting axes and chisels by increasing the tin content in them. Such implements had to be frequently hammered and annealed. Since cold-working had to be depended upon to produce the final hardness of such objects, more than one heating was needed in forging the blades and this process necessitated a low tin content. Necessarily they employed a formula for combined copper and tin which has impressed archaeologists, only familiar with the chemical analysis of Inca bronzes, as being that which is unsuited for axes, chisels and large knives. It was only after a metallographic study of Inca bronzes, involving the mutilation of the pieces examined that Professor Matthewson learned the structure of such objects, the methods of their manufacture and the reasons for the variation that has been found to exist. The Inca metallurgists cast their bronze knives generally in one piece and then cold-worked them. Such reheating as took place was solely for the purpose of softening the metal to facilitate cold-working, which was probably done at less than red heat. Some Inca bronzes are found to have been repeatedly hammered and reheated. This hammering might have been done with the stone tools with which the Incas were familiar.

The knife blades appear to have been worked and hammered so as to extend the metal more or less uniformly in several directions. Chisels and axes, on the other hand, were cast practically in the shape finally desired.

The Inca metallurgists were sufficiently ingenious to use more than one variety of bronze in the construction of artistic knives. Their knives were in the shape of an inverted "t." If it was desired to ornament the end of the handle with a llama's head or attractive bird, the ornament would be made of bronze with a high content of tin. The metal of the blade and the lower part of the handle on the other hand was of bronze of lower tin content because the blades had to be cold-worked.

The ornamental part of the knife handle was actually cast around the shank of the knife after it had been completed. The Inca artisan, anxious to make a good serviceable knife and at the same time make it attractive, had learned over the centuries to take infinite pains in doing it. If he wished to make a hole in the end of a knife or shawl-pin, he did it in the process of casting because he lacked steel tools for drilling it.

In making bronze *bolas* which could be used in capturing a flying parrot or many-hued macaw, he cast the ball with a pin already in so that the cord connecting the two parts of the *bolas* could be securely fastened without interfering with the smooth flight of the missile. The pin was not set into the *bolas* but was cast in place. It must have been a great sight to see an Inca hunter bring down a flying macaw with a skillful swing of the little bronze *bolas*, discharging them at just the right moment to entangle its wings and legs without damaging the beautiful captive.

Some axe blades bear evidence that they were used upon stone. Their structure shows severe damage of a character which could only result from very hard usage. They were probably used in cutting square holes in ashlars and in making sharp inside corners. It is difficult to conceive of any stone tools that could have been used successfully for this purpose. Some writers have assumed that the Incas used bronze implements to a large extent in finishing their best stone work. It seems to me, however, that even their best bronze was too soft to last long in such activities. It is not likely that it was often so employed. Experiments made in our National Museum have demonstrated that patience, perseverance, elbow grease and fine sand will enable stone tools of various shapes to work miracles in dressing and polishing both granite and andesite.

However, it is reasonably certain that the Inca builders used powerful little bronze crow-bars to get those ashlars in place which were too heavy to be lifted by hand. Called *champis*, these bars were sufficiently strong to be used in adjusting blocks of stone weighing ten or twenty tons. In a tensile test, made under the direction of Professor Matthewson, an old Inca *champi* of poor quality showed an ultimate strength of 28,000 pounds to the square inch. We found by experiment with a new bronze crow-bar of the same composition, that when hardened by methods known to the Inca metallurgists, it had still greater strength. The Incas could have used their little crow-bars for prying into place granite blocks weighing twenty tons without damaging the *champis*.

Inca bronze included not only such tools as axes, knives, chisels, and crow-bars but also such domestic utensils as tweezers, shawl-pins, and large needles, as well as such articles of adornment as rings, bracelets, spangles and bells. They even made ear spoons, the ends of whose handles were often decorated with figures of humming birds.

Perhaps the commonest bronze articles made by the Incas were shawl-pins. Early drawings made by the Spanish conquerors show that these pins were always used for fastening the front of the shoulder covering. This custom is still common in the Andes and I have noticed in many cases the head of the shawl-pin is made like a spoon. The Incas do not appear to have been familiar with spoons. The heads of their shawl-pins, which vary in length from three inches to nine inches, are generally flat and shaped like a half-moon. They were beaten very thin so that the edges were fairly sharp and appear to have been used for cutting purposes. As the Inca women were frequently occupied in spinning yarn by means of a hand spindle, or in weaving textiles, they would have found such little knives very useful and handy.

They made bronze mirrors similar to those found in ancient Egyptian tombs. They even succeeded in making a concave bronze mirror which, when polished, enabled the rays of the sun to be sufficiently concentrated on a bit of cotton as to set it on fire. One cannot help being impressed with the great skill of the Inca metallurgists and wondering how long it took them to learn this art.

They also made bronze bodkins or large needles with eyes sufficiently large to permit them to carry a fairly stout cord. Sometimes these eyes were made by flattening the head to a narrow strip, drawing this under, laying it against the shaft of the bodkin and hammering enough of the sides onto it to secure it. This process would readily have been accomplished by the use of one of the little braziers.

They made little bronze tweezers intended to take the place of the modern razor. Highland Indians seldom have any hair on their faces. The Incas were probably anxious to remove any stray hairs that did appear. The custom of pulling out undesired facial hairs by means of tweezers was even known among the tribes of Micronesia in the Gilbert Islands before it was thought of in New York or Paris. It is evident to the observer of manners and customs that the desire for beauty parlors is nothing new under the sun.

WEAVING

The Incas were fortunate in having as their subjects a hard-working race, accustomed to constant effort. Today while one encounters lazy men, one never sees Quichua women idle. While tending flocks or walking along the road they are almost always winding or spinning yarn. One often finds them engaged in the manufacture of shawls, girdles, ponchos, and blankets on hand looms. Even the men and older children are sometimes thus engaged.

As a matter of fact, ancient Andean weaving, as developed by the Incas, was one of the greatest textile arts the world has ever seen. We depend on silk and linen for our finest textiles. They did not know of the silk worm or of the flax plant. They had cotton and the soft wool of the alpaca but they also used the extremely fine and rare wool of the *vicuña*, the smallest American camel. They never took the trouble to domesticate it. They depended on what would be caught by the Inca hunters after being rounded up in huge annual drives.

Tourists in Peru are always anxious to secure rugs made of vicuña skins but these little animals have now become so scarce as to be protected. In the days of the Incas vicuña wool seems to have been reserved for the rulers and the nobles.

Examples of early Peruvian textiles amaze the beholder. Fine specimens may be seen in various museums of art in Boston, New York and Washington. They are as worthy of admiration as the finest specimens of Egyptian or Chinese weaving. The inventive-ness and resourcefulness of the Peruvian weavers created materials which indicate as long a period of artistic development as that of Egypt or China. These rare and beautiful stuffs which have been found in the coastal cemeteries of Peru, where they have been preserved by the dry desert air and the absence of rainfall, prove to the students of the history of art the very great age of Inca civilization. And none of it was borrowed from Asia.

We are told that the finest textiles were made in the convents connected with the Temples of the Sun, by the Chosen Women, sometimes called the Virgins of the Sun, who were carefully trained in this difficult art. Some of their products are as fine and soft as the finest silk.

THE PEOPLE

No one knows the origin of the people over whom the Incas ruled. Physical anthropologists assure us that the bony structure of the American Indian is closely related to that of the people of Northeast Siberia. However, that does not prove that the migration went from Asia to America any more than it proves that the people of Eastern Asia came from America. Whenever that migration took place, and in whichever direction, it happened so many thousands of years ago that archaeological evidence, as distinct from anthropological, is lacking. In other words, there appears to be no resemblance between the culture of Northeastern Asia and Central South America. Furthermore, since wheat, one of the most valuable crops in the world, was developed in Asia and was unknown in America, and since similar ignorance prevailed in Asia regarding two other enormously important crops, potatoes and maize, it appears fairly certain that the migration took place many thousands of years ago. This appears to be borne out by the recent discovery in North America of the remains of glacial man whose age is estimated to be about 20,000 years.

The Incas took such trouble to spread the Quichua language wherever they went that it is fair to assume that they descended from a Quichua tribe. The Quichuas are brown in color. Their hair is straight and black. Gray hair is seldom seen. It is still the custom among the men in certain localities to wear their hair long and braided. Beards are very rare and when they occur are extremely sparse. Bearded Indians are almost certain to give signs of traces of Spanish blood.

Among the Quichuas, bald heads are very rare. Teeth seem to be more enduring than with us. Throughout the Andes the frequency of well-preserved teeth is noteworthy, except on sugar plantations where there is opportunity to indulge freely in crude brown sugar nibbled from cakes or mixed with parched corn and eaten as a convenient ration. Since the Incas did not know how to make sugar, it is fair to assume that they had good teeth and were not troubled by having to chew the hard kernels of their favorite parched corn.

The Quichua face is broad and short. Freckles are not common, although a large proportion of the mountain Indians are pock-marked. Asiatic smallpox was probably not known in the Andes in prehistoric times. On the other hand, there is abundant evidence, both in prehistoric tombs and in the vivid records of coastal pottery, that syphilis did not come from the Old World, but was an aboriginal disease. In fact, it was probably taken from America to the Mediterranean by the sailors of the early discoverers and explorers. It was the worst gift the New World gave to the Old World in exchange for the "benefits" of European culture.

There is no evidence that the Incas were fat. One hardly ever sees a fat mountain Indian today. It is difficult to tell whether this is a racial characteristic or due to the necessity of hard exercise in the mountains. Certainly the abundant use of white potatoes is supposed to be fattening. The diet of the Incas did not contain much meat since both llamas and alpacas were far too useful to be used as food except in the case of animals that died of old age.

Although the Peruvian highlander made the best use he could of the llama, he was never able to develop its slender legs and weak back sufficiently to use it for loads weighing more than one hundred pounds. Consequently, for the carrying of heavy burdens he has had to depend on himself. As a result it is not surprising that while his arms are poorly developed his shoulders are broader, his back muscles stronger and the calves of his legs, larger and more powerful than those of almost any other race.

CUSTOMS

Among the Incas, practically every man was married at least once. Polygamy was general among the upper classes and was regarded as a desirable state for those who could afford it. The Inca rulers, the nobles and distinguished military leaders, were awarded concubines. They were usually taken from one of the national boarding schools or convents, where attractive young girls or Chosen Women, selected annually from all over the empire, were trained.

These Chosen Women, whose lives were consecrated to the service of the Sun, his representatives, the Incas and his priests, lived in sanctuaries which were scattered throughout the Inca Empire. It was deemed a great honor to a newly conquered province for the Inca to establish one within its borders.

According to the Spanish conquerors, the most important convent was at Cuzco adjoining the Temple of the Sun. Other women were forbidden to enter that holy place. Men were not allowed in the royal boarding schools. The most beautiful and best born maidens in each province appear to have been selected early in life when eight or nine years old. They were supervised by older women who had lived for years in the convents. The girls learned not only to weave skillfully the clothing worn by the nobles as well as the beautiful robes and elaborate hangings used on state occasions, they were also taught the preparation of special foods and beverages used in great ceremonials. Apparently the girls were kept in the convents until they were about sixteen years of age, when they were divided into three classes based on their degree of beauty. Probably the most beautiful and highly born became concubines of the Inca Emperor himself. It is believed that some were selected to be sacrificed in honor of the sun, or at all events, to be interned for life in one of the convents where they could act also as temple attendants and as instructors of the Chosen Girls. A third group seems to have been given by the emperor as wives to nobles or military captains whom he wished particularly to favor.

It was natural that the most desirable girls should be set aside for the worship of the sun, whom the Incas regarded as a benevolent and life-giving god. In the Andes, one is rarely comfortable except when the sun is shining. It is not surprising, therefore, that the worship of the sun involved such elements as propitiation, supplication and thanksgiving. It was important that the sun god should be pleased in every way possible and that the priests should be served by the most attractive young women of the kingdom.

Our knowledge of the Chosen Women, or, Virgins of the Sun, is derived, in part, from the writings of Cieza de Leon, the greatest and most illustrious of the contemporary historians of the period of conquest. He says that at the doors of the convents porters were stationed to keep guard over the virgins, many of whom were of noble birth, besides being beautiful and charming. He says that if one of them had any connection with a man she was killed by being buried alive and the same penalty was suffered by her paramour.

One of his contemporaries, Polo de Ondegardo, says that the convents were called *aclla-huasi,* meaning "the house of the Chosen Ones." He says they were selected by the governors in the provinces who had the power to choose girls of the proper age without limit as to number chosen. Their teachers were called *mama-cunas.*

He says the number of women set apart for this purpose was very great and their parents could not excuse or redeem them under any circumstances. Estates were set apart for the support of the convents.

He says, further, that great quantities of the cloth made in the convents were distributed among the Inca's favorite soldiers and given to his relations and attendants. Also enormous quantities were deposited in storehouses to be used as needed.

Religion

The religion of ancient peoples, as well as their manners and customs, depended, in large measure, on the climate of the region where they lived. If it was a warm region where the sun was oppressively hot in the middle of the day and the nights were pleasant and cool, there was less temptation to worship the sun.

On the other hand, there was a marked tendency to worship the stars and the moon. Familiarity with these heavenly bodies led to that knowledge of astronomy, and even astrology, which is so marked a feature of Arabian civilization as well as that of the Mayas in Central America.

On the other hand, in the high Andes, on the Peruvian plateau, where the rarefied atmosphere does not retain the sun's heat and the nights are bitterly cold, it is not surprising that little attention was paid to the stars, while the most profound worship was accorded the sun. Other natural phenomena such as thunder and lightning, high mountains, dangerous precipices, and water-falls, came within their ken and naturally were propitiated by offerings and a certain amount of worship so as to protect human beings from harm.

Most important of all, naturally, was the sun, without which crops would not grow, and life, generally, was intolerable. Its favor must be sought. As the sun went farther and farther north and the shadows lengthened in the month of June, it was natural to fear that the sun would continue its flight to the north and might leave them eventually to freeze and starve. Consequently the priests of the sun, able, on the twenty-first or twenty-second of June, to stop its flight and tie it to a stone pillar in one of their temples, were regarded with veneration. When the shadows ceased to lengthen and became shorter until the sun was once more overhead and his kingdom firmly established there would naturally be great rejoicing. The period of the summer solstice was one of joy just as that of the winter solstice was one of fear. It is probable that the priests of the Sun, whose lives depended on their being successful in appearing to control his actions, had learned to read the length of the shadows cast by the huge sundials called *intihuatana*, or, "the place to which the sun is tied."

One naturally expects to find these sacred stones within the enclosure of the sanctuary or temple where the sun was worshipped and where the Chosen Women were taught to become his hand-maidens. There they learned to be useful wives for priests and nobles who could depend on them to weave beautiful garments, cook toothsome dishes, and brew excellent *chicha* with which the heart of man might be made glad and his spirit raised from the heaviness caused by toil or fear.

One of the most important spots in the Andes would be the ruins of a sanctuary with its temples of the Sun, Moon and Stars, *its intihuatana*, its supply of good fresh water for *chicha*, its palaces for nobles and priests and its dormitories for the women who had been chosen to be Virgins of the Sun. Such a sanctuary had been encountered by Pizarro and the conquistadors when they entered Cuzco. We found one somewhere else. It was constructed with the utmost care by the most skillful architects and masons in the most inaccessible parts of the Andes.

2.

The Origin
of the
Incas

THE MORE ONE STUDIES
the remarkable civilization which the Spaniards found when they
conquered Peru, the more one wishes that the Incas and their
predecessors had learned the art of writing or at least of carving
hieroglyphics and had left behind them inscriptions which, in the
course of time might have been deciphered and translated to tell
us something of their history. Students of art and architecture
assure us that the period of time needed for the evolution of the
ability and skill shown by the Incas in creating objects of beauty
must have been as long as that required by the artistic Egyptians
and Greeks.

The historic chronicle of Egypt and the classic lands of the
Mediterranean was fortunately confided to tablets, inscriptions
and manuscripts. It was carved in stone or on clay and written
on papyrus or vellum. So we know something positively of the
centuries their evolution took. Students of ancient Peru on
the other hand have no such kindly aids on which to base their
investigations. We must piece together contradictory traditions
which were first written down at the time of the Spanish Conquest, hundreds of years after the events. We must rely on frag-

37

ments of cloth and pottery, ruins of temples and terraces, such material as can be obtained from graves and a study of what we know was achieved in agriculture, horticulture and animal industry. From all this material we must put together what will be at best a very fragmentary story, on the details of which no two experts ever will agree!

The best that one can do is patiently to study the evidence offered by the climate, the physical geography, and the anthropology of the region and use it to construct a reasonable account which is at least not capable of being destroyed by incontrovertible evidence. Anyone who has read the stories which have come down to us from the early Spanish conquerors and their descendants like Garcilasso Inca de la Vega, or the Christian missionaries, priests, monks and Jesuits, who learned the language of the Incas and made reports on what they saw and found as well as what they heard, knows that their statements are frequently so contradictory and conflicting that they can hardly ever be said to be incontrovertible. Where the Spanish chronicles run counter to the known habits of the highlanders and the physical evidence gained by exploration, excavation and observation it may be accepted as less likely to be true than statements not so substantiated.

The first comprehensive account in English of the civilization of the Incas is that of the heroic historian William H. Prescott who overcame the handicaps of his partial blindness and inability to travel, by a patient acumulation of all the books and manuscripts dealing with Peru which he could secure. His vivid stories of the conquest of both Peru and Mexico must ever remain delightful classics to charm generations of readers. Of necessity his account of the conquest of Peru was based largely on Garcilasso Inca de la Vega, born in Cuzco in the year 1539, the son of an Inca princess. Unfortunately for the accuracy of his famous book, "Royal Commentaries," Garcilasso left Peru when only a boy in his teens, never returned to the land of his birth, lived most of his life in Spain, and did not write his celebrated chronicles of the Incas until he was an old man.

During his years in Europe Garcilasso had undoubtedly suffered frequently from remarks made by his contemporaries who were inclined to be contemptuous of the descendant of the brown-skinned "heathen" of the Andes. He had presumably frequently repeated stories of his mother's people, their achievements, their civilization and their ancestry. He knew what pleased and astonished his European auditors, what seemed to them admirable and altogether worthy of praise. He knew what shocked them. It was, therefore, quite natural that in the course of the thirty or forty years of his life in Spain, before he began writing his book, he should come to believe that his mother's people were much more like Europeans than they really were. He wanted Europeans to admire his maternal ancestors and he wrote his book accordingly. Consequently there are many pages in his book and many statements in Prescott's account, based on Garcilasso, which have a decidedly European atmosphere.

Another writer, an ecclesiastical lawyer of the Seventeenth Century, who has recently begun to come into his own, wrote a different sort of book. His name was Fernando Montesinos. In 1629, the century following the conquest, he appears to have gone to Peru as an adviser of a viceroy, the Count of Chinchon, whose name is remembered because his wife was cured of malaria by the use of one of the very few specifics in the world, a most important discovery of the Incas, a bark which they called *kina* and which we call quinine or "Peruvian bark." Since the Count of Chincon was instrumental in the introduction of this extraordinary medicine into Europe, the plant from which its bark is taken was called after him, *chincona*.

The Viceroy's secretary, Montesinos, was well educated and appears to have been devoted to historical research. He traveled extensively in Peru and published several books. He wrote a history of the Incas, "Memorias Antiguas Historiales del Peru," which was spoiled by the introduction in which, as might be expected of an orthodox ecclesiastic, he contended that Peru was peopled under the leadership of Ophir, the great-grandson of

Noah! Nothwithstanding his clerical prejudices his work appears to be of great value. The late Sir Clements Markham, foremost English student of Inca history, was inclined to place considerable credence in the statements of Montesinos. From the wise old men whom he was able to consult in Inca Land he secured a very long story of pre-Inca kings called Amautas who seem to have been responsible for many of the achievements which we naturally ascribe to the Incas because we use that term to cover the culture and the civilization found in the Peruvian highlands. Montesinos says that "the fifty-third of the Kings of Peru" was named Huilcanota or Vilcanota. *Huilca* is the name of a plant from which the aborigines obtained a narcotic snuff whose effects were startlingly intoxicating and produced visions. Whether he was the first to discover the virtue which lay in the seeds from which they made their powerful snuff we have no means of knowing.

However, he did give his name to the pass that is now called La Raya which is on the watershed between the Amazon basin and Lake Titicaca; at least the pass was called Vilcanota by the Incas. Montesinos was of the opinion that the king was named after the pass because of a great victory he had there. His capital was at Cuzco where he learned from the reports of his provincial governors that great hordes of people, barbarians, were coming up from the plains of Argentina and invading the Bolivian plateau and the basin of Lake Titicaca.

King Vilcanota sent out spies to get the details of the enemy forces. Learning that they were in two large armies, he assembled a powerful army himself and took up his stand in the high, snowy pass of La Raya and fortified it. Montesinos says, there "He gave battle to the first army, which he conquered easily on account of its being in disorder. The second army, hearing the news, came very confusedly to aid their fellows, and it also was conquered. The King entered Cuzco triumphant, bearing before him the vanquished, naked and with their hands tied. From this event the ancients call this king Huilcanota."

Montesinos says that this King Vilcanota was successful in

pacifying his kingdom, had a very long reign and left many sons. One of them, named Tupac Yupanqui, "rich in all the virtues," also had many sons and was a wise ruler. He had the good will of friends and neighbors with whom he exchanged gifts. He taught his sons the art of government and surrounded them with experienced counsellors. His great-grandson, Huaman Tacco, was the sixty-first Amauta. In his day there were bad omens, comets and earthquakes. His heir and successor was called Pachacuti.

Pachacuti was neither wise nor strong. Unfortunately in his time the barbarian migrations began again, "great armies of very fierce people" from the east and south. "Full of dismay and melancholy" on account of the earthquakes, comets and other bad omens and the somber prognostications of the wizards and soothsayers, he offered sacrifices to his gods and tried to make what preparations he could by fortifying camps and strong points. Learning from his spies that hordes of warriors were again marching north through the basin of Lake Titicaca he became panicky, scattered his forces, sent some captains to the Bolivian plateau, sent others to defend various passes and went himself with the main body of his army to the pass of La Raya which his famous ancestor Vilcanota had once fortified. There he built a fortress, the remains of which can still be seen.

Instead of waiting behind his walls and terraces for the enemy to attack at a disadvantage, he sallied out, against the advice of his captains, and gave battle. His troops were armed with slings, clubs and spears. The enemy had bows and arrows. The contest was terrific. Carried aloft on a golden litter, Pachacuti did his best to encourage his troops. Unfortunately he was an easy mark for an enemy archer. Fatally wounded by an arrow, his death caused consternation among his troops. Losing courage, the soldiers fled to a fortress with the body of their king.

Then, secretly, at night they carried it away to a place of safety called Tampu-tocco, or "a place of temporary abode where there were windows" or "Window Tavern." Here they were joined by the remnants of Pachacuti's army.

After this debacle, says Montesinos, "the Provinces of the Kingdom, learning of the death of the king, all rose up in rebellion, and the people of Tampu-tocco had many dissensions among themselves as to the choosing of a king."

"Thus was the government of the Peruvian monarchy lost and destroyed. It did not come to its own for four hundred years, and the knowledge of letters was lost. In each province they elected their own king, and he to who it was given to be the heir of Pachacuti was Titu Huaman Quicho, a very young boy. The loyal men were few, and could not bear comparison with the other peoples. They went to Tampu-tocco, and there they raised him up to be their king, because, on account of the revolts, none could live in Cuzco, all being in turmoil. And, as men came little by little to live at Tampu-tocco under the protection of the king, Cuzco became almost deserted, and only the ministers of the temple remained there."

"The faithful vassals were happy in Tampu-tocco with the boy king, for there, according to the legends of the amautas, is the very celebrated cave where the Incas had their origin, and they affirm as a certainty that there have never been seen there earthquakes, pestilence nor earth-tremors. And if evil fortune should pursue the boy king, they could hide him in the cave as in a holy place. The king came of age, and lived with much moderation for many years. He called himself king of Tampu-tocco, not of Cuzco, although on certain days he went to worship in the temple (at Cuzco). He left as his heir Cozque Huaman Titu, who lived twenty-five years. Of him and his successors nothing of note is related until the return to Cuzco."

Montesinos gives the name and length of reign of quite a number of the Kings of Tampu-tocco covering a period of some four hundred years. Then came the reign of one called Pachacuti VII who began to recover some of the cities and provinces which had been lost at the time of the barbarian invasion. "As the people obeyed him with so little certainty, and as they were so greatly corrupted in the matter of religion and customs, he took steps to

Part of the Cordillera Vilcabamba, a glimpse of which from Choqquequirau made me want to "Go and look behind the ranges," where we were sure there was "something lost."

We learned long afterwards that the name of this glacier-covered dome is Panta and that its elevation is 18,320 feet above sea level or 2500 feet higher than Mont Blanc. We found the remains of an Inca road in this valley. It was probably used by Manco's soldiers in their raids out of Vitcos to the highway from Cuzco to Lima.

A section of the great Inca fortress of Sacsahuaman, the most unbelievable achievement of ancient man in America. The caravan of loaded llamas in the foreground is on its way to the old Inca capital of Cuzco which lies at the foot of the hill on which the fortress is located. Many of the irregular blocks in the lower wall of Sacsahuaman weigh more than ten tons but they were worked without the use of iron tools by engineers who had no derricks or pulleys and knew only the principal of the lever and the incline plane. They fit together so closely a knife blade cannot find a space between them.

In the gable end of this well-built house we discovered a device, invented by the Incas to help support the purlins of the roof, which had not previously been observed by archaeologists. We called it an eye-bonder because it consists of a long narrow stone slab, in one end of which a chamfered hole had been drilled, firmly bonded into the gable at right angles to its slope. Four of them can be seen in the picture. Sometimes more were used. At Choqquequirau the gables each have nine eye-bonders instead of four. Near the eye-bonder and on the outside of the gable end is a roughly cylindrical block of stone, firmly bonded into the wall, which we call a roof-peg because it was intended to hold a rope that would tie the thatched roof firmly down. That part of the roof-peg which is in the wall is roughly squared so as to hold better. The outer end of the peg was rounded so as not to chafe the rope. Eye-bonders and roof-pegs were unique inventions of Inca architects. Modern Peruvian huts occasionally have wooden roof-pegs.

A general view of the valley of Ollantaytambo. The town and
ruins lie on the slopes on the left-hand of the flat valley floor.
Note the broad, low-walled agricultural terraces on the alluvial
bottomlands and the steep, narrow terraces on the sides of the
valley.

In order to cultivate their fields the Incas invented a foot plow which is still in use in the Andes. With its two handles and a foot rest it is quite efficient in loosening up the ground but the sods have to be turned over by hand. It appears that that is the women's job. Labor was lightened by being done in common with many shouts and songs of cheer. Frequent rests, when a drink of chica would be followed by the preparation of a quid of coca leaves, enabled a lot of hard work to be done even at high altitudes. These farm hands were cultivating a field at an elevation of more than 14,000 feet above sea level.

*The upper part of the Urubamba valley in which lies the charm-
ing Yucay where Sayri Tupac made his last home. Peaches,
apples, and strawberries flourish here as well as roses and lilies.*

Large jars used by the Incas for the manufacture and storage of chica, *the favorite native beer, made usually from sprouted corn. These were found by Saavedra in the jungles of the Pamapaconas river near the Pampa of Ghosts and used by him in the manufacture of brown crude sugar. The nubbins are a characteristic of all the huge aryballi and served a double purpose—to keep the rope from slipping when the jar was being carried on a person's back and also as a useful handle to grasp when pouring liquid out of the jar.*

A Beaker-shaped Olla *or Cooking Pot*

A Jug decorated with the Necklace or Royal Fringe of Sovereignty Pattern

A Brazier for Annealing Bronze Articles

*An Aryballus or Chica Jar found in a Burial Cave at Machu
Picchu*

Dishes and Drinking Ladles found in the Burial Caves at Machu Picchu

Dishes and Drinking Ladles found in the Burial Caves at Machu Picchu

A water bottle made by one of the Peruvian coast tribes which were conquered by the Incas. It was not found at Machu Picchu but is depicted here as a striking example of the difference between Inca pottery and Chimu or coast pottery. The artist has here given a record of human sacrifice. Two figures above the altar are hanging forward ready to be decapitated by the demon who has just completed his task with the first victim whose face has a decidedly Inca profile. There is no evidence that human sacrifice was ever practiced at Machu Picchu.

Bronze Shawl-Pins and Bronze Knives found in the Excavations and Caves of Machu Picchu.

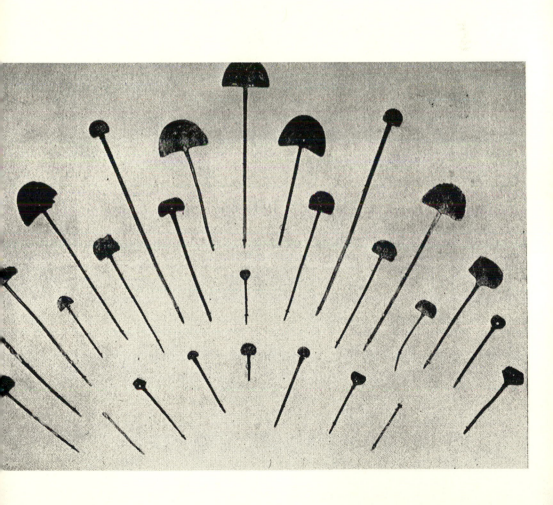

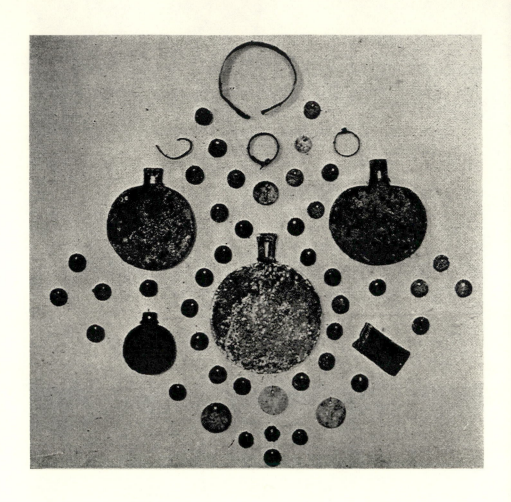

Silver and Bronze Spangles, Rings, Mirrors, and a Bracelet found at Machu Picchu

conquer them, because he said that if those people communicated with his they would corrupt them with the great vices to which they had given themselves up like ungovernable beasts. Therefore he tactfully sent messengers in all directions, asking the chiefs to put a stop to superstition and to the adoration of the many gods and animals which they adored; and the outcome of this was but a slight mending of their ways and the slaying of the ambassadors. The king dissembled for the time being and made great sacrifices and appeals to Illatici Huira Cocha. One reply was that the cause of the pestilence had been the letters, and that no one ought to use them nor resuscitate them for, from their employment great harm would come. Therefore Tupac Cauri commanded by law, that under the pain of death, no one should traffic in *quilcas*, which were the parchments and leaves of trees on which they used to write, nor should use any sort of letters. They observed this oracular command with so much care that after this loss the Peruvians never used letters. And, because in later times a learned amauta invented some characters, they burnt him alive, and so, from this time forth, they used threads and *quipos*."

One cannot help wondering whether it is true that there was a time when the ancient Peruvians, so skillful in so many lines, so inventive in developing art and agriculture and in breeding new plants and animals, also conceived the idea of making a written record but were prevented from doing it by the superstition of the people and the fear of the priests and soothsayers. It is not an impossibility.

It was currently believed in Cuzco at the time that Montesinos was writing, that Tampu-tocco, the "Window Tavern," was about twenty miles from Cuzco at a place known then and now as Paccari Tampu or the Tavern of the Dawn. So we are not surprised to find Montesinos saying that the king built there a "sort of University where the nobles attended the exercises of the soldiery and the boys were taught the manner of counting by the *quipos*, adding together the different colours, which served as letters, by means of which they were increasing their slight learning. The soldiery, and the loyalty of his people being assured, he determined to conquer the rebels. For this purpose, all his men were placed under arms, but the attack did not take place because there were remarkable earthquakes which ruined many buildings all through the region of Cuzco, and rivers sprang up in dry beds and ran for many days through dry gullies where no water had been seen before, and destroyed many villages. After this, a pestilence took place, of which innumerable people died, and the amautas say that only in Tampu-tocco was no pestilence seen; a fact which led Manco Capac to establish his court there." And there they lived for more than five hundred years until it became too small for an active, growing nation.

The significant part of this story of what happened before Manco Capac, the first ruler to be called an Inca, established his court at Tampu-tocco, is that it was far enough away from Cuzco so that neither earthquakes nor pestilence reached it. It must have been much farther away than the little village of Paccarictampu where the climate is too cold for windows and the distance from Cuzco only a few leagues.

There are many stories of the rise of Manco Capac, who, when he had grown to man's estate, assembled his people to see how he could secure new lands for them. Pachacuti Yamqui Salcamayhua, a descendant of a long line of Incas, whose great-grandparents lived in Cuzco at the time of the Spanish Conquest, wrote in 1620 an account of the antiquities of Peru in which he gives the history of the Incas as it was handed down to the descendants of the former rulers of Peru. We are informed by him that Manco Capac, after consultation with his brothers, determined to set out with them "towards the hill over which the sun rose," and that he and his brothers succeeded in reaching Cuzco and settled there. Manco married one of his own sisters in order that he might not lose caste and that no other family be elevated by this marriage to an equality with his. He made good laws, conquered many provinces, and is regarded as the founder of the Inca dynasty. The highlanders of Peru soon came under his sway with good grace and brought him rich presents. The Inca, as he now came to be called, was recognized as the most powerful chief, the most valiant fighter, and the luckiest warrior in the Andes. His captains and soldiers were brave, well disciplined, and well armed. All his affairs prospered greatly. "Afterward he ordered works to be executed at the place of his birth, *consisting of a masonry wall with three windows*, which were emblems of the house of his fathers whence he descended." The windows were named for his paternal and maternal grandparents and his uncles. We shall have occasion to refer to these three windows again.

His descendants gradually extended their power and sway until by the time of the Spanish Conquest they had subdued almost all the tribes and kingdoms of the Andes and the West Coast from Quito in Ecuador to northern Argentina and central Chile in the south. Their rule was a benevolent despotism. Their armies were powerful. Their people were taught to speak the Quichua tongue. They were essentially agriculturists and delighted in practising the arts of peace rather than war. They did not like soldiers. As has been pointed out they called them "enemies." Finally, after some three centuries, the rulers became soft and luxury loving.

Then one day there appeared out of the north a small group of stocky warriors, wearing armor and carrying weapons "which used thunder and lightning" to carry death to soldiers at incredible distances. With them were strange animals, twice as large and strong as a llama, heavy enough to carry the armed cavaliers into battle. To a superstitious people the Spanish conquistadors appeared to be supernatural—possibly foreign gods with mysterious and dreadful powers.

The Emperor of the time, the Inca Atahualpa, a weak and vacillating monarch, was captured by Pizarro, threatened with death unless he would fill a room full of gold. To the Incas, gold was a precious metal, secured at great expense from the placer mines of the eastern Andes. The gold vessels they produced were extremely thin and disappointingly light in weight, so far as the avaricious conquerors were concerned. Furthermore, Pizarro learned that millions of Indians regarded Atahualpa as a god, a supreme ruler able to command their lives, but without whom they were uncertain what to do or how to act. Consequently the Inca was put to death, and Peru with its millions of people and its untold wealth fell into the hands of a small company of Spanish soldiers like manna from heaven. The story is one of the strangest miracles of history. It has been romantically told by the historian Prescott and others * and need not be repeated here as our story deals chiefly with the Incas who were set on the throne by Pizarro himself.

* NOTE: A new account, based on hundreds of hitherto unpublished documents and a scientific exploration of the route taken by Pizarro and his companions, is being prepared by the distinguished historian and biographer, Dr. Victor Wolfgang von Hagen.

3.

The Story
of the Last
Four Incas

We are told by Pedro Sancho, who was one of the secretaries of the great Pizarro, that as soon as Cuzco was captured by the Spaniards in 1533 the conqueror selected a young nobleman named Manco, who was prudent and active and seemed to him the best of the Incas. Conquistador Pizarro placed him on the throne of his ancestors in order that the Inca nobles and the military chieftains should not flee to their own lands and set up independent provinces, and should not join the northern Indians who were inclined to rebel against the rule of Atahualpa, whom Pizarro had just put to death. To prevent incipient rebellion and keep the disaffected Caciques from organizing hostile bands, he gave orders that they were to obey young Manco II and accept him as their emperor. As the grandson of the famous emperor Huyana the Great, he could be legally regarded as entitled to rule over the aborigines.

The young man was naturally very much pleased to be placed on the throne and crowned with the sacred fringe, which among the Incas, constituted the principal badge of sovereignty. He soon learned, however, that he was not his own master but was merely a puppet, obliged to take orders from the new conquerors. His ambition and his restless spirit led him to stage a revolt. After all, he knew he could command the services of thousands of Inca warriors. He knew that the Spanish conquerors were really only a handful of armed men, less than two hundred in number, and far from their base of supplies. He reckoned, however, without full conception of the difference between heavily armed men able to use weapons infinitely more efficient than the bows and arrows, spears, clubs, and sling stones on which his own soldiers had to depend. His men were brave and devoted but they were naturally terrified by the sounds of the Spanish field pieces and blunder-busses, as well as amazed at their ability to kill at a far greater distance than any weapon ever seen before. Manco was also grievously disappointed to find that the Spanish were able to secure the services of large numbers of disaffected Indians who had no feeling of loyalty to the new Inca. In 1536, after several bloody encounters, Manco's troops were routed and fled with him from the vicinity of Cuzco down into the Urubamba Valley.

A contemporary who wrote a graphic account of the wars of Peru a few years later says that Manco took with him a great quantity of treasure, including gold ornaments and "many loads of rich clothing of wool, delicate in texture and very beautiful and showy." The Spaniards believed that he had also burdened himself with much silver and gold. *We do know that he took with him the largest and most valuable of the gold images of the sun which had been in the principal temple in Cuzco.*

Manco also took with him his three sons. His second son Titu Cusi, seems to have been his favorite, although it was claimed that he was illegitimate because his mother was one of the concubines and was not the Empress or First Lady.

Some years later Titu Cusi dictated to a *mestizo*, whose father was a Spanish soldier and whose mother was a Quichua, an account of the life and death of the Inca Manco II. It appears that the *mestizo*, who spoke both his father's and mother's tongue, was able to prepare a crude translation, which, as it was intended to be sent to the King of Spain, was revised by an Augustinian missionary, Friar Marcos Garcia.

According to Titu Cusi's story, he was a little boy of six years when they fled from Cuzco into the Urubamba Valley. He remembers that his father, becoming aware that the Spaniards would soon descend from the plateau into the lovely temperate valley near Yucay, which was the favorite residence of the Incas, decided to take refuge in the lower Urubamba Valley beyond the Cordillera de Vilcabamba in one of the most inaccessible parts of the Andes. He remembers that when his father bade a tender and affectionate farewell to the soldiers who had been with him in his unsuccessful campaigns against the Spaniards they replied with great shouts which "seemed as if they would sink the hills."

Manco gave permission to all who wished to return to their own homes. Many, however, followed him, including some of his bravest captains who had survived the fierce battles fought during the revolt.

The last important town in the temperate valley they were about to leave is called Ollantaytambo. Before they left it to go their separate ways, Titu Cusi tells us, his father invited all the Indians of the region to come to a great feast. Apparently many of the soldiers got drunk and left their arms in their houses and were unable to defend themselves when a group of Spaniards took advantage of the farewell party to stage an attack. Titu Cusi says that the Spaniards seized some of the mummies of his ancestors who were being carried away from Cuzco, together with many jewels and precious objects. He claims that they drove off 50,000 head of llamas and alpacas. If this is true the number must have included many of the flocks and herds which the Inca Manco could rightfully claim as his own even though they were not at Ollantaytambo.

Titu Cusi says that his father escaped as best he could but that the Spaniards captured him with his mother and many of the royal family and carried them back in triumph to Cuzco with the booty they had taken.

The Spanish soldiers who attempted to follow Manco and the remains of his army found their position impregnable. Every one is familiar with the story of how hazardous it was for Hannibal and Napoleon, in different epochs, to bring their armies into Italy through the comparatively low passes of the Alps. It is not surprising that Pizarro found it impossible to follow the Inca Manco over passes which were higher than the very summit of Mont Blanc. In no part of the Peruvian Andes are there so many very beautiful snow peaks. Veronica (elevation 19,340 ft.), Salcanty (elevation 20,565 ft.), Soray (elevation 19,435 ft.), and Soiroccoha (elevation 18,197 ft.), are outstanding features of the landscape. Some of them are visible for a hundred miles. None of them have been climbed so far as is known.

On the shoulders of these mountains are scores of glaciers that have scarcely ever been visited except by some hardy prospector or inquisitive explorer. The valleys between them are to be reached only through passes 15,000 feet high where the traveler is likely to be halted by violent storms of hail and snow. During the rainy season a large part of the region beyond these mountains is impenetrable. Even in the dry season the difficulties of transportation are very great. The sure-footed mules of modern Peruvians are frequently unable to use the mountain trails without assistance. It will be easily recognized that this region was a natural fortress where the Inca Manco and his followers were defended by nature in one of her profoundest moods.

Manco's army fled over the Pass of Panticalla, went down the Lucumayo River, crossed the lower Urubamba on an Inca suspension bridge at a place called Chuquichaca. There they were able to enter one of the affluents of the Urubamba which to-day is called the Vilcabamba, and passing up that valley establish themselves in a pleasant region where their favorite crops could be grown and their llamas and alpacas find adequate pasturage.

Manco established himself on top of a mountain where he built a long "palace" and characteristic Inca structures. The place was called Vitcos or possibly Uiticos. Manco's refuge was also referred to by contemporary writers as Vilcapampa. The common name of the province was Vilcabamba. Of this I shall have more to say in a later chapter. Here, safe from the armed forces of his enemy, he was able to enjoy the benefits of a dry climate in a well-watered region where corn and potatoes, as well as the fruits of the temperate and sub-tropical zones grow rapidly.

Titu Cusi tells us that using Vitcos as a base, Manco and his captains were accustomed to sally forth against the Spaniards frequently and in unexpected directions. It was relatively easy for him, with a handful of followers, to dash out of the mountain fastnesses, cross the great river Apurimac on primitive rafts and reach the high road between the Spanish capital of Lima and the ancient city of Cuzco. As time went on, officials and merchants whose business forced them to use this road, the principle route across the Andes, found it becoming more and more precarious. Manco was able to encourage his followers by making them realize that in these raids they were taking sweet revenge on their conquerors. Even one of the Spanish chroniclers justifies Manco in these activities, remarking that the Spaniards had indeed stolen his inheritance and forced him to leave his native land and live in exile.

Manco's success in securing such an excellent place of refuge and in using it as a base from which he could make frequent raids led many Inca nobles to follow him and take up residence in the Cordillera Vilcabamba. While they had none of the weapons or armor used by the Spaniards, they were very efficient with the *bolas* and with slings. The Spaniards reported that the *bolas* were frequently thrown at their horses, binding their legs together and enabling them to be captured. They said that sometimes the bolas even pinned a man's arms to his side. They reported that the Incas, using large slings, could hurl heavy stones with sufficient force to kill a horse and even break a sword at a distance of thirty paces.

Manco's raids finally became so annoying that Pizarro sent

from Cuzco an expeditionary force to attempt to capture him, disperse his army and destroy his castles.

The Spanish soldiers found it impossible to use their horses and attempted to make a successful raid on foot. As might have been expected, while they were suffering from fatigue, exhausted by their difficult march and the *Soroche*, or mountain sickness which is very likely to affect Europeans at altitudes of more than 13,000 feet, they were ambushed by Manco's soldiers and almost all of them perished. To anyone who has climbed over the Pass of Panticalla, it is not surprising that Pizarro's expedition was a failure or that the Inca, warned by keen sighted Indians, posted according to their custom, on appropriate vantage points where they could signal with beacon fires, succeeded in defeating a small force of weary soldiers clad in armor and carrying the heavy blunderbuss of those days. Pizarro's men were probably stoned to death by the skillful operators of slings before they could even prepare their clumsy weapons for firing. The survivors returned to Cuzco with a vivid story of disaster and the conviction that the Pass of Panticalla was not to be used easily by an invading force. The affect of their story on Pizarro and his advisers and the importance of this reverse will be better appreciated if one remembers that the original size of the expedition which conquered Peru and captured Atahualpa was less than two hundred, only a few times larger than the company which had been wiped out by Manco's little band estimated by the Spaniards at only about eighty Indians. Possibly there were not even that many.

News of the disaster to his men was so startling, and so likely to cause further trouble among the thousands of Indians whom he was attempting to govern, that Pizarro himself hastily set out with a body of soldiers determined to punish young Manco who had inflicted such a blow on the prestige of Spanish arms. This attempt, however, also failed even though they succeeded in using the Pass of Panticalla because the Inca had withdrawn across the rivers and mountains destroying bridges and trails, safely reaching the inaccessible region around Vitcos.

Gonzalo Pizarro, the brother of the great Francisco, undertook the pursuit of the Inca and occupied some of the passes and bridges but was also unsuccessful in penetrating the mountain labyrinth. He did not come into actual conflict with Manco. Unable to subdue him or prevent disastrous raids on travelers between Cuzco and Lima, Francisco Pizarro established a fortified city called Ayacucho at a convenient point on the road so as to make it secure for travelers.

Francisco Pizarro was made a Marshal by the King of Spain, Charles V, but was bitterly opposed by Almagro, his original partner. In 1541 some of the followers of Almagro assassinated the Marshal, an event which must have brought joy to Manco in Vitcos. His joy did not last long, however, because the Almagrists were soon defeated and had to flee. Half a dozen of the refugees managed to get across the Apurimac and, protesting allegiance to the Inca, were kindly received by him in 1542. The leaders of the band were Gomez Perez and Diego Mendez, "rascals," says Father Calancha, "worthy of Manco's favor." (Father Calancha wrote a missionary chronicle from reports of Augustinian Friars who lived near Vitcos for some years.)

It is said that they instructed him in the use of firearms and in horsemanship. They may have been able to bring their horses with them. They also taught him how to play various games with which they were familiar, quoits, bowls and even chess and checkers—at least that is what we are told by the chroniclers. They took their games very seriously and occasionally violent disputes arose in which they were inclined to forget the rank of their host and how highly he was regarded by his people.

As long as Gonzalo Pizarro was in power they were glad to be Manco's guests, but one day they heard that Charles the Fifth had had enough of the rough conquistadors. In 1544 he sent out a Viceroy with a new code, the "New Laws," a result of the efforts of the good Bishop Las Casas to alleviate the sufferings of the Indians. The "New Laws" provided, among other things, that all the officers of the crown were to renounce their *repartimientos* or holdings of Indian serfs, and that compulsory personal service was to be entirely abolished. *Repartimientos* given to the conquerors were not to pass to their heirs, but were to revert to the king. In other words, the "New Laws" gave evidence that the Spanish crown wished to be kind to the Indians and did not approve of the Pizarros. This was good news for Manco and highly pleasing to the refugees. They persuaded the Inca to write a letter to the Viceroy, asking permission to appear before him and offer his services to the king. The Spanish refugees told the Inca that by this means he might some day recover his Empire, "or at least the best part of it." Their object in persuading the Inca to send such a message to the Viceroy becomes apparent when we learn that they "also wrote as from themselves desiring a pardon for what was past" and permission to return to Spanish dominions.

Gomez Perez, who seems to have been the most active leader of the little group, was selected to be the bearer of the letters from the Inca and the refugees. Attended by a dozen Indians whom the Inca instructed to act as his servants and bodyguard, he left Vitcos, presented his letters to the Viceroy, and gave him "a large relation of the State and Conditions of the Inca, and of his true and real designs to do him service. The Vice-king joyfully received the news and granted a full and ample pardon of all crimes, as desired. And as for the Inca, he made many kind expressions of love and respect, truly considering that the interest of the Inca might be advantageous to him, both in war and peace. And with this satisfactory answer Gomez Perez returned both to the Inca and to his companions." The refugees were delighted with the news and got ready to return to king and country. Their departure, however, was prevented by a tragic accident, thus described by Garcilasso Inca de la Vega:

"The Inca, to humour the Spaniards and entertain himself with them, had given directions for making a bowling-green; when playing one day with Gomez Perez, he came to have some quarrel and difference with this Perez about the measure of a Cast, which often happened between them; for this Perez, being a person of a hot and fiery brain, without any judgment or understanding, would take the least occasion in the world to contend with and provoke the Inca . . . Being no longer able to endure his rudeness, the Inca punched him on the breast, and bid him consider with whom he talked. Perez, not considering in his heart and passion either his own safety or the safety of his Companions, lifted up his hand, and with the bowl struck the Inca so violently on the head, that he knocked him down. (He died three days later.) The Indians hereupon, being enraged by the death of their Prince, joined together against Gomez and the Spaniards, who fled into a house, and with the swords in their hands defended the door; the Indians set fire to the house, which being too hot for them, they sallied out into the Marketplace, where the Indians assaulted them and shot them with their Arrows until they had killed every man of them; and then afterwards, out of mere rage and fury they designed either to eat them raw as their custom was, or to burn them and cast their ashes into the river, that no sign or appearance might remain of them; but at length, after some consultation, they agreed to cast their bodies into the open fields, to be devoured by vultures and birds of the air, which they supposed to be the highest indignity and dishonour that they could show to their Corps." Garcilasso concludes: "I informed myself very perfectly from those chiefs and nobles who were present and eye-witnesses of the unparalleled piece of madness of that rash and hair-brained fool; and heard them (he was five years old) tell this story to my mother and parents with tears in their eyes."

Garcilasso's story, written sixty years after the event, is redolent of punishments he doubtless became acquainted with during the years he served in the army of Spain.

There are many versions of the tragedy. One version is that the quarrel was over a game of chess between the Inca and Diego Mendez, another of the refugees, who lost his temper and called the Inca a dog. Angered at the tone and language of his guest, the Inca gave him a blow with his fist. Diego Mendez thereupon drew a dagger and killed him.

A totally different account from the one obtained by Garcilasso from his informants is that given by an eye-witness, Manco's son, Titu Cusi, twenty years after the event.

He says that his father "because he did not like to be without me, sent to Cuzco for me. The messengers took me and my mother secretly to the town of Vitcos, where my father had come for fresh air, it being a cold land. There I and my Father stayed for many days. At different times seven Spaniards arrived, saying that they were fugitives owing to having committed offences, and they protested that they would serve my Father with all their power, for the remainder of their lives. They prayed that they might be allowed to remain in that land and end their days there. My father, thinking that they came with good intentions, ordered his captains to do them no harm, for he wished to keep them as his servants, and that they should have houses in which to live. The captains would much rather have put an end to them, but obeyed my father's orders. My father had them with him for many days and years, treating them very well, and giving them all that they needed, even ordering his own women to prepare their food and their beverage, and taking meals with them. He treated them as if they were his own brothers."

"After these Spaniards had been with my father for several years in the said town of Vitcos they were one day, with much good fellowship, playing at quoits with him; only them, my Father, and me, who was then a boy. (He was about fifteen years old.) In this game, just as my father was raising the quoit to throw, they all rushed upon him with knives, daggers, and some swords. My father, feeling himself wounded, strove to make some defense, but he was one and unarmed, and they were seven fully armed; he fell to the ground covered with wounds, and they left him for dead. I, being a little boy, and seeing my Father treated in this manner, wanted to go where he was to help him. But they turned furiously upon me, and hurled a lance which only just failed to kill me also. I was terrified and fled amongst some bushes. They looked for me, but could not find me. The Spaniards, seeing that my father had ceased to breathe, went out of the gate, in high spirits, saying, 'Now that we have killed the Inca we have nothing to fear.' But at this moment the Captain Rimachi Yupanqui ('rich in all virtues') arrived with some Antis, and presently chased them in such sort that, before they could get very far along a difficult road, they were caught and pulled from their horses. They all had to suffer very cruel deaths and some were burnt. Notwithstanding his wounds my father lived for three days."

SAYRI TUPAC

On the death of the Inca Manco in 1545, his oldest son, Sayri Tupac, still a minor, ruled in his father's stead. He was not at all warlike but on the other hand seems to have been fond of luxury and comfort. With the aid of the nobles and chieftains who had been his father's friends and supporters he reigned for ten years without disturbing his Spanish neighbors or arousing their hostility.

In 1555 a new Viceroy from Spain decided to attempt to make a peaceful conquest of this difficult region by inviting young Sayri Tupac to come out of the inaccessible wilds of the Cordillera Vilcabamba and live in the fertile and attractive valley of Yucay, not many miles from Cuzco. It has a temperate climate, produces lovely flowers and luscious fruits, and has frequently been called one of the beauty spots of the world.

The Viceroy undertook to accomplish this matter through an aunt of the young man who was living in Cuzco. She sent a trusted ambassador, one of her relatives of the blood royal, attended by faithful retainers. Sayri Tupac's counselors permitted the messenger to enter Vitcos and deliver the Viceroy's invitation. But with their knowledge of the Conquistadors, who had not built up much of a reputation for integrity and honor, the Inca nobles were not inclined to advise Sayri Tupac to place himself in the Viceroy's hands. Accordingly they kept the visitor as a hostage and sent a messenger of their own to Cuzco to ask that a more trusted cousin be sent as ambassador.

In the meantime the Viceroy had become annoyed with this delay and sent from Lima a priest, and a soldier who had married the daughter of the unfortunate Inca Atahualpa and had learned to speak Quichua. They started off quite confidently on their mission, taking with them as presents for the young Sayri Tupac and his friends, silver cups and Spanish velvet. They traveled as fast as they could but were detained at the bridge of Chuquichaca which was the key to the valley in which Vitcos was situated. Here they were joined by the Inca's cousin, who had been sent for by the nobles and who arrived at the bridge a few days after them. He was welcomed by the Inca nobles and did his best to encourage Sayri Tupac to accept the Viceroy's offer. At his suggestion the Viceroy's messengers were admitted to the presence of the Inca. They offered the presents which the Viceroy had sent, but were disappointed to find that Sayri Tupac seemed to prefer to remain free and independent in his secluded valley. He asked them to take back the silver cups to the Viceroy. A few days later, however, after listening to the many interesting stories of life in Cuzco as told by his cousin, the young Inca finally decided to reconsider the matter and accept the Viceroy's invitation, notwithstanding the advice of his nobles.

Anxious to see something of the world, only known to him by rumor, Sayri Tupac even went to Lima, traveling in regal state, carried in a litter by faithful retainers and accompanied by some 300 Indians. He was kindly received by the Viceroy and sent back to Cuzco where for a time he lodged in one of the old Inca palaces. His cousin, Garcilasso, says that he himself as a young boy went to see Sayri Tupac, found him playing games and was invited to stay and enjoy a few cups of excellent *chicha*.

The Viceroy, carrying out his original plan, now ordered that Sayri Tupac should publicly receive the sacred red fringe of Inca sovereignty, embrace Christianity, be married to a princess of the Blood Royal, and take up his abode as planned, in beautiful Yucay. Here, Sayri Tupac's fondness for comfort and luxury was readily gratified. He was surrounded by devoted retainers who took delight in attending to the wants of the wearer of the sacred red fringe. He was seemingly well contented with his lot and neither ambitious nor restless. Of course he might have served as the focus for an uprising against the Spaniards but so far as we know there is no evidence that he wished to do so. Nevertheless he only lived in Yucay for about two years. The Viceroy said he died of disease. The nobles in Vitcos believed he was poisoned. At all events in 1560 his half brother, Titu Cusi, the favorite, if illegitimate, son of Manco, immediately assumed the throne, not at Cuzco or Yucay but in the wilds of Vilcambamba.

Titu Cusi

Thanks to Titu Cusi's own narrative, already referred to in the account of his father's life and violent death, and to Father Calancha's chronicle, we know more about Titu Cusi than about any of his brothers or his father.

It will be remembered that he had lived for some years as a little boy in Cuzco but had managed to escape from his captors and was with his father Manco, living in Vitcos at the time of the fatal game of quoits or bowls which resulted so badly for the Spanish refugees as well as for the Inca.

We do not know where he was at the time of Sayri Tupac's death but we are told that as soon as he heard of it he fled into the inaccessible valleys of the Cordillera Vilcabamba, put his younger brother Tupac Amaru "into the House of the Sun with the Chosen Virgins and their Matrons" and assumed the throne of the now greatly shrunken Inca Empire. Titu Cusi was then about thirty years old.

Captain Baltasar de Ocampo, a contemporary Spanish soldier who went to the Vilcabamba valley after gold a few years later prepared an account of the Province. In it he says that Tupac Amaru "was the natural and legitimate Lord of these lands . . . but the elder brother by his management and cunning kept him secluded and imprisoned on account of his want of experience, usurping the government for himself." However he also says that to place him with the Virgins of the Sun was "a most ancient custom among all the rulers of these kingdoms before the arrival of the Spaniards."

A great sanctuary, provided well with temples, baths and trained handmaidens must have been an ideal place for the young man. He probably spent most of the next ten years among its temples and palaces. Since its whereabouts were unknown to the Spaniards it would also have been a favorite residence for Titu Cusi himself where he would have been well taken care of by the Chosen Women. His mother seems to have stayed there also. But it was necessary for him to spend a good part of his time with his councillors and his army at Vitcos.

One of his first visitors at Vitcos was Don Diego Rodriguez de Figueroa, who, acting under the Viceroy's orders, attempted to convert Titu Cusi to Christianity and persuade him to leave Vilcabamba. Fortunately Rodriguez wrote a full account of his trip. His narrative is entertaining and shows clearly the precautions which Titu Cusi took to keep out strangers.

Unlike so many of our sources of knowledge of the Incas it was not written from hearsay or long after the event. So it is worth quoting at some length.

Rodriguez, according to Sir Clements Markham's translation, wrote as follows:

"I left Cuzco on the 8th of April 1565, after having received letters from Judge Matienzo to the Inca Titu Cusi Yupanqui, with leave to make an entrance, after having offered my services to go by that route. I went to sleep at Ollantaytambo, where they gave me seven Indian carriers to show me the way." He then went over the Pass of Panticalla and down the Lucumayo river to an ancient suspension bridge.

"On the 5th day of May ten (Inca) captains came to the bridge, richly dressed with diadems of plumes, and lances in their hands which they brandished, and wearing masks on their faces. They came to the passage of the bridge where I was, and asked me if I was the man who had the audacity to want to come and speak to the Inca. I said yes. They replied that I could not fail to be much afraid, and if I felt fear I could not come, because the Inca was a great enemy of cowards. To this I answered that if he was an elephant or a giant I might be afraid, but as he was a man like myself I had no fear, but I would offer him respect. If he would let me enter under his word, I would do so, for I knew that he would keep it." Apparently he did not like the bridge or they were afraid to let him use it, because he says that, "On the 6th day of May I crossed the river in a basket travelling along a cable, and seven Indians came with me. The ten Indians of the Inca helped me to cross, and accompanied me. That night I slept at the foot of a snowy mountain."

"I set out on the 12th of May and went on to Vitcos where the seven Spaniards killed the Inca, and their heads are exposed. The Indians told me that those Spaniards had killed him to raise the land, and that they determined to kill him while playing at *la herradura* (horse-shoe quoits). One Mendez did it with four or five stabs behind him until he killed him; and to Titu Cusi, the Inca who is now, they would have done the same, but he escaped down some rocks, which they showed me. If they had wanted to kill some Indians they could have done so, but their object was to kill the Inca. Then many Indians and captains assembled, who seized the Spaniards and killed them."

It will be noticed that this version differs from the one told by Garcilasso and by Titu Cusi himself. They made it sound more like an accident in a quarrel. Since the regicides were renegades and outlaws, it was perhaps natural that Rodriguez as an official of the vice-regal government, should have felt no compunction in accusing them of treachery to their host.

Rodriguez continues: "On the 13th of May I sent two of my Indians to the Inca with some refreshments of raisins, figs, and other things. The Inca received them well, and gave them two baskets of peanuts which they were to take to me, with a message that next day he would arrive, so that we should see each other soon, and that I need not travel further."

"On the 14th of May the Indians of Bambacona had made me a large house on a strong height surrounded by entrenchments. Below were the houses of the inhabitants. The road by which he was to come was very clean and passed over a great plain. The three hundred Indians with their lances, and others from the surrounding country, had made a great theatre for the Inca, of red clay. They were awaiting his arrival, and wished me to go out to meet him. They told me that the people of the village would wait on the plain, and that they would show me a place where they had brought two loads of straw, half a stone's throw from the rest of the people. They told me to wait there, and see the entry of the Inca, and not to move until the Inca sent for me."

"Many lances were drawn up on a hill, and messengers arrived to say that the Inca was coming. Presently the escort of the Inca began to appear." Rodriguez now does us the great service of describing as accurately as he can, the formal dress deemed appropriate for the Emperors of Peru in the days of Inca power and majesty. "The Inca came in front of all, with a head-dress of plumes of many colours, a silver plate on his breast, a golden shield in one hand, and a lance all of gold. He wore garters of feathers and fastened to them were small wooden bells. On his head was a diadem and another around the neck. In one hand he had a gilded dagger, and he came in a mask of several colours." From this description, the Spanish artists of the XVI and XVII Centuries drew their pictures of Inca Emperors they had never seen. Copies may be seen in Cuzco.

"Arriving on the plateau where the places of the people were, and his seat was set up, and mine, he gazed where the sun was, making a sort of reverence with his hand, which they call *mucha*, (a kiss) and then went to his seat. There came with him a *mestizo* with a shield and sword, and in a Spanish dress, a very old cloak. Presently he turned his eyes in the direction where I was, and I took off my hat. The Indians did not notice this. I held up an image of Our Lady which I carried in my bosom, and though the Indians saw it, they took no notice. Then two *orejones* (big-ears, nobles)

came near the Inca with two halberds, dressed in diadems of
plumes with much adornment of gold and silver. These made
obeisance and reference to the sun and then to the Inca. All the
rest were standing near his seat, encircling him in good order.
Presently the governor came, named Yamqui Mayta, with sixty
or seventy attendants with their silver plates, lances, belts of gold
and silver, the same dresses as were worn by all who came with the
Inca. Then came the Master of the Camp with the same gaily
dressed following; and all made obeisance first to the sun and then
to the Inca, saying, 'Child of the Sun thou art the child of the
day.' Then they took up their position round the Inca. Then
another captain entered, named Vilcapari Guaman, with about
thirty Indians bearing lances adorned with feathers of many
colours. Then twenty men with axes, making reverence to the
sun like the rest. All wore masks of different colours, which they
put before their faces. Next a little Indian entered who, after
making reverences to the sun and the Inca, came towards me,
brandishing a lance, and raising it with great audacity. He then
began to cry out in Spanish 'Get out! get out!' and to menace me
with his lance. Next another captain entered named Cusi Puma,
with about fifty archers, who are Antis eating human flesh.
Presently all these warriors took off their plumes of feathers and
put down their lances. With their daggers of bronze and their
shields of silver, or leather, or of feathers, each one came to do
reverence to the Inca who was seated, and then returned to their
places."

"Presently he sent for me, and passing through that multitude
of Indians, I took off my hat and made a speech to him. I said that
I had come from Cuzco solely to know and serve him. If I wore a
sword and dagger it was to serve him with them and not to offend
him. To this he answered that it was for men to bear arms and
not for women or cowards, and he did not, therefore, hold me in
more esteem for that. But he said he was pleased at the trouble I
had taken to come from such a distance to him, adding that he had
come forty leagues only to see and converse with me. Then he

gave me a cup of chicha, asking me to drink it for his service. I drank a quarter of it, and then began to make faces and wipe my mouth with a handkerchief. He began to laugh, understanding that I did not know that liquor."

"The Inca was a man of forty years of age, of middle height, and with some marks of smallpox on his face. His mien rather severe and manly. He wore a shirt of blue damask, and a mantle of very fine cloth. He is served on silver, and there are also twenty or thirty good-looking women, waiting behind him. He sent for me to eat where he was with his women and his governor. The food consisted of maize, potatoes, small beans, and the other products of the country, except that there was very little meat, and what there was consisted of venison, fowls, macaws, and monkeys, both boiled and roasted. When night came on he asked me whether I had made the acquaintance of his captains. I replied in the affirmative and he then took leave of me. He went to the house that had been prepared for him, in exactly the same order as when he arrived, with music of silver flutes and trumpets. That night there was a guard of a hundred Indians who were divided into watches, and flutes and drums were played to call each watch. They placed a guard of fifteen Indians over me with their lances, I being in a house outside the village. I calculate that all the Indians who came with the Inca, and those of the village numbered 450.

"In the morning of the 15th of May the Inca sent for me to his house, for it was raining. The greater part of his troops were seated round a large fire. The Inca was seated, dressed in a shirt of crimson velvet, with a mantle of the same. All his captains had taken off the masks they wore on the day before. . . ."

"As daylight was now appearing, and they had all drunk freely, I asked permission of the Inca to return to my lodging and get something to eat, and that another day I would state frankly what I had come for. So I departed, leaving them to boast loudly, but all much disturbed in their minds."

"Soon afterwards they sent me a sheep of Castille, (evidently, the result of a successful raid on a Spanish colonial sheep ranch), many fowls and partridges, and other food which their country produces. To those who brought them I gave some trinkets, needles, and other Spanish things. Presently the Inca sent for me. I went there, and was there until night, without a word being spoken, when I returned to my lodging. The reason for this appeared to be that too much *chicha* had been drunk." Even today the Quichuas are noticeably not talkative after consuming much *chicha*.

Rodriquez had brought presents for the Inca, silver bracelets, crystals, and pearls. With the Inca's permission, he was permitted to deliver a discourse on Christianity and suggested the propriety of setting up crosses as evidence of faith. This pleased the Inca not at all and he said he had a good mind to order the intruder killed.

"From the top of a rising ground," says Rodriguez, "I saw the festivities made for the Inca, and heard the songs. The dances were war dances with spears in their hands, throwing them from one to another. I believe that they did such things by reason of the quantity of *chicha* they had drunk."

"The Inca sent for me late in the afternoon and I went against my will. He told me to sit down and began to boast, saying that he could himself kill fifty Spaniards and that he was going to have all the Spaniards in the kingdom put to death. He took a lance in his hand and a shield and began to act a valiant man, shouting 'Go at once and bring me all the people that are behind those mountains; for I want to go and fight the Spaniards and to kill them all, and I want the wild Indians to eat them.' "

"Then there marched up about 600 or 700 Antis Indians, all with bows and arrows, clubs and axes. They advanced in good order, making reverence to the sun and to the Inca and took their positions. Then the Inca again began to brandish his lance, and said that he could raise all the Indians in Peru, he had only to give the order and they would fly to arms. Then all those Antis made an offer to the Inca that, if he wished it, they would eat me raw. They said to him, 'What are you doing with this little bearded one here, who is trying to deceive you? It is better that we should eat him at once.' Then two renegade Inca *orejones* came straight to me with spears in their hands, flourishing their weapons and saying, 'The bearded ones! Our enemies.' I laughed at this, but at the same time commended myself to God. I asked the Inca to have mercy and protect me, and so he delivered me from them, and hid me until morning." Apparently Titu Cusi was a little bit afraid his nobles might go too far in their desire to take revenge on one of the hated Spaniards.

"On the morning of the 16th of May the Inca sent for me to come to the open square which he entered in the same order as before, and as I came in I saluted the Inca and sat down. The Inca and all the captains then began to laugh heartily at what had happened the day before, and they asked me what I thought of yesterday's festival. I replied that I thought it rather exceptional, and that to have treated me so was wrong, seeing that I had come on serious business. They explained that it was only their fun, and that they could not give it up. . . ."

Apparently to please his visitor, Titu Cusi permitted a cross to be set up near where he was staying. Then Rodriguez told Titu Cusi of the might and power of Charles V of Spain.

"To this he replied that the power of the king was great, and though he had so many nations, as well black men as Moors, subject to him, yet he, the Inca, like Manco Inca his father before him, knew how to defend himself in those mountains . . . Presently he sent to Vilcapampa for more men." The first lot of soldiers had apparently come up the Pampaconas valley from the warm jungles and were savages with bows and arrows. Now, to impress Rodriguez, Titu Cusi sent to the ancient sanctuary, his other capital called Vilcapampa, for some highland warriors.

"On the 25th of May one of his generals arrived with 300 men, armed with lances, who entered the open place where the rest were drawn up, and made obeisance to the Sun and to the Inca. Then a hundred captains of those who came from Vilcapampa went to where Yamqui Mayta was standing and asked why he had consented to have the cross planted in their land, seeing that it had not been set up in the time of Manco Inca. Why then was it there now? If I had persuaded the Inca to do this, they intended to kill me. The Inca replied that it was done by his order, and that it was well that they should accept the cross of the creator of all things. Having received this answer they went to their seats, and the festival proceeded."

Rodriguez was a man of courage and profound convictions and carried himself with so much bravery and tact that he succeeded to a large extent in arousing the Inca's admiration and respect and made him almost willing to assent to the proposal that he follow in the footsteps of Sayri Tupac, leaving Vitcos and going to Yucay to live in comfort, surrounded with all due honor.

Sufficient progress was reported by Rodriguez to encourage another ambassador, accompanied by thirty Spanish soldiers and a number of Indian guards, to reach the key bridge at Chuquichaca. The sight of this armed force, which included twenty harquebusiers, so alarmed Titu Cusi, however, that he caused the bridge to be torn down, sent Rodriguez and all the Spanish envoys back to Cuzco and retired to Vitcos.

Nevertheless he appears to have kept as his Secretary, a *mestizo*, one Martin Pando, who probably spoke both Spanish and Quichua.

Martin Pando seems to have lived in Vitcos or the neighboring village of Puquiura for the next five years and to have won the confidence of Titu Cusi to such an extent that the Inca decided to carry on a correspondence with the Spanish authorities. It may have been due to his influence that about three years later, Titu Cusi apparently became convinced that he might be better off if he adopted the religion of the conquerors.

One cannot help wondering whether the news of the abdication of Charles the Fifth and the accession of his intensely zealous and intolerant son Philip II to the throne of Spain and the Indies in 1565 may not have penetrated to Vitcos and led some of Titu Cusi's advisers—and possibly his relatives in Cuzco—to suggest the wisdom of his adopting the forms of Christianity, welcoming the monks, and finally appealing to Philip II to recognize his right to sit on his father's throne and wear the sacred fringe of Inca sovereignty. At all events, in a letter to Don Lopez Garcia de Castro, the Governor of Cuzco and a Member of the Council of the Indies, in which it certainly looks as though they were trying to please that bigoted monarch, Titu Cusi said:

"Having received letters from your Lordship, asking me to become a Christian and saying that it would conduce to the security of the country, I enquired of Diego Rodriguez and Martin de Pando, as to who was the principal monk among those who were in Cuzco, and who were the most approved and of most weight among the religious orders. They replied that the most flourishing were those of St. Augustine, and their Prior was the most important priest in Cuzco. Having heard this, I became more attached to the order of St. Augustine than any other. I wrote letters to the Prior, requesting him to come in person to baptize me, because I would rather be baptized by him than by anyone else. He took the trouble to come to my country and to baptize me, bringing with him another monk, and Gonzalo Perez de Vivero and Atilano de Anaya who arrived at Rayangalla (Huarancalque?) on the 12th of August, 1568, whither I came from Vilcapampa to receive baptism. There, in that village of Rayangalla, were the said Prior named Juan de Vivero and his companions. I was instructed in the things of the faith for a fortnight, at the end of which time, on the day of the famous St. Augustine, the Prior baptized me." He was given the name of Diego, and the family name of Governor de Castro. "My godfather was Gonzalo Perez de Vivero and my godmother Dona Angelina Zica Ocllo. After I was baptized the Prior remained for eight days to instruct me in the Holy Catholic Church and to initiate me into its mysteries. He then departed with Gonzalo Perez de Vivero, leaving me a companion named Friar Marcos Garcia, that he might little by little instill into my mind what the Prior had taught, that I might not forget, and also to teach the word of God to the people of my land. Before he departed I explained to my followers the reason why I had been baptized, and had brought these people into my land. All replied that they rejoiced at my baptism, and that the friar should remain. In effect the friar did remain with me."

How two Augustinian Friars almost got inside the walls of the great Inca sanctuary then called Vilcapampa is told in Father Calancha's long "Moralizing Chronicle of the activities of the Order in Peru." From occasional sentences in its hundreds of folio pages has been gathered a story which throws an interesting light on some of the things that took place behind the snowy passes of the Cordillera Vilcabamba during the reign of Titu Cusi.

Father Calancha was chiefly interested in providing material for the sermons preached by his fellow monks, so more than nine-tenths of his Chronicle is taken up with references to the lives of the Saints and their Teachings. Consequently it has not been reprinted since 1639, and probably never will be.

Of the "Province of Vilcabamba" he says: "It is a hot country of the Andes and is mountainous and includes parts that are very cold, intemperate bleak uplands. It has hills of silver from which some quantity has been taken and it produces gold of which in those days much was found . . . It is a land of moderate comfort, large rivers and almost ordinary rains." (!) As a matter af fact, it is far more rainy than most of the Peruvian cities.

"To these Andes and highlands came the Father Friar Marcos Garcia in the year 1566 after he had been a missionary for three years in the city and valley of Capinota." Capinota does not appear on any map but it may have been the town now called Qquente or Patallacta and the valley variously known as Pampacahuana or Chamana, a few miles down the Urubamba valley below Ollantaytambo, where there are a large number of ruined sites. While there, he would have been likely to have heard about the Inca Sanctuary at Vilcapampa. At all events, Calancha says that the results of Friar Marcos' work in Capinota "fired him with the desire to seek souls where not a single preacher had entered and where the gospel message had not been heard."

"He communicated his holy impulse to the worthy Father Friar Juan de Vivero who was the Prior of the Augustinian Monastery in Cuzco and the Supervisor of those territories. The Prior approved his plan, gave him the authority of a direct mandate, as well as the sacred vestments and whatever he needed for his journey, and sent him to convert those infidels. He found the journey full of difficulties because the Inca had cut the bridges, walled up the passes and flooded the roads. When Friar Marcos asked directions as to the road from passing Indians they replied either that they did not know—which was what they had been instructed by the King to say—or else they said that they believed the route was practically impassable and the difficulties so great as to leave no hope of using it 'unless one had the wings of a bird'. However, he arrived, after many trials, in the presence of the Inca "who received him badly and was vexed and grieved to see that Spaniards had been able to penetrate his retreat, particularly to see one arrive to preach against his idolatries in his own towns."

This, it will be noticed, is quite a different story from the one told by Titu Cusi himself in his letter to the Governor of Cuzco, in which he says that he invited the Prior of the Monastery to come to "Rayangalla" where Juan de Vivero baptized him and then departed leaving Friar Marcos as his chaplain.

Calancha's story naturally differs from the version which Titu Cusi wanted the authorities to believe. Nevertheless, Father Marcos gained the good will of the Inca and secured license to preach. Accordingly "he abandoned caution and unfurled the standard of the cross." He built a church in Puquiura, "two long days journeys from Vilcapampa." Puquiura was a town "in which the Inca King held his court and his armies." Friar Marcos was disappointed to find it so far from the great sanctuary. Nevertheless, "he set up crosses in the land and in the forests."

Finally it was decided by the Cuzco Prior to send Friar Diego to join Friar Marcos in the valley of the Vilcabamba river. He made his journey alone, "suffering much on the way, not so much because of leagues and distances—for from Cuzco to the first lands of Vilcabamba it is little more than ten leagues," (actually about forty miles) as because of having to find detours and "having no guides for entering the mountains; and because, the rivers had no bridges, and the roads shifted in position with every freshet." He penetrated into the Inca's retreats, and accompanied by Friar Marcos entered his presence. If the Inca was not overjoyed to see the new preacher, he at least was pleased because he knew that Friar Marcos wished to return to Cuzco and he thought that Friar Diego, "would not try to reprimand him." Father Marcos was a crusading preacher who was angry at his inability to make much of any impression on Titu Cusi.

Friar Diego, a gentler soul, a medical missionary, much liked by the Indians, "within a few days, so gained the Inca's good will that he gave him a feast whenever the father visited him, saying that he loved him like a brother." He sent him presents of fowls and food from his own stores (though this was done in order to make Friar Marcos envious). "However, as the spirit of this blessed man was not seeking of gifts, but the winning of souls and dissemination of the faith, he asked the Inca's permission to found another church and to indoctrinate another different pueblo." Titu Cusi granted him the permission, and he chose the pueblo of Guarancalla, probably the village of Huarancalque. "It was a distance of two or three days' travel from one convent to the other." Friar Diego built a church, a dwelling, and arranged a hospital, "all of them being poor edifices which the Indians, with love and ardor, completed quickly. He went about the country erecting tall crosses, and those sacred trees were planted throughout the mountains and on the (heathen) temples, the idols being thrown down. The sorcerers (echizeros) raged, but the other Indians rejoiced at his actions, for they loved him devotedly, influenced not so much by the virtues which they recognized in him, as by the continuous benefactions with which he won them, curing them, clothing them, teaching them. He assembled many children and became their schoolmaster, their numbers increasing every day; and many of both sexes and all ages asked for baptism.

The Christian community increased gloriously within a few months, the blessed Friar Diego bringing Indians from the depths of the forest jungles, attracting them with kindness, controlling them by prayer and holding them by his benefactions . . ." Huarancalque is near a pass which leads down into the warm valley of the Pampaconas, still the abode of savage Indians.

Calancha says that while Friar Diego was busy with the advancement of his church, beloved by all, Friar Marcos "was suffering persecution, because he, with Catholic courage, rebuked some superstitions among the principal Indians, and some heathen actions on the part of the Inca, exhorting them to put an end to the drunkenness which is the cause of all the misfortunes of these Indians. It precipitates them into incest, sodomy and homicide, and there is rarely a drinking bout that is not mixed with heathen rites, the Devil often being visibly present, disguised in the person of an Indian." Friar Marcos carried on such a violent crusade against the bibulous habits of Titu Cusi and his nobles as greatly to irritate the Inca and his caciques. They even attempted to kill the father secretly, "by giving him deadly herbs and powders. Notwithstanding that secrecy was imposed, there was one who pretended to hate Father Marcos, in order not to anger the Inca, but was a Catholic and secretly the Father's friend. He warned him that they wished to kill him and that he should be careful. The afflicted monk remained in his place, but seeing that the poisoners stayed near him, he determined to go to Cuzco."

He notified Father Diego of his decision, "entrusted to him the ornaments of the church, and alone, on foot, with two fragments of bread, he advanced slowly through the country, planning to travel more rapidly after dark and enter a less dangerous valley at daybreak, reaching Cuzco in two to four days. The Inca learned of it. The news must have been given to him by the Indian with whom the Father left the church ornaments, not through enmity but in order that the father, whom the poor and lowly Indians loved so devotedly, might not leave them. The Indians would not have known that they were attempting to kill him."

The Inca was angry and sent five of his captains with lances to fetch the father. Titu Cusi gave him "an insulting reprimand, abusing him for leaving his province without permission." Father Marcos prudently replied, "Señor, the Indians whom you have in this pueblo do not desire to receive the faith, nor to hear the word of God; they run away from me and insult the holy doctrines which I preach to them, most of those who requested baptism being already enemies of Christ our Creator. If your Indians had received the faith, or if those who did receive it had not apostatized, I would remain among them until death. Those who now accept the faith and are baptized are Indians who came from Cuzco; others fear to come to me." The Inca then told him to return to his church.

One day Friar Marcos and Friar Diego were with Titu Cusi when he said that he was willing to take them to the city of Vilcapampa, his "principal seat" which neither of them had seen. He said, "Come with me; I desire to entertain you." They left the next day with the Inca who was accompanied by a small party of his captains and caciques. "They came to a place called Ungacacha, and there perpetrated the infamy they had plotted, which was that they covered the roads with water, the country being inundated by turning the river from its course, because the fathers desired and had often attempted to go to Vilcapampa to preach, because it was the chief town and the one in which was the University of Idolatry and the professors of witchcraft, teachers of the abominations."

"The Inca, in order to frighten them, so that they would not attempt to live or preach in Vilcapampa, but would leave the province, plotted a sacrilegious and diabolical scheme. Shortly after daylight, on descending to a plain, the monks thought they had come to a lake. The Inca said to them, 'all of us must pass through this water.' O cruel apostate! [The Inca did not take his Christian baptism as seriously as the monks wished he had.] He traveled in a litter and the two priests on foot, without shoes! The two ministers went into the water and proceeded joyfully, as if they were treading on fine carpets, for they knew they were receiving these insults and torments because of the Inca's hatred of their preaching." Waist-deep in water and chilled through, they slipped and fell "and there was no one to help them up. They held each other's hands while those sacrilegious ones shouted with laughter and amused themselves by insulting them. With their habits soaked in water, and in bitter cold weather, these servants of God traveled on, not showing signs of anger or irritation."

"Cold and covered with mud, they came out on dry land and there the Inca told them that he had come by that difficult route because he thought it would so disgust them with the attempt to settle in Vilcapampa that they would go from thence to Cuzco. . . ." It is three days' journey from Puquiura to Machu Picchu.

It is important to remember that the missionaries reported that it was a terribly cold and tiresome journey of three days' duration between the two capitals of Titu Cusi, the headquarters of his army at Puquiura and his principal seat, the great sanctuary of Vilcapampa the Old, a place the Spaniards never found or saw. Nevertheless Father Calancha says the monks finally reached its vicinity and continued preaching for three weeks. "The Inca did not wish the fathers to live in the town and ordered that they be given lodging outside so that they might not see the worship, ceremonies and rites in which the Inca and his captains participated daily with their socerers."

Undoubtedly, since this was the principal city in the whole province and admittedly a great sanctuary, it must have had fine temples and palaces as well as priests and Virgins of the Sun but the Inca kept the missionaries from seeing the sacred city or even having any idea of its beautiful buildings. Titu Cusi had no intention of allowing the Friars to enter his "University of Idolatry" or desecrate the precious sanctuary. He had done his best to keep them away and discourage them from ever wanting to come again. Nothing daunted, the monks took advantage of their situation to preach against the idols, emphasizing their abomination. Since the

great mass of the common people were not admitted to the sanctuary but lived in its vicinity, the friars had a large audience whom
they attempted to convert. This naturally put the Inca and his
captains in a rage, and set them to plotting revenge. He consulted
his sorcerers as to what could be done to subdue the friars and
silence them. "The sorcerers asked for a day in which to consult
on the matter with the demons that they called idols or Gods."

"The result of the infernal conference was that since their
enemies, the friars would not succumb to offers of gold or silver,
they must be subdued by being made to violate their vow of
chastity." Titu Cusi and his advisers selected among the Chosen
Women the very handsomest, not only those from the highlands
but particularly ones from the warm and humid valleys in the
coastal provinces where modesty and chastity were unknown,
women regarded as the "most beautiful and pleasing of those
regions, the most elegantly adorned and doubtless the most seduc-
tive."

The Chosen Women were "assured that they could subdue
these servants of God and thus win the Inca's praise." They "made
use of all that the devil knew how to teach them, practicing all the
arts of sensuality and the most dangerous gifts of seduction. But
these apostolic men defended themselves so valiantly that the
women returned, defeated and abashed, the friars remaining
humble and victorious."

"The Inca and his socerers, irritated by their failure and raging
at the affront, went again to consult the Devil and from this conference came another and more outrageous expedient. They made
habits from black and white blankets, dressed many of the most
beautiful and dissolute Indian women in them, and sent them (to
the friars) in this order: two went out wearing black habits and
came to where the priests were, pretending that it was a gesture
to amuse and entertain them. There they did what the demons
had instructed them, but the servants of God thrust them out with
reproaches." At an unseemly hour two others came wearing white
habits, who looked like friars. Since neither the Indians' rooms

nor their taverns had any keys or doors, the women were able to reach the friars' beds. However, these "emissaries of hell, novices of deceit and devotees of lust made no impression on the friars. . . . If they came by day to their infernal battle, they reproached them; if by night, they preached to them until, seeing that they were defeated, they did not return. . . . This battery of women continued day and night, the habits being changed and different Indians always being sent. If the monks left their houses and went into the country, they sought them out. The attackers did not cease to contrive new wiles and to present terrible temptations."

While the efforts of the Inca and the Priests of the Sun were in vain, the Friars finally became discouraged, realized that they were not making any headway and were not to be allowed in the sanctuary of Vilcapampa. So they asked the Inca's permission to go back to their churches and schools in Puquiura and Guarancalla.

Notwithstanding the unpleasant experiences in the neighborhood of Vilcapampa the Old, they still were willing to try to please Titu Cusi. Matters seem to have gone along smoothly for a time and Titu Cusi even went so far as to dictate to Friar Marcos the account of the life and death of his father Manco which already has been referred to several times. He in turn dictated it to Martin Pando, the educated young *mestizo*, trusted by the Inca, who got into the Vilcabamba valley with Rodriguez. He says he wrote it with his very own hands in the presence of Father Diego Ortiz and three of Titu Cusi's captains. He gives the location as "San Salvador de Vilcabamba," a place not known today, possibly the residence of Friar Marcos. The account was signed by Titu Cusi and witnessed by both the Augustinian monks, in February, 1670. It was in the nature of a memorial addressed to Philip II that he "may show favor to me (Titu Cusi) to my sons and my descendants." He wrote:

"I Don Diego de Castro Titu Cusi Yupanqui, natural son of Manco Inca, rich in all virtues, late Lord of these kingdoms of Peru, declare that, as it is necessary for me to make this statement to the King Don Philip our Lord, containing things of importance to me and my successors, and not knowing the style and manner used by Spaniards in such reports, I requested the very Reverend Father Friar Marcos Garcia and Martin de Pando that, in conformity with the usage on such occasions, they would order and compose the above narrative, for the very illustrious Lord, the Licentiate Lope Garcia de Castro, to send to Spain; that for me, in my name, holding, as I do hold, my power, all may be explained to his Majesty Don Philip our King and Lord."

After this literary task was completed, Titu Cusi probably went back to his principal court at Vilcapampa where he and his mother could be well taken care of by the Chosen Women. His "apostacy," however, convinced Father Marcos that something drastic should be done to discredit the Inca's gods and encourage the Indian converts. So he and Father Diego decided to invade a Temple of the Sun which was "near a great white rock over a spring of water." According to Father Calancha, this was the principal center of Sun worship where the people went to adore, to reverence and to kiss their hands to the sun, probably in June at the time of *their* winter solstice, to beg for its eagerly desired return.

The author of the Book of Job quotes him as referring to an act of adoration of the Gentiles who "when the sun rises resplendent or the moon shines clear, exult in their hearts and extend their hands toward the sun and throw kisses to it." It was one of the most natural and widespread forms of religious worship in the ancient world.

As has already been said, Friar Marcos and Friar Diego decided to make a spectacular attack on the particular devil who could be encountered there. They took advantage of the absence of the Inca and his mother and chief councillors, and probably his bodyguards, to summon such converts as they had to gather at one of the churches, bringing with them stacks of firewood in order that they might burn up this devil who had tormented them.

Father Calancha asks us to believe that the converted Indians were most anxious to get even with this devil who had slain their friends and inflicted wounds on themselves. Doubters were curious to see the result. Inca priests were there to see their god defy the Christians. While, as may be readily imagined, the rest of the population came to see the excitement.

It took great courage on the part of the two Augustinians thus to desecrate one of the chief shrines of the Inca and the people among whom they were dwelling. It is almost incredible that in this remote valley, far from the protecting hand of any Spanish officials, they should have dared to insult so wantonly the religion of their hosts.

Nevertheless, Friars Marcos and Diego marched over here with their converts from Puquiura, each carrying a stick of firewood. Calancha says the Indians worshipped the water as a divine thing, that the Devil had at times shown himself in the water. The Augustinian monks here raised the standard of the cross, recited their orisons, and piled firewood all about the rock and temple. Exorcising the Devil and calling him by all the vile names they could think of, the friars commanded him never to return. Setting fire to the pile, they burned the temple, scorched the rock, making a powerful impression on the Indians and causing the poor Devil to flee, "roaring in a fury." "The cruel Devil never more returned to the rock nor to this district." Whether the conflagration temporarily dried up the source or interfered with the arrangements of the water supply so that the pool disappeared for the time being is a matter for speculation.

It is possible that the Inca Titu Cusi and his mother may have been visiting the University of Idolatry when this happened. At any rate, as soon as they heard of it they were furious and immediately returned to Vitcos. The nobles wished to kill the missionaries and probably would have done so had it not been for the regard in which Friar Diego was held due to his skill in curing disease. Friar Marcos, however, did not fare so well and was stoned out of the province and threatened with death if he should return.

Friar Diego, beloved by the Indians who came from the fever stricken jungle in the lower valley, was not only allowed to remain but finally became a trusted friend and adviser of Titu Cusi.

It is possible that Friar Diego may have advised Titu Cusi to accept an invitation of his cousin Carlos Inca who lived in Cuzco and whose son was given a splendid christening. Captain Ocampo, who was living in Cuzco at the time, says the ceremony was accompanied by "festivals, rejoicings, fireworks, dances, and many newly invented and costly conceits." Invitations were sent out throughout the region "for more than 40 leagues around Cuzco" to all places where Incas were living. Ocampo says that "among the rest there went to the christening Titu Cusi Yupanqui Inca and his young brother Tupac Amaru Inca, who came from the province of Vilcapampa." We are told that the infant's godfather was none other than the new Spanish Viceroy who had just arrived in Cuzco, Don Francisco de Toledo. If they came, as was reported by Ocampo, they did not make their presence known and remained in seclusion at the Colcampata home of their relatives on the hill above Cuzco. As the good Captain Ocampo was obviously only reporting rumour and gossip, it is very doubtful if the story merits belief. But there is no doubt that after Father Marcos had been driven out of the valley, Friar Diego made good progress and won the esteem of the Inca notwithstanding the hostility of the priests of the Sun.

"It happened," says Calancha, that "one day there entered into the Province of Vilcabamba, a Spaniard called Romero. He sought a license from the Inca to permit him to hunt for gold and silver since he thoroughly understood metals and all that pertains to mining. The Inca gave him permission. His prospecting was very successful. He found a rich vein and in a few days took out quantities of gold. It seemed to Romero that it would be a good plan to flatter the Inca, so he showed him the gold and asked for a new permit and additional time in which to take out a quantity. As soon as the Inca saw the gold he realized that it would prove very attractive to greedy Spaniards and would bring thousands of them so he would lose the Province that sustained him." Accordingly he ordered Romero to be killed.

"The unfortunate avaricious miner tried to defend himself. His loud cries for help and the resulting disturbance came to the attention of Friar Diego who flew on the wings of charity to the Inca's house in order to ransom that life, begging the Inca to pardon him, or permit the unfortunate one to confess. The Inca was advised that Friar Diego was coming running at full speed. Knowing what his purpose was he sent to tell him to return to his church and let him kill that man, because if he begged for him he would kill him too. The holy man returned weeping that the miner would have to die without confessing his sins. . . . They killed Romero and cut off his head. . . ."

"Friar Diego sent to ask the Inca to give him the corpse so that it might receive Christian burial, since justice had already been done. His request was denied because the Inca wished the birds of the air and the beasts of the field to eat the body. He ordered it thrown in the river and prohibited any one under pain of his displeasure to bury it or recover it."

Nevertheless, Friar Diego went out several times at night in an effort to find the body and bury it. When the Inca learned of this he was very angry and threatened to kill the Friar if he left his church at night.

Not very long after this, according to Calancha, Titu Cusi gave a large and very wet party which Friar Diego who "disliked noise and boisterous revelry" was urged to attend. His failure to accept the Inca's invitation is said to have caused much annoyance to the royal court. After the party it appears that the Inca had an attack of double pneumonia. Unfortunately Friar Diego attended his sick bed in the mistaken hopes of effecting a cure with his simple remedies or at any rate getting Titu Cusi to confess and secure absolution. Titu Cusi died. The nobles and one of the Inca's wives then charged Friar Diego with the fatal end of the Inca's illness.

The Friar was put to death with great cruelty. Many pages of the Chronicle are filled with gruesome details.

The *mestizo* Martin Pando who was Titu Cusi's secretary was also put to death by the Inca chieftains. Friar Marcos, on hearing of the death of his friend Friar Diego tried to return to the valley from which he had been driven by Titu Cusi but was drowned in attempting to cross one of the rivers.

So ended the first attempt of Christian missionaries to convert the last of the warlike Incas.

Captain Baltasar de Ocampo gives a story of what was told him by those who were present at Titu Cusi's funeral.

He says that the Inca's insignia, battle axes, lances, bracelets, the scarlet fringe and a shield were carried in the hands of the greatest lords, in deep mourning, with muffled drums, and sounds of grief. Then they "proceeded to the House of the Sun, where was the Inca Tupac Amaru, the true and legitimate Lord, with the *Acllus* under the *Mama-cunas*, who were matrons to keep guard over them, for they were very beautiful."

Tupac Amaru

So now in 1571, it became the turn of Manco's third son, Tupac Amaru, brought up as a playfellow of the Chosen Women of the Sun and now happily married to one of them, to rule the little kingdom of Vilcapampa. His brows were then decked with the scarlet fringe of sovereignty.

Unfortunately, due to the jealousy and fear of his half brother Titu Cusi, his training had not been that of a wise ruler or even of a soldier.

Naturally he expected to continue to live in the great sanctuary surrounded by devoted followers and safe from any intruders. However, part of the time must be spent at Vitcos with his captains and his little army. His councilors had reason to fear the Spanish conquerors.

Unfortunately for the Incas, the Viceroy, Don Francisco de

Toledo, an indefatigable soldier and very able administrator, was savagely bigoted, cruel and pitiless. His master, Philip II, with the approval of the Council of the Indies, had decided that every effort must be made to secure the submission of the Indians who lived in the province of Vilcapampa, where Spaniards were not welcome and where, as Father Marcos could have assured him, missionaries were in danger of their lives. Accordingly, not knowing that Titu Cusi was dead or Father Diego a martyr, the Viceroy determined to induce the Inca to come and live where he would be accessible to Spanish authority. He dispatched a highly trusted ambassador to carry out this mission.

News of what was taking place in Cuzco traveled very fast to Vilcapampa even though the bad news of what had happened in Vitcos was slow in reaching the Viceroy. The captains and councillors of the young Inca learned what was on foot, undoubtedly from their relatives in the Spanish city. They had seen the great Inca Empire reduced to a mere province in rugged mountains where their ancestors had sought refuge in centuries past and where they hoped to be able to outwit the conquistadors. They believed that their Inca Sayri Tupac had been poisoned while he was the guest of the Spaniards at Yucay. They remembered that Manco had been murdered by the Spanish refugees he was befriending. They knew that Titu Cusi had died while being treated by a Spanish monk. So, when they heard that the Viceroy was sending an ambassador to Vitcos with the express purpose of persuading the young and inexperienced Tupac Amaru to leave the security of the Cordillera Vilcapampa and go to Cuzco they determined to take no chances of his being weak enough to accept a sinister invitation.

So they sent seven warriors to waylay the ambassador on the road and kill him. Whether Tupac Amaru knew of their plan we do not know. A wiser and more experienced young ruler would have realized that such an act was merely to court disaster. They probably knew it would cause trouble and so sent the young ruler down into the warm valley of the Pampaconas where his brother Titu Cusi had built a country house near the savage Antis who were very faithful to him. At least the Spanish soldiers could not reach him there.

The Viceroy, Francisco de Toledo, learned of the murder of his ambassador at the same time he heard of the martyrdom of the Augustinian Father Diego. A blow had been struck at the very heart of Spanish rule. If a faithful representative of the Vice-regent of Heaven and the messenger of the Viceroy of Philip II were not inviolable, then who was safe. Accordingly the energetic Toledo determined to make war on the unfortunate young Tupac Amaru and to give a reward to the soldier who would effect his capture. Furthermore, it was hoped that by his imprisonment all the lost Inca treasure might be found, treasure which was supposed to include a chain of gold which the great Inca Huayna had commanded to be made for himself to wear on great occasions, and which actually did include the gold image of the Sun from Cuzco. Furthermore, the Council naturally claimed that the chain of gold and the remaining treasure "belonged" to Philip II "by right of conquest." Anyhow, the Inca royal family must now be exterminated.

The expeditionary force was divided into two parts, one to capture the Inca in case he should attempt to cross the Apurimac by one of the routes which had been used by his father in his marauding expeditions on the Spanish caravans; the other to go via Ollantaytambo, the route followed by Rodriguez. This company went down the Urubamba Valley as far as the great precipices of the granite canyon which blocked the way for centuries, climbed out of the canyon through the Pass of Panticalla, where they found no Inca defenders at all. Thirty-five years before, a similar company, it will be remembered, had been met and destroyed by the slingstones of the well trained soldiers of the active Inca Manco II.

Accordingly, they were able to reach the keybridge of Chuquichaca over the lower Urubamba without mishap.

The narrow suspension bridge, built in accordance with Inca

engineering practice, of native fibers, sagged deeply in the middle and swayed so threateningly over the gorge of the Urubamba that only one man could use it at a time. The rapid river was too deep to be forded and there were no canoes. It would have been a difficult matter to have constructed rafts as most of the trees in this vicinity are of very hard wood that will not float. When the expedition reached the bridge they found to their surprise that it had not been destroyed. Young Tupac Amaru had had no experience in warfare and his chieftains apparently relied on their ability to take care of one Spanish soldier at a time and so prevent the invading force from crossing the narrow, swaying structure. They little knew what was in store for them for the Spaniards had brought with them one or two light mountain guns, with which the raw troops of the Inca were not acquainted. The sides of the valley near the Chuquichaca bridge rise very steeply from the river and the reverberations caused by gunfire would be fairly terrifying to those who had never heard anything like it before. A few volleys from the harquebuses and a few salvos from the guns and the Inca's soldiers fled pell mell, leaving the bridge quite undefended.

The Spanish soldiers were commanded by a Captain Garcia, who had married a niece of Tupac Amaru and who presumably spoke the Quichua language. His men now found the road a mere footpath, very narrow with a jungle on one side and a deep ravine on the other. It was barely wide enough for two men to pass. Garcia, with the customary bravery of the conquistadors, marched at the head of the company. Suddenly out of the jungle an Inca chieftan named Hualpa, endeavoring to protect the flight of his master, jumped on Garcia and tried to hurl him over the cliff. The Captain's life, however, was saved by a faithful Indian servant who was following immediately behind him carrying his sword. Quickly drawing it from the scabbard the servant killed Hualpa and saved Garcia's life.

So they marched up the valley of the Vilcabamba, swept

through Puquiura where Friar Marcos had had his church, and stormed several Inca forts. "Then," wrote Captain Garcia, "having arrived at the principal fortress, Guaynapucara which the Incas had fortified, we found it defended by the Prince Philip Quispetutio, a son of the Inca Titu Cusi, with his captains and soldiers. It is on a high eminence surrounded with rugged crags and jungles, very dangerous to ascend and almost impregnable. Nevertheless, with my aforesaid company of soldiers I went up and gained the young fortress, but only with the greatest possible labor and danger."

"The young fortress," seems to have been another name for Vitcos. Perhaps the Inca's "palace" was known as Vitcos while the fortifications which surrounded it were called Guaynapucara.

Captain Garcia hoped to catch the young Inca Tupac Amaru here but was disappointed to find that he and his immediate guards and captains had left, taking with them the golden image of the Sun which had been brought from Cuzco by his father Manco.

The Spanish soldiers followed them through Huarancalla and down into the Pampaconas Valley. Garcia's expedition was well provided with arms and ammunition. They had a remorseless and determined master back in Cuzco who would tolerate no failure and who was willing to reward success. And they were led by a very brave officer.

Nothing daunted by the dangers of the jungles, the rapids of the river or the hostility of the people, Garcia finally succeeded in penetrating deep into the forest. At length they captured Tupac Amaru, who chose to trust the Spaniards rather than perish in the Amazon jungles, either at the hands of the savages or because of the great hardships of the region.

Probably he thought that he would be treated with some respect, but in this he was doomed to disappointment. With his wife and children he was carried in triumph to Cuzco where the Viceroy, Francisco de Toledo, went to enjoy the spectacle of a mock trial and cruel punishment. The captured Inca chiefs were tortured to death with fiendish brutality. Tupac Amaru's wife was mangled before his eyes. His own head was cut off and placed on a pole in the great plaza at Cuzco. His little boys did not long survive. So, in 1572, perished the last of the Incas, descendants of some of the wisest rulers America has ever seen.

Part 2
The Search

1.

My Introduction to the Land of the Incas

PEOPLE OFTEN SAY TO
me: "How did you happen to discover Machu Picchu?" The answer is, I was looking for the last Inca capital. Its ruins were believed to be in the Cordillera Vilcabamba. My search for it began this way.

Some forty years ago, in a desire to qualify myself to teach South American history, and to write about the great General Simon Bolivar, I followed his route across the Andes from Venezuela to Colombia. Elihu Root, then Secretary of State, was interested in my trip and closely questioned me about what I had seen. He liked my report and the next year very graciously gave me the opportunity to see a lot more of South America by appointing me a delegate to the First Pan American Scientific Congress which was held in Santiago de Chile in December 1908.

My experiences in Venezuela and Colombia had taught me the great advantage it was to an explorer to have government backing so I determined to take advantage of my position as a *Delegado Official de los Estado Unidos*, to penetrate the Central Andes and follow the old Spanish Trade Route from Buenos Aires to Lima.

From Cuzco, accompanied by my friend, Clarence L. Hay, I undertook to cross Inca Land on mule back.

It was the month of February. Unfortunately we knew nothing of the usual weather in the Central Andes during the so-called summer months. The climate of Argentina had been pleasantly warm. That of Chile had been agreeable. We expected Peru to treat us as well. As a matter of fact, February is the very worst month in which to explore the highlands where the Incas flourished. The rains commence in November and continue well into April. This particular February turned out to be "the rainiest month of the rainiest season" that anyone remembered having experienced in Peru for a quarter of a century, so that we saw the mountain trails at their worst. It was an unfortunate introduction to exploration in Inca Land. The continuous downpour frequently overcame the conscientious scruples of local dignitaries who wished to escort us in and out of town. However, the Prefect, or chief official, of the Province of Apurimac, the Honorable J. J. Nuñez, had taken the trouble to come to Cuzco and urge me to visit his province, and particularly to explore the ruins of Choqquequirau. He said it had been the home of the last of the Incas. Since Choqquequirau means "Cradle of Gold," a number of attempts had been made in fairly recent times to explore the ruins in order to discover the treasure which it was believed the Incas had hidden there instead of allowing it to fall into the hands of the Spanish Conquerors.

Owing to the very great difficulty of reaching the site, it had only been seen three times in a hundred years by bold mountain climbers. It was generally believed among the officials and sugar planters of the Abancay region that Choqquequirau had once been a great city, "containing over 15,000 inhabitants" and that the buried treasure was well worth the expense of an adequate expedition.

The Prefect told us that a small party of adventurers had once succeeded in reaching the ruins with enough food to last them for two days. They had dug two or three holes in vain efforts to find the buried treasure. The tale of their sufferings, which lost nothing in the telling, kept anyone from following their example for many years, although they brought back reports of "palaces, temples, prisons and baths," all covered by dense jungles and luxuriant tropical vegetation.

A local magistrate, dreaming of hidden gold, had once endeavored to construct a path by which it might be possible to reach Choqquequirau and maintain a service of Indian carriers who could provide the workmen with food while a systematic effort was made to explore the "Cradle of Gold." Although the official had at his disposal the services of a company of soldiers and as many mountain Indians as he could use, he only succeeded in reaching a pass at the top of the range, which is 12,000 feet above the Apurimac River. The great valley is at this point a canyon two miles deep. He was unable to pass the precipices that protect Choqquequirau.

Others tried to utilize the path he had made. The latest of these was our new friend, Prefect Nuñez of the Department of Apurimac. Under the patronage of this ambitious and energetic official, who later greatly improved conditions in the city of Cuzco, a company of treasure seekers was formed and several thousand dollars subscribed for the new venture.

The first difficulty that they had encountered was in the construction of a bridge over the frightful rapids of the great river Apurimac. Nevertheless, due to the courage of an aged Chinese peddler who have braved the terrors of the rugged Andes for many years and who succeeded in swimming across the river when it was low in the "dry season" with a string tied to his waist, a suspension bridge made of six strands of telegraph wire was finally constructed. A trail that could be used by Indian bearers was made through twelve miles of mountain forest and over torrents and precipices. The task which had defied all comers for centuries was finally accomplished.

The results, however, had not been satisfactory, at least so far as securing any valuable treasure was concerned. The only metal articles that had been found were several ancient bronze shawl-pins and a small crowbar. The latter had a yellowish tinge that gave rise to the story that it was pure gold. Unfortunately, however, it was only bronze, made of copper hardened with tin. So the Prefect was particularly anxious that I should visit the ruins and be able to report their importance to the President of Peru.

He insisted that as I was a "Doctor" (Ph.D.) and a Government Delegate to a Scientific Congress I must know all about archaeology and could tell him how valuable Choqquequirau was as a site for buried treasure and whether it had been as he believed, Vilcapampa the Old, the Capital of the last four Incas. My protest that he was mistaken in his estimate of my archaeological knowledge was regarded by him merely as evidence of modesty rather than as a true statement of fact.

My previous studies of South American history had been limited largely to the Spanish Colonial days, the wars of independence, and the progress made by the different republics. Archaeology lay outside my field and I knew very little about the Incas except the fascinating story told by Prescott in his famous "Conquest of Peru." My efforts to avoid visiting the ruins of Choqquequirau were also laid partly to the very inclement weather and partly to the extreme difficulty of reaching that site.

Secretary Root had impressed upon us the importance of developing international good will by endeavoring in every way to please the officials of the countries we visited. Accordingly, I agreed to the Prefect's proposal, not knowing that it was destined to lead me into a fascinating field. It was my first introduction to prehistoric America.

Had it not been for Prefect Nuñez and his very practical interest in Choqquequirau I should probably never have been tempted to look for Inca ruins and thus find the two cities which had been lost to geographical knowledge for several centuries.

We left Cuzco on the morning of the first of February. The day promised ill. Rain fell in torrents. The preceding day we had received calls from a number of local dignitaries, all of whom assured us that they would be on hand in the morning to escort us out of town. But the continuous downpour overcame their sense of appropriate courtesy. Even the Prefect's polite aide de camp, who had been unremitting in his attentions, was glad enough to take our hint that we were sufficiently honored by his accompanying us for three blocks from the hotel.

The Prefect had been very solicitous about our welfare, and, although we assured him that we preferred to travel without a military escort, he insisted that a sergeant and at least one soldier should accompany us as long as we were in his Department. I never discovered why he was so insistent. There was no danger, and highway robbery is unheard of in Peru. Possibly he was afraid that the *delegados* might otherwise go hungry at villages where inhospitable, half-starved Quichuas would say that there was no food on hand; or he may have thought it undignified for us to travel without an escort. Whatever his reasons, he meant well and it was not a case of graft, for the soldiers were ordered to accompany us at the expense of the government.

We started off in a northwesterly direction, leaving the marvelous Cyclopean fortress of Sacsahuaman on our right. We were amazed to find that some of the polygonal blocks in it, as has been said, weighed over 200 tons! After climbing out of the Cuzco valley we descended gradually to the great plain of Anta, famous as the scene of numerous battles in the wars of the Incas. We crossed it by the ancient Inca road, a stony pathway five or six feet wide, with ditches and swamps on either side. It had been allowed to fall into decay, and for a good part of the distance it had disappeared. We had to make long detours in order to avoid the swamps and ponds that in the wet season cover the road. Skirting the hills north of the Plain of Anta, we passed several great terraces a third of a mile long and fourteen or fifteen feet high, and towards evening entered Zurita, a small Indian town. Here we were directed to the house of a hospitable Gobernador.

We left Zurita the next morning, accompanied by the Gobernador and his friends, leaving our muleteer and his pack mules to follow in charge of our military escort, we pushed on at a good pace and found ourselves at noon at Challabamba on the divide that separates the waters of the river Urubamba from those of the Apurimac. In marked distinction to the grassy, treeless plain of Anta from which we had just ascended, we saw before us deep green, wooded valleys.

The trail, a rocky stairway not unlike the bed of a mountain torrent, led us rapidly into a warm tropical region whose dense foliage and tangled vines were grateful enough after the bleak mountain plateau. Beautiful yellow broom flowers were abundant. The air was filled with the fragrance of heliotrope. Parti-colored lantanas ran riot through a maze of agaves and hanging creepers. We had entered a new world.

A steep descent brought us to the town of Limatambo where there are interesting terraces and other evidences of the Inca fortress which was used in Pizarro's day. The valley of the Limatambo River is here extremely narrow and the fortifications were well placed to defend an enemy coming against Cuzco from the west and north. An exceptionally bloody encounter took place there between the Spanish conquerors and the Inca forces.

Rain had been falling most of the day and the river Limatambo had risen considerably. The ford was quite impassable, and we were obliged to use a frail, improvised bridge over which our mules crept very cautiously sniffing doubtfully as it bent under their weight. Soon afterwards we crossed the river Blanco and left the old trail, which goes through the Indian village of Mollepata, described by Squier as "a collection of wretched huts on a high shelf of the mountain with a tumble-down church, a drunken Governor who was also keeper of a hovel which was called a post-house, and a priest as dissolute as the Governor . . . a place unsurpassed in evil repute by any in Peru." Fortunately for us, since the days of Squier's visit, an enterprising Peruvian has carved a sugar plantation out of the luxuriant growth on the mountain side, at La Estrella. Here we were given an extremely cordial welcome although Sr. Montes, the owner,—the fame of whose hospitality had reached Cuzco,—was not at home. Our military escort did not arrive until nearly three hours later, with a sad story of wretched animals and narrow escapes.

The next morning we descended from the cane-fields of La Estrella by an extremely precipitous winding trail. In places it seemed as though our heavily-laden mules must surely lose their footing and roll down the fifteen hundred feet to the raging Apurimac River below. At length, however, we came to Tablachaca, an excellent modern bridge which we were actually able to cross without dismounting, something that rarely happened to us on that journey.

In the old days a wonderful, lofty suspension bridge made by the Indians in the Peruvian fashion, was the only means of crossing this river. Vivid pictures of it, no two alike, are given in such famous books of travel as Squier's "Peru," Markham's "Cuzco and Lima" and Lt. Gibbon's "Exploration of the Valley of the Amazon." Although they all differ as to its height above the water and its length, all were greatly impressed by the remarkable canyon that it crossed. Gibbon says "the bridge was . . . 150 feet above the dark green waters," Sir Clements Markham, who crossed the bridge two years later says, "the bridge spanned the chasm in a graceful curve at a height of full 300 feet above the river." As he crossed it in the middle of March just at the end of the rainy season when it may be supposed the waters were high, while Lt. Gibbon crossed it in August, the middle of the dry season, when the river is very low, the contrast between their estimates of the height of the bridge above the river is all the more striking. Unfortunately it has disappeared and travelers can no longer dispute over its dimensions. Squier's picture of it was one of the reasons why I decided to take this trip at a time when I was tempted to go down the Amazon from La Paz by way of the Beni. So I was disappointed, but not for long.

The scenery today was superb; the great green mountains piling upon one another, their precipitous sides streaked with many lovely waterfalls. Green parrots overhead and yellow iris underfoot lent additional color to the scene. To add to our joy the sun shone all day long. A comparatively easy journey over steep but well-traveled mountain trails brought us to the town of Curahuasi where we were met by Lt. Caceres, aide de camp to Prefect Nuñez, who had been directed to act as our escort, and who proved to be a most genial and exceptionally high spirited young Peruvian, a member of an old and distinguished family.

Immediately on our arrival at Curahuasi we were taken to the local telegraph office where Caceres sent off an important message announcing the approach of "distinguished visitors"! To recompense us for waiting while he wrote the messages, bottles of stout were opened and toasts solemnly proposed. We expected to spend the night in the town, but found that the Gobernador, who desired us to be his guests, lived a couple of miles up the valley at Trancapata on the road to Abancay, the capital of the Province of Apurimac.

Although his establishment was a primitive one, it was charmingly situated on the edge of a deep ravine. The dining-room was an old verandah overlooking the gorge, and we enjoyed the view and the generous hospitality quite as much as though the villa had had all modern conveniences. In fact, neither of us had ever before experienced such a cordial welcome from a total stranger. We were to learn, however, before we left the Department, that such friendliness was characteristic of nearly every village and town that enjoyed the over-lordship of the genial Prefect of Apurimac.

The next morning we finally managed to bid our cordial host goodby, but it was not until he had accompanied us for a long distance up the deep valley. The weather had been unspeakably bad and heavy clouds had hemmed us in. Today, as we climbed the ascent under a bright sun, a wonderful panorama spread itself out behind us, the snowy peaks of Mt. Salcantay and Mt. Soray gleaming in the distance.

However, we soon left the region of luxurious vegetation, lantanas, cacti, and tropical plants, and again ran into a chilly drizzle at an elevation of thirteen thousand feet. Then we descended, came out of the rain, and had a delightful ride over a trail lined with masses of blue salvia. We were on the border line between the tropics and the temperate zone. We were in sight of the climate of the poles and the equator. We could see great glaciers and snow fields as well as the lovely light green fields of sugar-cane that have made Abancay famous throughout Peru. To one familiar with the broad canefields of Hawaii or the great plantations of Cuba and Puerto Rico, the fame of this rather small district was surprising. But after spending weeks in the bleak highlands of the Central Andes and experiencing the chill of the mountain climate, one readily appreciates why a warm, rich valley, eight thousand feet above the sea, where sugar can be easily raised, is a matter for profound congratulation.

A long descent down a very bad road brought us into a charming countryside. A mile from Abancay itself we were met by the sub-Prefect and a dozen sugar planters and *caballeros* who had taken the trouble to saddle their horses and come out to give us a fitting welcome. After an interchange of felicitations, we clattered gaily into town and were taken at once to the Prefecture. Here the genial Prefect gave us a cordial reception and apologized for the fact that he could not give us suitable sleeping quarters in the Prefecture, since he had quite a large family. As it was, he placed the local club entirely at our disposal. We were only too glad to accept, for the club's two pleasant rooms overlooked the little plaza and commanded a very pretty view of the ancient church and steep hills beyond.

That night Prefect Nuñez gave us an elaborate banquet to which he invited fifteen of the local notables. After dinner we were shown the objects of interest that had been found at Choqquequirau, including several Inca shawl-pins and a few nondescript metallic articles. The most interesting was a heavy bronze *champi* fifteen inches long and rather more than two inches in diameter, square, with round corners, much like the wooden clubs with which the Hawaiians beat *tapa*.

The next afternoon, amidst a heterogeneous mess of canned provisions, saddles, rugs, and clothes, we packed what we expected to need on our little excursion, and received distinguished guests. Almost everyone who called told us that he was going to accompany us on the morrow, and we had visions of a general hegira from Abancay.

In the evening we were most hospitably entertained at one of the sugar estates. To this dinner a genial gathering came from far and near. The planters of Abancay are a fine class of *caballeros*, hospitable, courteous, and intelligent, kind to their working people, interested both in one another's affairs and in the news of the outside world. Many of them spend part of each year or two in Lima. A few have traveled abroad.

The next morning, accompanied by a large cavalcade, we set out. Most of our escort contented themselves with a mile or so, and then wishing us good luck, returned to Abancay. We did not blame them. Owing to unusually heavy rains, the trail was in a frightful state. Well-nigh impassable bogs, swollen torrents, avalanches of boulders and trees, besides the usual concomitants of a Peruvian bridle-path, cheered us on our way.

All day long through the rain and heavy mist that broke away occasionally to give us glimpses of wonderfully deep green valleys and hillsides covered with rare flowers, we rode along a slippery path that grew every hour more treacherous and difficult. In order to reach a little camp on the bank of the Apurimac River that night, we hurried forward as fast as possible although frequently tempted to linger by the sight of acres of magnificent pink begonias and square miles of blue lupins. By five o'clock we began to hear the roar of the great river seven thousand feet below us in the canyon.

The Apurimac, which flows through the Ucayali to the Amazon, rises in a little lake near Arequipa, so many thousands of miles from the mouth of the Amazon that it may be said to be the parent stream of that mighty river. By the time it reaches this region, it is a raging torrent two hundred and fifty feet wide, and at this time of the year, over eighty feet deep. Its roaring voice can be heard so many miles away that it was long ago given by the Indians its Quichua name, Apu-rimac, which means the "Great Speaker."

Our guide, the enthusiastic Lieutenant Caceres, declared that we had now gone far enough. As it was beginning to rain and the road from there on was "worse than anything we had as yet experienced," he said it would be better to camp for the night, in an abandoned hut near by. His opinion was eagerly welcomed by two of the party, young men from Abancay, who were having their first real adventure, but the two *Yankis* decided it was best to reach the river if possible. Caceres finally consented, and aided by the dare-devil soldier, Castillo, we commenced a descent that for tortuous turns and narrow escapes beat anything we had ever seen. We were about to be initiated into what it means to go exploring in the wild region where the Incas were able to hide away from the conquistadors in 1536.

The sun had long since set behind the walls of the canyon when we encountered a large tree which had fallen across the path so as completely to block all progress. An hour's work enabled us to pass this obstacle, only to reach a part of the hillside where an avalanche had recently occurred. Here even the mules and horses trembled with fright as we led them across a mass of loose earth and stones which threatened to give way at any moment. To cheer us up, we were told that two weeks previously two sure-footed mules attempting to cross here had started a renewal of the avalanche which had swept the poor animals along with it down into the bottom of the canyon.

An hour after dark we came out on a terrace where the roar of the river was so great that we could scarcely hear Caceres shouting that our troubles were now over and that "all the rest was level ground." This turned out to be his little joke. We were still a thousand feet above the river. A path cut in the face of a precipice had yet to be negotiated. In broad daylight we should never had dared to ride down the tortuous trail that led from the terrace to the bank of the river, but as it was quite dark and we were innocent of any danger, we readily followed the cheery voice of our guide. The path descended the wall of the canyon by means of short turns, each twenty feet long. At one end of each turn was a precipice while at the other was a chasm, down which plunged a small cataract which had a clear fall of 700 feet. Half way down the path my mule started trembling and I had to dismount, to find that in the darkness he had walked off the trail and slid down the cliff to a ledge. How to get him back was a problem. There was no way to back him up the steep hill and there was scarcely room in which to turn him around. It was such a narrow escape that when I got safely back on the trail I decided to walk the rest of the way and let the mule go first, preferring to have him fall over the precipice alone, if that were necessary. Two-thirds of the way down the descent the path crossed the narrow chasm, close to and directly in front of the little cataract. There was no bridge. To be sure, the waterfall was only about three feet wide, but in the darkness I could not see the other side of the chasm. I did not dare jump alone, so remounted my mule, held my breath, and gave him both spurs at once. His jump was successful.

Ten minutes later we saw the welcome light of the master of the camp who came out to guide us through a thicket of mimosa trees that grew on a lower terrace just above the river. The "Great Speaker" made so much noise we could not hear a word our host said. But we were glad to have arrived safely.

The camp consisted of two huts, six feet by seven, built of reeds. Here we passed a most uncomfortable night, and the next day our explorations of Manco Inca's hideout began.

We had arrived at the river bank in the night and could see nothing although the terrific roaring of the "Great Speaker" made us wonder what lay before us. We were told the river was over a hundred feet deep. As soon as it was light we scrambled out of the tiny hut and stood in complete amazement at the sight of its tumultuous rapids, two hundred and fifty feet across, tearing through the canyon at a fearful pace, throwing up great waves like the ocean in a north-east storm. An incredible mass of water was dashing past us at a dizzy speed. We learned that the river had risen more than fifty feet on account of the recent heavy rains. When the frail little bridge was built it was eighty feet above the surface of the current. Now it was scarcely twenty-five.

The bridge was less than three feet wide but two hundred and seventy-three feet long. It swayed in the wind on its six strands of telegraph wire. To cross it seemed like tempting fate. So close to death did the narrow cat-walk of the bridge appear to be, and so high did the rapids throw the icy spray, our Indian bearers crept across one at a time, on all fours and obviously wishing they had never been ordered by the Prefect to carry our luggage to Choqquequirau. It had been brought as far as the bridge on pack animals but mules could not possibly use the new trail.

As has been said, the Incas had learned a thousand years ago to build good suspension bridges, using the tough lianas of the jungle to make powerful cables. Otherwise they never could have extended their empire as they did in the Andes where bitterly cold water from the glaciers makes it extremely difficult to cross the streams that unite to form the great affluents of the Amazon. No one thinks of learning to swim in the Central Andes. A misstep in fording one of the small rapidly flowing rivers usually means death. The mountain Indians are very cautious about taking such risks. So the behaviour of our carriers was understandable, especially as they were not acquainted with the tenacity of tele-graph wire. It must have seemed to them the height of folly for any one voluntarily to use this bridge. The river at this point is about 5000 feet above sea level. Our guide pointed out that the ruins were more than a mile above us. We had had little practice in mountain climbing, except on mule-back, for many months. It seemed like a pretty serious undertaking to attempt to climb up a slippery little trail for six thousand feet, to an elevation twice as high as the top of Mount Washington. This sounds tame enough to the experienced mountain climber although it was anything but easy for us.

Our patient, long-suffering Quichua bearers, coming of a race that is in the habit of marching great distances at these altitudes bore their burdens most cheerfully. At the same time even they gave frequent evidence of fatigue which was not at all to be wondered at under the circumstances. Our aide, the enthusiastic Lieutenant Caceres, kept shouting "Valor" at the top of his lungs as evidence of his good spirits and in an effort to encourage the others. The two *Yankis* had a hard time of it and were obliged to stop and rest nearly every fifty feet. Anyone who has attempted to walk fast at an elevation of 8000 feet will know how we felt trying to climb at 10,000 feet.

At times the trail was so steep that it was easier to go on all fours than to attempt to walk erect. Occasionally we crossed streams in front of waterfalls on slippery logs or treacherous little foot-bridges. Roughly constructed ladders led us over steep cliffs. Although the hillside was too precipitous to allow much forest growth, no small part of the labor of making the path had been the work of cutting through dense underbrush and bamboo thickets.

As we mounted, the view of the valley became more and more magnificent. Nowhere had I ever witnessed such beauty and grandeur as was here displayed. The white torrent of the Apurimac raged through the canyon thousands of feet below us. Where its sides were not sheer precipices or scarred by recent avalanches, the steep slopes were covered with green foliage and luxuriant flowers. From the hilltops near us other slopes rose six thousand feet above to glaciers and snow-capped summits. The whole range of the White Mountains or the Great Smokies of Tennessee and North Carolina could have been placed on the floor of this great valley and not come much more than half way to the top. In the distance, as far as we could see, a maze of hills, valleys, tropical jungle and snow peaks held the imagination as though by a spell. Such were our rewards as we lay panting by the side of the little path when we had reached its highest point.

After getting our wind, we followed the trail westward, skirting more precipices and crossing other torrents, until, about two o'clock, we rounded a promontory and on the slopes of a bold mountain headland 6000 feet above the river we caught our first glimpse of the ruins of Choqquequirau. Between the outer hilltop and the ridge connecting it with the snow-capped mountains, a depression or saddle had been terraced and levelled so as to leave a space for the more important building of the Inca stronghold.

At three o'clock we reached a glorious waterfall whose icy waters, coming probably from the glaciers on Soray, cooled our heads and quenched our thirst. We had now left our companions far behind, and were pushing slowly along through the jungle, when shortly before four o'clock we saw terraces in the near distance. We clambered up to a little bit of flat ground, to enjoy the view. Here we were discovered by a huge condor who proceeded to investigate the invaders of his domain. Apparently without moving a muscle, he sailed gracefully down in ever narrowing circles until we could see clearly not only his cruel beak and great talons, but even the whites of his eyes. We had no guns and not even a club with which to resist his attack. It was an awe-inspiring moment, for he measured about twelve feet from tip to tip of wing. He finally decided not to disturb us, and seemingly without changing the position of a feather, soared off into space. We were told afterwards by the Prefect's aides that they had been greatly bothered by condors when they first commenced operations here. Shepherds in the high Andean pastures have to wage a constant battle with condors who have no difficulty in carrying off a sheep.

Since we had no knapsacks or loads of any kind we arrived ahead of our carriers. The day had been warm, and in our efforts to make climbing as easy as possible, we had even divested ourselves of all warm clothes. Night came on and as usual the air became intensely cold. Our Indians had taken their time and failed to put in an appearance. So we spent an uncomfortable night in the smallest of the little thatched huts which workmen had erected for their own use while engaged in clearing the ruins. It was scarcely three feet high and about six feet long by four feet wide. Notwithstanding the fact that a shelter tent was pulled down and wrapped around us for warmth, and stacks of dry grass piled about us, we were scarcely able to close our eyes for the cold and chilling dampness.

During the four days that we spent on the mountain the humidity was usually 100%, so we were in clouds or mist most of the time, when it was not actually raining. It was not a pleasant introduction to archaeological reconnaissance, especially as I was inexperienced and unacquainted with my duties.

Fortunately I had with me that extremely useful handbook "Hints to Travellers," published by the Royal Geographical Society. In one of the chapters I found out what should be done when one is confronted by a prehistoric site—take careful measurements and plenty of photographs and describe as accurately as possible all finds. On account of the rain, our photographs were not very successful but we took measurements of all the buildings and made a rough map.

We found that the ruins were clustered in several groups both of terraces and on natural shelves and could be reached by stairways or winding paths. The buildings appear to have been placed close together, probably in order to economize all the available space. It is likely that every square yard that could be given to agriculture was cultivated.

Magnificent precipices guard the ruins on every side and render Choqquequirau virtually inaccessible to an enemy. Every avenue of ascent, except such as the engineers determined to leave open, was closed and every strategic spot was elaborately fortified. Wherever it might have been possible for a bold mountaineer to gain a foothold, the Incas had built well-faced walls of stone so as to leave an adventurous assailant no support. The terraces thus made served the double purpose of military defense and of keeping the soil from sliding away from the gardens down the steep hillside.

The ruins consist of three distinct groups of buildings. All had been more or less completely hidden by trees and vines during the centuries of solitude. Fortunately for us the treasure-seeking company had done excellent work in clearing away from the more important buildings the tangled mass of vegetation that had covered them. Dynamite had also been used in various likely spots where treasure might have been buried. But the workmen had found no gold and only a few objects of interest including, besides those we saw at Abancay, a few clay pots and two or three rocking pestles or grinding stones of a pattern still in use in this part of the Andes and as far north as Panama.

At the top of the southern and outer precipice, five thousand eight hundred feet immediately above the river, stands a parapet and the walls of two buldings without windows. The view from here, both up and down the valley surpasses the possibilities of language for adequate description. Far down the gigantic canyon one catches little glimpses of the Apurimac, a white stream shut in between guardian mountains, so narrowed by the distance that it seems like a mere brooklet. Here and there through the valley are marvellous cataracts, one of which has a clear fall of over one thousand feet. The panorama in every direction is wonderful in variety, contrast, beauty and grandeur.

North of this outer group of buildings is an artificially truncated hill. It is probable that on this flattened hilltop, which commands a magnificent view up and down the valley, signal fires could be built to telegraph to the heights overlooking Cuzco, intelligence of the approach of an enemy from the Amazonian wilds.

We noticed on this hilltop that small stones had been set into the ground, in straight lines crossing and recrossing at right angles as though to make a pattern. So much of it was covered by grass, however, that we did not have a chance to sketch it in the time at our disposal. It might have been the floor of a hut used by sentries 400 years ago.

North of the lookout and on the saddle between it and the main ridge is located the main group of ruins. In general, all the walls appear to have been built entirely of stone and clay. The construction, compared with that of the Inca palaces in Cuzco, is extremely rude and rough and no two niches or doors are exactly alike. Occasionally the lintels of the doors were made of timber, the builders not having taken the trouble to provide stones wide enough for the purpose. One such lintel was still standing, the wood being of a remarkably hard texture. Probably the ruins today present a more striking appearance than they did when they were covered with thatched roofs.

In one of the niches I found the small stone whirl-bob of a spindle-wheel, in size and shape like those made from wood and used today all over the Andes. This simple spinning apparatus consists of a stick about as large around as the little finger and from ten to twelve inches long. Its lower end is fitted with a whirl-bob of wood to give it proper momentum when it is set in motion by a twirl of the forefinger and thumb grasping the upper end of the spindle. It is in universal use by Indian women from Colombia to Chile. One rarely sees a woman tending sheep or walking along the high road who is not busily engaged in using this old-fashioned spindle. In the tombs of Pachacamac near Lima have been found spindles fitted with similar whirl-bobs of stone, more than 500 years old.

The third group of buildings is higher up on the spur, a hundred feet or more above the second group. Near the path from the lower to the upper plaza are the remains of a little *azequia* or water-course, now dry, lined with flat stones. The Incas never failed to provide water for all their fields and towns.

The southeast corner of the third group is marked by a huge projecting rock twenty feet high and twelve or fifteen feet in diameter. Beside it, facing the eastern slope, is a giant stairway. It consists of fourteen great steps roughly made and of varying dimensions. It is possible to ascend these stairs by means of small stone steps erected on one side or the other. Walls on each side, two feet wide serve as a balustrade. A peculiarity of the construction is the locating of a huge flat stone in the centre of the riser of each step. The view to the eastward from this stairway is particularly fine. Perhaps the rising sun, chief divinity of the Incas, was worshipped here. Mummies may have been brought out here on feast days to dry in the sun.

Beyond the stairway are terraces, alley-ways, walls and story-and-a-half houses, filled with niches and windows. Two of the houses have no windows and one of them contains three cells. Our military escort said they were used for the detention of prisoners. They were more likely storehouses. On the north side of the plaza is a curious little structure built with the utmost care and containing many niches and nooks. It may possibly have been the place in which criminals, destined to be thrown over the precipice, according to the laws of the Incas, awaited their doom.

Above it the hillside rises steeply, and on the crest of the ridge runs a little conduit which we followed until it entered the impenetrable tropical jungle at the foot of a very steep hill. The water in this little *azequia*, now dry, coming straight down the spur, was conducted over a terrace into two well-paved tanks on the north side of the plaza. Thence it ran across the plaza to a little reservoir on the south side. A small outlet had been provided at the end of this basin so that the water could flow underneath the floor of the tank house and then proceed on its way down the ridge to the buildings below.

As the western slope of the Choqquequirau spur is a sheer precipice, little attempt at fortification was made on that side. The eastern slope, however, is not so steep. On this side were enormous terraces hundreds of feet long faced with perpendicular walls twelve feet high. Two narrow paved stairways lead from one terrace to another.

In the jungle immediately below the last terrace, under ledges and huge boulders, were dug little caves in which the mummified bodies of the dead were placed. I found that the bones were heaped in a little pile as though they had been cleaned before being interred. No earth had been placed on them, but on top of the little pile on one grave I found a small earthenware jar about one inch in diameter. There was nothing in the jar, although it had retained its upright position during all the years of its internment. The natural entrance to the little tomb had been walled up with wedge-shaped stones from the inside in such a way as to make it difficult to enter the cave from the front. I found, however, that by digging away a little on one side of the huge boulder, I could easily remove the stones which had evidently been placed there by the grave-digger after the bones had been deposited in the tomb. Graves dug in the sandy deserts of the coast of Peru usually contain mummies in fairly good condition but here in the rain-soaked mountains of the eastern Andes, mummies are seldom found intact.

The workmen had excavated under a dozen or more of the projecting ledges and in each case had found bones and occasionally sherds of pottery. In no case, however, had they found anything of value to indicate that the dead were of high degree. If any of the officers of the garrison or Inca nobles were ever buried in this vicinity, their tombs have not yet been discovered, or else the graves were rifled years ago. But of this there is no evidence.

All conspicuously large rocks below the terraces were found to cover graves. The skulls were not found alone but always near the remainder of the skeleton. The larger bones were in fairly good condition but the smallest ones had completely disintegrated. Some of the largest bones could be crumbled with the fingers and easily broken, while others were white and hard; all that we found were those of adults, although one or two of them seemed to be of persons not over twenty years of age. So far as has been observed, no superincumbent soil was placed on the skeleton. The Quichua Indian carriers and workmen watched our operations with interest, but they became positively frightened when we began the careful measurement and examination of the bones. They had been in doubt as to the object of our expedition up to that point, but all doubts then vanished and they decided we had come there to commune with the spirits of the departed Incas.

In one of the buildings we found several slabs of slate on which visitors had registered their names. According to these inscriptions Choqquequirau was visited in 1834 by a French explorer, M. Eugene de Sartiges, and by two Peruvians, Jose Maria Tejada and Marcelino Leon; and in 1861 by Jose Benigno Samanez ("pro Presidente Castilla") Juan Manuel Rivas Plata, and Mariana Cisneros. On July 4, 1885, three Almanzas, Pio Mogrovejo and a party of workmen did what they could to find the buried treasure but in vain.

After my return to New Haven I learned that M. de Sartiges, writing under the nom de plume "E. de Lavandais," published an account of his visit in the *Revue de Deux Mondes*, in June, 1850. His route, the only one possible at the time, was exceedingly circuitous. From Mollepata, a village near the sugar plantation of La Estrella, he went north across the very high pass between Mts. Salcantay and Soray to the river Urubamba, to a village called Yuatquinia (Huadquiña). Here, without knowing it, he was within a few miles of Machu Picchu, then unheard of. He engaged Indians to cut a trail to Choqquequirau. After three weeks he found that the difficulties of making a trail were so great that it would take at least two months to finish the undertaking. So he and his companions made their way through the jungle and along the precipices as best they could for four days. On the fifth day they arrived at the ruins. In his projects for exploration, he had failed to take into account the fact that tropical vegetation had been at work for centuries covering up the remains of the Inca houses, and as he was only able to stay at Choqquequirau for two or three days, he failed to see some of the most interesting ruins. The giant stairway escaped his attention entirely. He seems to have spent most of his time hunting for treasure. He had expected to spend eight days here, but the difficulties of reaching the place were so great and the food supply so limited that he had to hurry back without seeing more than the buildings of the lower plaza, the lower terraces, and a grave or two. It was his opinion that fifteen thousand people lived here once. One wonders what they lived on. Nevertheless every available foot of arable land had been conserved by extensive terraces. No soil was allowed to escape. Corn and potatoes could grow here.

M. de Sartiges' description made us realize how much we were indebted to the labors of the treasure-seeking company for uncovering buildings whose presence otherwise would never have been suspected.

Apparently Choqquequirau was a frontier fortress that defended the upper valley of the Apurimac, one of the natural approaches to Cuzco, from the country occupied by the Chancas and the Amazonian Antis.

There were undoubtedly several less important outlying fortresses lower down the river, situated in such a way as to be able to prevent the incursions of small parties of wild savages and give notice of any large expeditions that might attempt to march on Cuzco.

The Prefect of Apurimac was much disappointed that I was unable to indicate to him the possible whereabouts of any buried treasure. The chief satisfaction derived by the local gentry who had invested several thousand dollars in the unsuccessful enterprise was due to the claim that they had laid bare the capital of the Last of the Incas. For this they took considerable credit.

Peruvian writers like Paz Soldan and the great geographer Raimondi, were positive that Choqquequirau was really Manco Inca's "Vilcapampa." They based their belief on the fact that Father Calancha says Puquiura was "Two long days' journey from Vilcabamba." Raimondi calls attention to the fact that Choqquequirau is in fact two or three long days' journey from the present village of Puquiura and therefore must have been the last Inca Capital.

This belief was not shared by Don Carlos Romero, one of the

chief historians of Lima, who assured me that the Spanish Chronicles contained enough evidence to show that the last Inca capital was not at Choqquequirau but was probably over beyond the ranges in the region where I had seen snow-capped peaks.

As a matter of fact those snow-capped peaks in an unknown and unexplored part of Peru fascinated me greatly. They tempted me to go and see what lay beyond. In the ever famous words of Rudyard Kipling there was "Something hidden! Go and find it! Go and look behind the ranges—Something lost behind the Ranges. Lost and waiting for you. Go!"

2.

The Search for Vitcos

IN THE SUMMER OF 1910 while I was reading the proof sheets of "Across South America," my friend, the late Edward S. Harkness, asked me when I was going on another expedition to South America and said he would be glad to contribute the cost of sending a geologist with me. That was an exciting idea. Just about that time I had been asked to review professor Adolph Bandelier's scholarly book on "The Islands of Titicaca and Koati." In one of his footnotes he casually remarked that he believed it "likely" that Mount Coropuna in the Peruvian Coast range near Arequipa "is the culminating point of the continent." He said that "it exceeds 23,000 feet in height" whereas Aconcagua is only 22,763 ft.

My father had taught me to love mountain climbing. He took me for my first steep climb when I was just four years old. Later we had climbed together a number of mountains in the suburbs of Honolulu. So I knew the thrill of that great and hazardous sport. My sensations when I read Bandelier's footnote are difficult to describe for I did not remember ever having heard of Coropuna. On many maps it did not exist but I finally found it on one of Raimondi's large scale sheets and was thrilled to find that that great explorer gave its height as 8 meters higher than Aconcagua which is actually the highest mountain in the Western Hemisphere. It lay about a hundred miles north of Arequipa, near the 73rd meridian, almost due south of Choqquequirau and the hidden lands "behind the ranges" where possibly Manco II had had his last capital.

So I said to myself why would it not be a good idea to make a cross-section of Peru along the line of the 73rd meridian from the head of canoe navigation on the Urubamba river to tide water on the Pacific, exploring the hinterland for historical and archaeological remains and climbing Coropuna.

That winter at a Class dinner at the Yale Club in New York I was called upon for a "speech." Naturally I spoke of what was on my mind. To my great surprise one of my classmates, the late Herbert Scheftel, came to me offering to pay the expenses of a topographer on the expedition now fairly launched in my mind's eye! Other friends soon offered to furnish a surgeon, a naturalist and a mountain-climbing engineer. An undergraduate offered to go along as an assistant. And so the Yale Peruvian Expedition of 1911 was organized in the hope that we might climb the highest mountain in America, collect a lot of geological and biological data and above all try to find the last capital of the Incas.

At my invitation Professor Isaiah Bowman became our Geologist-Geographer; Professor Harry W. Foote, our Naturalist; Dr. William G. Erving, our Surgeon; Kai Hendrikson, our Topographer; H. L. Tucker, our Engineer and Paul B. Lanius our Assistant. We left New York early in June. In Lima Señor Carlos Romero showed me some paragraphs in Calancha's chronicle about Vitcos.

As soon as we got to Cuzco I began to ask the planters of the Urubamba river about the places mentioned in Calancha. They had never heard of most of them but two or three did say there were Inca ruins in various places down the valley. And one old prospector said there were interesting ruins at Machu Picchu. But his statements were given no importance by the leading citizens; and the professors in the University of Cuzco knew nothing of any ruins down the valley. They thought Choqquequirau was the old Inca capital although, as has been said, the historian Carlos

Romero did not think so. He placed Vitcos "near a great white rock over a spring of fresh water."

We had with us the sheets of Antonio Raimondi's great map which covered the region we proposed to explore. His map contained references to Inca ruins but none at all in the Urubamba valley below Ollantaytambo or in the Vilcabamba valley. In 1865 this remarkable explorer, who spent his life crossing and recrossing Peru went deep into the heart of the Cordillera Vilcabamba; yet found no Vitcos. He did locate a small town bearing the name Vilcabamba, but obviously it was not Inca and had been built by the first Spanish settlers, who were interested in working a gold mine in that vicinity. We did not know until after our return to New Haven that the French explorer Charles Wiener had heard there were ruins in Huayna Picchu and Machu Picchu which he was unable to reach. Naturally we did not have with us the 1000 page folio volume of Father Calancha's Chronicle of the Augustinians. We only had a few notes that I had been able to make in Lima under the guidance of Romero. These referred to the places in the vicinity of Vitcos.

The last refuge of the Incas lies about one hundred miles from the Cuzco palace of the Spanish Viceroy, in what Prescott calls "the remote fastnesses of the Andes." One looks in vain for Vitcos on modern maps of Peru, although several of the ancient maps give it. In 1625 "Vitcos" is marked on de Laet's map of Peru as a mountainous province northeast of Lima and three hundred and fifty miles northwest of Vilcabamba! This error was copied by some later cartographers, including Mercator, until about 1740, when "Vitcos" disappeared from all maps of Peru. The map makers had learned that there was no such place in that vicinity. Its real location was lost for about three hundred years.

It was in July that with the aid of Don Cesar Lomellini, a courteous Italian merchant, we organized a good mule train, left Cuzco and its wonderful Inca ruins and went over to the Urubamba Valley, little suspecting what was in store for us.

We saw snow peaks ahead of us but were totally unprepared

for the wonderful view that suddenly breaks on the traveller as he comes to the end of the arid plateau and finds himself on the edge of an enchanting great valley, 3,000 feet deep.

Uru is the Quichua word for caterpillars or grubs, *pampa* means flat land. *Urubamba* is the "flat-land-where-there-are-grubs-or-caterpillars." Had it been named by people who came up from a warm region where insects abound, it would hardly have been so denominated. Only people not accustomed to land where caterpillars and grubs flourished would have been struck by such a circumstance. Consequently, the valley was probably named by the plateau dwellers who were working their way down into a warm region where butterflies and moths are more common.

Notwithstanding its celebrated caterpillars, we found Urubamba's gardens to be full of roses, lilies, and other brilliant flowers. There were orchards of peaches, pears, and apples; there were fields where lucious strawberries are raised for the Cuzco market. Apparently, the grubs do not get everything. This is the valley of Yucay where Sayri Tupac lived. No wonder it was a favorite resort of the Incas.

The first day down the Urubamba Valley brought us to romantic Ollantaytambo, described in glowing terms by Castelnau, Marcou, Wiener, and Squier many years ago. It has lost none of its charm, even though Marcou's drawings are imaginary and Squire's exaggerated. Here, as at the town of Urubamba, there are flower gardens and highly cultivated green fields. The brooks are shaded by willows and poplars. Above them are magnificant precipices crowned by snow-capped peaks. The village itself was once the capital of an ancient principality whose history is shrouded in mystery. There are ruins of Inca gabled buildings, storehouses, "prisons," or "monasteries," perched here and there on well-nigh inaccessible crags above the village. Below are broad terraces which will stand for ages to come as monuments to the energy and skill of a bygone race, who were great agriculturists.

The "fortress" is on a little hill, surrounded by steep cliffs, high walls, and hanging gardens so as to be difficult of access.

Centuries ago, when the tribe which cultivated the rich fields in this valley lived in fear and terror of their savage neighbors, this hill offered a place of refuge to which they could retire. It may have been fortified at that time. As centuries passed in which the land came under the control of the Incas, whose chief interest was the peaceful promotion of agriculture, it is likely that this "fortress" became a royal garden. The six great slabs of reddish granite weighing fifteen or twenty tons each, and placed in line on the summit of the hill, were brought from a quarry several miles down the valley and at a lower level, so they had to be dragged up hill with an immense amount of labor and pains. They were probably intended to be a record of the magnificence of an able ruler. His name may have been Ollantay, a celebrated Prince.

Fortunately for those who are interested in ancient Peru, Ollantaytambo can now be reached from Cuzco both by train and automobile. The scenery en route alone makes the trip memorable.

Before the completion of the Urubamba River road, about 1895, travelers from Cuzco to the lower valley had a choice of two routes. One was by way of the Pass of Panticalla, followed by Wiener in 1875. Near this pass are two groups of ruins. One of them, extravagantly referred to by Wiener as a "granite palace, whose structural plan resembles the more beautiful parts of Ollantaytambo," was only a storehouse. The other was probably a *tampu*, or inn, for the benefit of official Inca travelers. The other route was by way of the pass between Mts. Salcantay and Soray, followed by the Count de Sartiges in 1834 and Raimondi in 1865. Both passes are higher than the top of Pike's Peak. Both are dangerous during the rainy season when they lie under deep snow and violent storms are frequent. The mountainous wilderness between these two routes was practically unknown and had been inaccessible for almost four centuries. Up to the time of our visit it had not been described in the geographical or archaeological literature of southern Peru. Thanks to the new road we were able to avoid the high passes and go straight down the Urubamba

River, asking all the local Indians to show us Inca ruins, and in particular a place where there was a "great white rock over a spring of water."

At Salapunco, (*sala*—ruins; *punco*—gateway), the road skirts the base of precipitous cliffs. They are the beginnings of a wonderful mass of granite mountains which have made Vilcapampa more difficult of access than the surrounding highlands which are composed of schists, conglomerates, and limestone. This is the natural gateway to the ancient province, but it was closed for centuries by the combined efforts of nature and man. The Urubamba River, in cutting its way through the granite range, forms rapids too dangerous to be passable and precipices which can be scaled only with great effort and considerable peril, if at all. At one time a footpath probably ran near the river, where the Indians, by crawling along the face of the cliffs and sometimes swinging from one ledge to another on hanging vines, were able to make their way to the alluvial terraces down the valley. Another path may have gone over the cliffs above Salapunco, where we noticed, in various inaccessible places, the remains of walls built on narrow ledges. They were too narrow and too irregular to have been intended to support agricultural terraces. They may represent the foundations of an old trail. To defend these ancient paths we found that the Incas or their predecessors had built, at the foot of the precipices, close to the river, a small but powerful fortress, fashioned after famous Sacsahuaman and resembling it in the irregular character of the large polygonal building blocks and also by reason of the salients and reentrant angles which were intended to prevent the walls from being successfully scaled.

Passing Salapunco, we skirted high granite cliffs and verdure-clad precipices and entered a fascinating region, where we were surprised and charmed by the extent of the ancient terraces, their length and height, the presence of many Inca ruins, the beauty of the deep, narrow valleys, and the grandeur of the snow-clad mountains which towered above them.

Across the Urubamba River at Qquente, and near the mouth

of the Pampacahuana River, on top of a series of terraces, we saw an extensive ruined city. It looked as though it had possibilities, so I asked Mr. Herman Tucker, one of our topographers to cross the Urubamba and see what he could find out about it. He spent several days in that vicinity and reported that the name of the city was Patallacta (*pata*—height or terrace; *llacta*—town), an Inca town of importance. It contains about one hundred houses. One wonders why it was abandoned. Above it, in the valley he visited, are several important sites at Paucarcancha, Huayllabamba, Incasamana or Ccolpa Mocco, and Hoccollopampa, which we later surveyed. None of the places in this vicinity fitted in with the accounts of Vitcos. Their history can only be surmised. Their identity remains a puzzle, although the symmetry of the buildings, their architectural idiosyncrasies such as niches, stone roof-pegs, barholds, and eye-bonders, indicate an Inca origin. At what date these towns and villages flourished, who built them, why they were deserted, we do not yet know; and the Indians who live hereabouts are ignorant, or silent, as to their history. It is entirely possible that this region was fully occupied and cultivated before the Incas were able to control the Cuzco valley and other more accessible arable lands. The original inhabitants must have been hard put to it for room, to have spread into the upper valleys of this inhospitable region. In a way it fits in with the theory which will be advanced in a later chapter that the original inhabitants of Cuzco were pushed out of their fertile valleys by a horde of barbarians coming from the Bolivian altoplanicie, found a refuge for several hundred years in this mountainous country where they finally became too crowded to be comfortable and fought their way back to Cuzco.

On the other hand, since the architecture appears to be "Late Inca," the chances are that they were occupied at the time of the Conquest and were abandoned when the Viceroy Toledo in 1573 wiped out a large part of the population. At all events we found practically no one living in these ancient towns.

Father Calancha's Chronicle gives a story of mass slaughter which followed the martyrdom of Friar Diego and the death of the Viceroy's ambassador. Toledo was led to take fearful revenge on the hapless Indians.

At Torontoy, the end of the cultivated temperate valley, we found another group of interesting ruins, possibly once the residence of an Inca noble. Some of the buildings showed very fine stone cutting, the work of patient artisans.

Torontoy is at the beginning of the Grand Canyon of the Urubamba, and such a canyon! The river road ran recklessly up and down rock stairways, blasted its way beneath overhanging precipices, spanned chasms on frail bridges propped on rustic brackets against granite cliffs. Under dense forests, wherever the encroaching precipices permitted it, the land between them and the river was terraced and once cultivated. We found ourselves unexpectedly in a veritable wonderland. Emotions came thick and fast. We marveled at the exquisite pains with which the ancient folk had rescued incredibly narrow strips of arable land from the tumbling rapids. How could they ever have managed to build a retaining wall of heavy stones along the very edge of the dangerous river, which it is death to cross! On one sightly bend near a foaming waterfall some Inca chief built a temple, whose walls tantalize the traveler. He must pass by within pistol shot of the interesting ruins, unable to ford the intervening rapids. High up on the side of the canyon, several thousand feet above this temple, are the ruins of Corihuayrachina (*kori*—"gold"; *huayra*—"wind"; *huayrachina*—"a threshing-floor where winnowing takes place."). Possibly this was an ancient gold mine of the Incas. Half a mile above us on another steep slope, some modern pioneer had recently cleared the jungle from a fine series of ancient Inca terraces.

Then we reached a hut called "*La Maquina*," where travelers frequently stop for the night. It is at present the end of the new narrow gauge railroad from Cuzco. The name comes from the presence here of some large iron wheels, parts of a "machine" destined never to overcome the difficulties of being transported all the way to a sugar estate in the lower valley, and years ago left here to rust in the jungle.

As there was little fodder, and there was no good place for us to pitch our camp, we pushed on over the very difficult road, which had been blasted out of the face of a great granite cliff, two thousand feet high. Part of the cliff had slid off into the river. The breach thus made in the road had been repaired temporarily by means of a frail-looking rustic bridge built on a bracket composed of rough logs, branches, and reeds, tied together, and surmounted by a few inches of earth and pebbles to make it seem safe to the cautious cargo mules who picked their way gingerly across it. No wonder "the machine" rested where it did and gave its name to that part of the valley.

Dusk falls early in this deep canyon, the sides of which are considerably over a mile in height. It was almost dark when we came to a little sandy plain two or three acres in extent, which in this land of steep mountains is called a *pampa!* Were the dwellers on the *pampas* of Argentina—where a railroad can go for 250 miles in a straight line, to see this little bit of flood-plain called *Mandor Pampa,* they would think some one had been joking or else grossly misusing a word which means to them illimitable space with not a hill in sight. However, to the ancient dwellers in this valley, where level land was so scarce that it was worth while to build high stone-faced terraces to enable two rows of corn to grow where none grew before, any little natural breathing space in the bottom of the canyon is called a *pampa.*

The story of our stay at Mandor Pampa, of its sole resident, Melchior Arteaga, and of the ruins he showed me above the precipices on the slopes of Machu Picchu mountain, I shall relate in detail in Chapter I, of Part III, which tells of the discovery of Machu Picchu. Suffice it to say that the ruins he showed me were not near a "great white rock over a spring of water" and that there was no presence that this was Vitcos, Manco's capital for which we were looking. So a few days later we crossed the river on the fine new bridge of San Miguel and pushed on down the

Urubamba Valley asking for ruins, offering cash prizes for good ones—and a double bonus for any that would fit the description of the Temple of the Sun which Father Calancha had said was "near Vitcos."

Our first stop was at the hospitable plantation of Huadquiña which once belonged to the Jesuits. They planted the first sugar cane and established the mill. After their expulsion from the Spanish Colonies at the end of the eighteenth century, Huadquiña was bought by a Peruvian. It was first described in geographical literature by the Count de Sartiges, who stayed here for several weeks in 1834 when on his way to Choqquequirau. He says that the owner of Huadquiña "is perhaps the only landed proprietor in the entire world who possesses on his estates all the products of the four parts of the globe. In the different regions of his domain he has wool, hides, horsehair, potatoes, wheat, corn, sugar, coffee, chocolate, *coca*, many mines of silver-bearing lead, and placers of gold." Truly a royal principality.

Our hosts, Señora Carmen Vargas and her family, read with interest my copy of those paragraphs of Calancha's "Chronicle" which referred to the location of the last Inca capital. Learning that we were anxious to discover Vitcos, a place of which they had never heard, they ordered the most intelligent tenants on the estates to come in and be questioned. The best informed of all was a sturdy *mestizo*, a trusted foreman, who said that in a little valley called Ccollumayu, a few hours' journey down the Urubamba, there were "important ruins" which had been seen by some of Señora Carmen's Indians. Even more interesting and thrilling was his statement that on a ridge up the Salcantay Valley was a place called Yurak Rumi (*yurak*—white; *rumi*—stone) where some very interesting ruins had been found by his workmen when cutting trees for firewood. We all became excited over this, for among the paragraphs which I had copied from Calancha's "Chronicle" was the statement that "close to Vitcos" is the "white stone of the aforesaid house of the Sun which is called Yurak Rumi." Our hosts assured us that this must be the place, since no one hereabouts had ever heard of any other Yurak Rumi. The foreman, on being closely questioned, said that he had seen the ruins once or twice, that he had also been up the Urubamba Valley and seen the great ruins at Ollantaytambo, and that those which he had seen at Yurak Rumi were "as good as those at Ollantaytambo." Here was a definite statement made by an eyewitness. Apparently we were about to see that interesting rock where the last Incas worshipped. However, the foreman said that the trail thither was at present impassable, although a small gang of Indians could open it in less than a week. Our hosts immediately gave orders to have the path to Yurak Rumi cleared for our benefit.

Meanwhile we spent a few days exploring the ruins of Ccollumayu only to meet with disappointment as there was little besides the foundations of some very primitive huts.

Finally the trail to Yurak Rumi was reported finished. It was with a feeling of keen anticipation that I started out with the foreman to see those ruins which he had just revisited and now declared were "better than those of Ollantaytambo." It was to be presumed that in the pride of discovery he might have exaggerated their importance. Still it never entered my head what I was actually to find. After several hours spent in clearing away dense forest growth which surrounded the walls I learned that this Yurak Rumi consisted of the ruins of a single house! No effort had been made at beauty of construction. The walls were of rough, unfashioned stones laid in clay. The building was without a doorway, although it had several small windows and a series of ventilating shafts under the house. The lintels of the windows and of the small apertures leading into the subterranean shafts were of stone. It was really only intended by the Inca builders to be a useful storehouse to provide food for travelers.

Yurak Rumi is on top of the ridge between the Salcantay and Huadquiña Valleys, probably on the ancient road which crossed the province of Vilcapampa. As such it was interesting, but to compare it with Ollantaytambo, as the foreman had done, was to liken a cottage to a palace or a mouse to an elephant. It seems incredible that anybody having actually seen both places could have thought for a moment that one was "as good as the other." To be sure, the foreman was not a trained observer and his interest in Inca building was probably of the slightest. Yet the ruins of Ollantaytambo are so well known and so impressive that even the most casual traveller is struck by them and the natives themselves are enormously proud of them.

Obviously, we had not yet found Vitcos. So, bidding farewell to Señora Carmen, we crossed the Urubamba on the bridge of Colpani and proceeded down the valley past the mouth of the Lucumayo and the road from Panticalla, to the hamlet of Chauillay, where the Urubamba is joined by the Vilcabamba River. Both rivers are restricted here to narrow gorges, through which their waters rush and roar on their way to the lower valley. A few rods from Chauillay was a fine bridge. The natives call it Chuquichaca! Steel and iron have superseded the old suspension bridge of huge cables made of vegetable fiber, with its narrow roadway of wattles supported by a network of vines. Yet here it was in 1572 the military force sent by the Viceroy, Francisco de Toledo, under the command of Captain Garcia, found the forces of the young Inca drawn up to defend Vitcos.

Eventually we reached the town of Santa Ana at the head of canoe navigation on the Urubamba and the site of fine sugar and *coca* plantations, which had formerly been a Jesuit Mission. Two hundred Indians are employed here in raising sugar cane, making *aguardiente*, "fire water," cultivating *coca* and drying the leaves to be sold in the markets of the highlands.

We were most kindly welcomed here by Don Pedro Duque who took great interest in enabling us to get all possible information about the little-known region into which we proposed to penetrate. Born in Colombia, but long resident in Peru, Don Pedro was a gentleman of the old school, keenly interested, not only in the administration and economic progress of his plantation, but also in the intellectual movements of the outside world. He entered with zest into our historical-geographical studies. The name Vitcos was new to him, but after reading over with us our extracts from the Spanish chronicles he was sure that he could help us find it. And help us he did. Santa Ana is less than thirteen degrees south of the equator; the elevation is barely 2000 feet; the "winter" nights are cool; but the heat in the middle of the day is intense. Nevertheless, our host was so energetic that as a result of his efforts a number of the best-informed residents were brought to the conferences at the great plantation house.

Of Vitcos as well as most of the places mentioned in the chronicles, none of Don Pedro's friends had ever heard. It was all rather discouraging, until one day, by the greatest good fortune, there arrived at Santa Ana another friend of Don Pedro's, the *Teniente Gobernador* of the village of Lucma in the valley of the River Vilcabamba—a crusty old fellow named Evaristo Mogrovejo. His brother, Pio Mogrovejo, had been a member of the party of energetic Peruvians who, in 1884, had searched for buried treasure at Choqquequirau. Evaristo Mogrovejo could understand searching for buried treasure, but he was totally unable otherwise to comprehend our desire to find the ruins of the places mentioned by Father Calancha. Had we first met him in Lucma he would undoubtedly have received us with suspicion and done nothing to further our quest. Fortunately for us, his official superior was the sub-prefect of the province who lived near Santa Ana, and was a friend of Don Pedro's. The sub-prefect had received instructions from the prefect of Cuzco, to further our undertaking, and accordingly gave particular orders to Mogrovejo to see to it that we were given every facility for finding the ancient ruins and identifying the places of historic interest.

Our present objective was the Vilcabamba valley. So far as we have been able to learn, only one other explorer had preceded us—the distinguished cartographer, Raimondi. His map of the Vilcabamba is fairly accurate. He reports the presence here of mines and minerals, but with the exception of an "abandoned *tampu*" at Maracnyoc ("the place which possesses a millstone"), he makes no mention of any ruins. Accordingly, although it seemed from the story of Baltasar de Ocampo and Captain Garcia's other contemporaries that this was the valley of Vitcos, it was with feelings of considerable uncertainty that we proceeded on our quest.

A new road had recently been built along the Vilcabamba river by the owner of the sugar estate at Paltaybamba to enable his pack animals to travel more rapidly. Much of it had to be carved out of the face of a solid rock precipice and in places it pierces the cliffs in a series of little tunnels. My *gendarme* missed this road and took the steep old trail over the cliffs. As Ocampo said in his story of Captain Garcia's expedition, "the road was narrow in the ascent with forest on the right and on the left a ravine of great depth." We reached Paltaybamba about dusk.

We had a long talk with the manager of the plantation and his friends that evening. They had heard little of any ruins in this vicinity, but repeated one of the stories we had heard in Santa Ana, that way off somewhere in the great forests of the *montaña* was "an Inca city." None of them had been there, but if their accounts should prove to be correct that would account for the presents of a macaw and some peanuts which the Inca Titu Cusi sent to Rodriguez and also for young Tupac Amaru's flight into the jungle when he was surprised by the forces sent by Viceroy Toledo.

The Vilcabamba valley above Paltaybamba is very picturesque. There are high mountains on either side, covered with dense jungle. Its dark green foliage was in pleasing contrast to the light green of the fields of waving sugar cane. The valley is steep, the road is very winding, and the torrent of the Vilcabamba roars loudly, even in July. What it must be like in the rainy season, we could only surmise.

Our next stop was at Lucma, the home of *Teniente Gobernador* Mogrovejo. We offered to pay him a *gratificacion* of a *sol*, or Peruvian silver dollar for every ruin to which he would take us, and double that amount if the locality should prove to contain particularly interesting ruins. This aroused all his business instincts. He summoned his *alcaldes* and other well-informed Indians to appear and be interviewed. They told us there were "many ruins" hereabouts! Being a practical man himself, Mogrovejo had never taken any interest in ruins. Now he saw the chance not only to make money out of the ancient sites, but also to gain official favor by carrying out with unexampled vigor the orders of his superior, the sub-prefect. So he exerted himself to the utmost in our behalf.

The next day we were guided up a ravine to the top of the ridge back of Lucma. This ridge divides the upper from the lower Vilcabamba. On all sides the mountains rose several thousand feet above us. In places they were covered with forest growth, chiefly above the cloud line, where daily moisture encourages vegetation. On the more gentle slopes recent clearings gave evidence of enterprise on the part of the present inhabitants of the valley. After an hour's climb we reached what were unquestionably the ruins of Inca structures, on an artificial terrace which commands a magnificent view far down toward Paltaybamba and the brige of Chuquichaca, as well as in the opposite direction. The contemporaries of Captain Garcia speak of a number of forts which had to be stormed and captured before Tupac Amaru could be found. This was probably one of those "fortresses." Its strategic position and the ease with which it could be defended point to such an interpretation. Nevertheless this ruin did not fit the "fortress of Vitcos," nor the "House of the Sun" near the "white rock over the spring." It is called *Incahuaracana*, "the place where the Inca shoots with a sling." Which Inca, we wondered.

We left Lucma the next day, forded the Vilcabamba River and soon had an uninterrupted view up the valley to a truncated hill a thousand feet high, its top partly covered with a scrubby growth of trees and bushes, its sides steep and rocky. We were told that the name of the hill was "Rosaspata," a word of modern hybrid origin—*pata* being Quichua for "hill," while *rosas* is the

Spanish word for roses." Mogrovejo said his Indians told him that on the "Hill of Roses" there were more ruins. We hoped it might be true, especially as we now learned that the village at the foot of the hill, and across the river, was called Puquiura.

When Raimondi was here in 1865 it was but a "wretched hamlet with a paltry chapel." Today it is more prosperous. There is a public school here, to which children come from villages many miles away. I doubt if the teacher knew that this was the site of the first school in this whole region. Yet it was to a Puquiura that Friar Marcos came in 1566. If this were his Puquiura, then Vitcos must be near by, for he and Friar Diego walked with their famous procession of converts from Puquiura to the "House of the Sun" which was "close to Vitcos."

Crossing the Vilcabamba on a footbridge that afternoon, we came immediately upon the Marocnyoc ruins which Raimondi had marked on his map but obviously these were not Inca. Examination showed that they were apparently the remains of a Spanish ore-crushing mill, probably intended to pulverize gold-bearing quartz on a considerable scale. Perhaps this was the ore referred to by Captain Baltasar de Ocampo who came to Puquiura shortly after the death of the last Inca. He says that his houses and lands were "in the mining district of Puquiura, close to the ore-crushing mill of Don Cristoval de Albornoz."

Near the mill the Tincochaca River joins the Vilcabamba. Crossing this on a footbridge, we followed Mogrovejo to an old and very dilapidated structure in the saddle of the hill on the south side of Rosaspata. They called the place Uncapampa, or Inca pampa. It was probably one of the forts stormed by Captain Garcia and his men in 1571.

Ocampo wrote: "the fortress of Pitcos was on a very high mountain whence the view commanded a great part of the province of Vilcapampa." Garcia, as will be remembered, says that the principal fortress was "on a high eminence surrounded with rugged crags and jungles, very dangerous to ascend and almost impregnable."

Leaving Uncapampa and following my guides, I climbed up the ridge and followed a path along its west side to the top of Rosaspata. It is indeed a "high eminence surrounded with rugged crags." The side of easiest approach is protected by a splendid, long wall, built so carefully as not to leave a single toe-hold for active besiegers.

Passing some ruins much overgrown and of a primitive character, I soon found myself on a pleasant *pampa* near the top of the mountain. The view from here does command "a great part of the province of Vilcapampa." It is remarkably extensive on all sides; to the north and south are snow-capped mountains, to the east and west, deep verdure-clad valleys.

On the very summit of the hill we found the ruins of a partly enclosed compound consisting of thirteen or fourteen houses arranged so as to form a rough square, with one large and several small courtyards. The outside dimensions of the compound are about 160 feet by 145 feet. The builders showed the familiar Inca sense of symmetry in arranging the houses. Due to the wanton destruction of many buildings by the natives in their efforts at treasure-hunting, as well as their natural desire to get good building stones, the walls had been so pulled down that it was impossible to get the exact dimensions of the buildings. In only one of them could we be sure that there had been any niches.

Ocampo says of Pitcos, "there is an extensive level space with a very sumptuous and majestic building erected with great skill and art, all the lintels of the doors, the principal as well as the ordinary ones, being marble elaborately carved."

Most interesting of all is the structure which caught the attention of Ocampo and remained fixed in his memory. Enough remains of this building to give a good idea of its former grandeur. It was indeed a residence fit for a royal Inca, an exile from Cuzco. It is 245 feet long by 43 feet wide. There were no windows, but it was lighted by thirty doorways, fifteen in front and the same in back. It contained ten large rooms, besides three hallways running from front to rear. It is easy to understand why the walls were built rather hastily and are not noteworthy, but the principal entrances, namely those leading to each hall, are particularly well made. To be sure, they are not of "marble" as Ocampo said—there is no marble in the province—but of finely cut white granite. The lintels of the principal doorways, as well as of the ordinary ones, are also of solid blocks of white granite, the largest being as much as eight feet in length. The doorways are better than any other ruins in the Vilcambamba valley thus justifying the mention of them made by Ocampo, who lived near here and had time to become thoroughly familiar with their appearance, although they are not "carved," in our sense of the word. A very small portion of the edifice is still standing. Most of the rear doors had been filled up with ashlars, in order to make a continuous fence.

At last we had found a place which seemed to meet most of the requirements of Ocampo's description of the "fortress of Pitcos."

In his account of the life and death of his father, Titu Cusi gives no definite clue to the location of Vitcos, nor a description of it, but as will be remembered, Calancha remarks that "close by Vitcos in a village called Chuquipalpa, is a House of the Sun and in it a white stone over a spring of water."

That night we stayed at Tincochaca, in the hut of an Indian friend of Mogrovejo. As usual we made inquiries. Imagine our feelings when in response to the oft-repeated question, our host said "yes" in a neighboring valley there was "a great white rock over a spring of water!" If his story should prove to be true our quest for Vitcos was over.

On the next day, I followed the impatient Mogrovejo—whose object was not to study ruins but to earn dollars for finding them —and went over the hill on its northeast side of the Valley of *Los Andenes* ("the Terraces"). Here, sure enough, was a large, white granite boulder, flattened on top, which had a carved seat or platform on its northern side. Its west side covered a cave in which were several niches. This cave had been walled in on one side and may have been a mausoleum for Inca mummies.

When Mogrovejo and the Indian guide said there was a *manan-*

tial de agua ("Spring of Water") near by, I became greatly interested. On investigation, however, the "spring" turned out to be
nothing but part of a small irrigating ditch. (*Manantial* means
"spring"; it also means "running water.") But the rock was not
"over the water." Although this was undoubtedly one of those
huacas, or sacred boulders, selected by the Incas as the visible
representations of the founders of a tribe and thus was an important accessory to ancestor worship, it was not the Yurak Rumi
for which we were looking.

When we learned that the present name of this immediate
vicinity is Chuquipalta we were excited. Leaving the boulder and
the ruins of what possibly had been the house of its attendant
priest, we followed the little water course past a large number of
very handsomely built agricultural terraces, the first we had seen
in a long time, and the most important ones in the valley. So scarce
are *andenes* in this region and so noteworthy were these in particular that this vale has been named after them. They were probably
built under the direction of an Inca and intended to be used for his
own special corn and potatoes. Near them there are a number of
carved boulders, *huacas*. One had an *intihuatana* or sundial nubbin,
on it; another was carved in the shape of a saddle.

Continuing, we followed a trickling stream through thick
woods until we suddenly arrived at an open place called Ñusta
Isppana. Here before us was a great white rock. Our guides had
not misled us. Beneath the trees were the ruins of an Inca temple,
flanking and partly enclosing the gigantic granite boulder, one
end of which overhung a small pool of running water.

Since the surface of the little pool, as one gazes at it, does not
reflect the sky, but only the overhanging rock, the water looks
black and forbidding, even to unsuperstitious Yankees. It is easy
to understand that simple-minded Indian worshippers in this
secluded spot could believe that they actually saw the Devil appearing "as a visible manifestation" in the water, and that Indians
came from the most sequestered villages of the dense forests to
worship here and offer gifts and sacrifices.

It was late on the afternoon of August 9, 1911, when I first saw this remarkable shrine. Densely wooded hills rose on every side. There was not a hut to be seen, scarcely a sound to be heard, an ideal place for practicing the mystic ceremonies of an ancient cult. The remarkable aspect of this great boulder and the dark pool beneath its shadow had caused this to become a place of worship. Here, without doubt, was "the principal *mochadero* of those forested mountains." It is still venerated by the Indians of the vicinity. At last we had found the place where, in the days of Titu Cusi, the Inca priests faced the east, greeted the rising sun, "extended their hands towards it," and "threw kisses to it," "a ceremony of the most profound resignation and reverence." We may imagine the sun priests, clad in their resplendent robes of office, standing on the top of the rock at the edge of its steepest side, their faces lit by the rosy light of the early morning, awaiting the moment when the Great Divinity should appear above the eastern hills and receive their adoration. As it rose we may imagine them saluting it and crying: "O Sun! Thou who art in peace and safety, shine upon us, keep us from sickness, and keep us in health and safety. O Sun! Thou who has said let there be Cuzco and Tampu, grant that these children may conquer all other people. We beseech thee that thy children the Incas may be always conquerors, since it is for this that thou has created them." This was their customary invocation we are told.

With the contemporary accounts in our hands and the physical evidence before our eyes we could now be fairly sure that we had located one of Manco's capitals and the residence known to the Spaniards, visited by the missionaries and ambassadors as well as by the refugees who had sought safety here from the followers of Pizarro and had unfortunately put Manco to death. While it was too near Puquiura to be his "principal capital," Vilcapampa, it certainly was Vitcos.

So we went back up the Hill of Roses to make further studies and do some excavating.

On the south side of the hilltop, opposite the long palace, is the ruin of a single structure, 78 feet long and 25 feet wide, containing doors on both sides, no niches and no evidence of careful workmanship. It may have been a barracks for Manco's soldiers, but the absence of any niches leads me to believe that it was built by Manco's order for the Spanish soldiers who had fled from Cuzco and taken refuge with him. Another reason for my belief is that between this building and the palace is a *"pampa"* which might have been the scene of those games of bowls or quoits, which were played by the Spanish refugees. Here may have occurred that fatal game when one of the players lost his temper and killed his royal host.

Our excavations yielded a mass of rough potsherds, a few Inca whirl-bobs and bronze shawl-pins, and also a number of iron articles of European origin, heavily rusted horseshoe nails, a buckle, a pair of scissors, several bridle or saddle ornaments, and three jews' harps. My first thought was that modern Peruvians must have lived here at one time, although the necessity of carrying all water supplies up the steep hill would make this unlikely. Furthermore, the presence here of artifacts of European origin does not of itself point to such a conclusion. In the first place, we know that Manco was accustomed to making raids on Spanish travelers between Cuzco and Lima. He might very easily have brought back with him a Spanish bridle. In the second place, the musical instruments as well as the saddle ornaments may have belonged to the refugees, who might have enjoyed whiling away their exile with melancholy twanging. In the third place, the retainers of the Inca probably visited the Spanish market in Cuzco, where there would have been displayed at times a considerable assortment of goods of European manufacture. Finally, Rodriguez de Figueroa speaks expressly of two pairs of scissors he brought as a present to Titu Cusi. That no such array of European artifacts has been turned up in the excavations of any other important sites in the province of Vilcapampa would seem to indicate that they were abandoned before the Spanish Conquest or else were occupied by natives who had no means of accumulating such treasures.

All our expeditions in the ancient province of Vilcapampa have failed to disclose the presence of any other "white rock over a spring of water" surrounded by the ruins of a possible "House of the Sun." Consequently it seems reasonable to adopt the following conclusions: Ñusta Isppana is the Yurak Rumi of Father Calancha. The Chuquipalta of today is the place to which he refers as Chuquipalpa. This is the "Viticos" of Cieza de Leon, a famous military chronicler, a contemporary of Manco, who says that it was to the province of Viticos that Manco determined to retire when he rebelled against Pizarro, and that "having reached Viticos with a great quantity of treasure collected from various parts, together with his women and retinue, the king, Manco Inca, established himself in the strongest place he could find, whence he sallied forth many times and in many directions and disturbed those parts which were quiet, to do what harm he could to the Spaniards, whom he considered as cruel enemies."

The "strongest place" of Cieza de Leon, the Guaynapucara of Garcia, is now called Rosaspata. Ocampo had called it "the fortress of Pitcos," where, he says, "there was a level space with majestic buildings," the most noteworthy feature of which was that they had two kinds of doors and both kinds had white stone lintels. Finally, the modern village of Pucyura in the valley of the river Vilcabamba is the Puquiura of Father Calancha, the site of the first mission church in this region, as assumed by Raimondi. The fact that the distance from the "House of the Sun," is not too great for the religious procession, and that its location is near the fortress, all point to the correctness of this conclusion.

Our identification of these localities mentioned by Calancha and the other Spanish chroniclers has now been accepted by Peruvian archaeologists and historians. Rosaspata is the present name of the military and political capital of the last four Incas, which is variously given in the chronicles as Vitcos, Pitcos, Viticos and Uiticos.

3.

The Search
for Vilcapampa

ALTHOUGH THE REF-
uge of Manco is frequently spoken of as Vitcos by the contemporary writers, the word Vilcapampa, or Uilcapampa, is used even
more often. In fact Garcilasso, the chief historian of the Incas,
himself the son of an Inca princess, does not mention Vitcos.
Vilcabamba was the common name of the province. Father
Calancha says it was a very large area, "covering fourteen degrees
of longitude," about seven hundred miles wide. It included many
savage tribes "of the far interior" who acknowledged the suprem-
acy of the Incas and brought tribute to Manco and his sons. "The
Manaries and the Pilcosones came a hundred and two hundred
leagues" to visit the Inca.

The name is derived from two Quichua words meaning the
pampa where the *huilca* grows. The *huilca* tree is sub-tropical in
habit, and does not live in the temperate zone. The Quichua dic-
tionaries tell us *huilca* is a "medicine, a purgative." An infusion
made from the seeds is used as an enema. Also from seeds of the
huilca a powder is prepared, sometimes called *cohoba*, a narcotic
snuff "inhaled through the nostrils by means of a bifurcated tube."
"All writers unite in declaring that it induced a kind of intoxication
or hypnotic state, accompanied by visions which were regarded by
the natives as supernatural." While under its influence the necro-

mancers, or priests, were supposed to hold communication with unseen powers, and their incoherent mutterings were regarded as prophecies or revelations of hidden things. In treating the sick, the physicians made use of it to discover the cause of the malady or the person or spirit by whom the patient was bewitched.

Clearly, from the point of view of priests and soothsayers, the place where *huilca* was first found and used in their incantations would be important. Mr. O. F. Cook found the *huilca* tree growing near the bridge of San Miguel, below Machu Picchu. It is not strange to find therefore that the Inca name of the Urubamba River was Vilca-mayu: The "*Huilca* river." The *pampa* on this river where the tree grew would likely receive the name Vilca-pampa. If it became an important city, then the surrounding region might be named Vilcapampa after it. This seems to be the probable origin of the name of the province. Anyhow, it is worth noting that denizens of Cuzco, coming down the river in search of this highly prized narcotic, must have found the first trees not far from Machu Picchu.

As has been said, until quite recently the Vilcabamba valley was an unknown land to most Peruvians, even to those who lived in the city of Cuzco. Had the capital of the last four Incas been in a region whose climate appealed to Europeans, whose natural resources were sufficient to support a large population, and whose roads made transportation no more difficult than in most parts of the Andes, it would have been occupied from the days of Captain Garcia to the present by Spanish-speaking *mestizos*, who might have been interested in preserving the name of the ancient Inca capital and the traditions connected with it. However, there was nothing to lead any one to visit the upper Vilcabamba Valley or to desire to make it a place of residence.

It is probable that after the gold mines ceased to pay, and before the demand for rubber caused the San Miguel Valley to be appropriated by the white man, there was a period of nearly three hundred years when no one of education or of intelligence superior to the ordinary Indian shepherd lived anywhere near

Puquiura or Lucma. And until Señor Pancorbo opened his new road to Lucma, Puquiura was extremely difficult of access. Nine generations of Indians lived and died in the province of Vilcapampa between the death of the last reigning Inca, Tupac Amaru, and the arrival of the first modern explorers. The great stone buildings constructed on the "Hill of Roses" in the days of Manco and his sons were allowed to fall into ruin. Their roofs decayed and disappeared. The names of those who once lived here were known to fewer and fewer of the natives. It was not until the renaissance of historical and geographical curiosity in the nineteenth century, that it occurred to any one to look for Manco's capital.

We felt sure we had found Vitcos; nevertheless it was quite apparent that we had not yet found all the places which were called Vilcapampa. Examination of the writers of the sixteenth century shows that there may have been several places bearing that name; one spoken of by Calancha as Vilcabamba Viejo ("the old"), another also called Vilcapampa by Ocampo, which was founded by the Spaniards.

The soldiers of the last expedition which came to capture Tupac Amaru spoke of it as being in the *montaña*, the jungle forests from which the savages with bows and arrows had come to serve Titu Cusi when Rodriguez de Figueroa visited him. At any rate I wanted to be sure and see what ruins, if any, could be found there and identified. We must try to find Vilcapampa.

The only town which bears this name on the maps of Peru is near the source of the Vilcabamba River, not more than three or four leagues from Puquiura. We determined to visit it.

We found the town to lie on the edge of bleak upland pastures, 11,750 feet above the sea. Its full name is San Francisco de la Victoria de Vilcabamba. Instead of Inca walls or ruins, Vilcabamba has three score solidly built Spanish houses. At the time of our visit they were mostly empty, although their roofs, of unusually heavy thatch, seemed to be in good repair.

The solidity of the stone houses was due to the prosperity of gold diggers, who came to work the quartz mines which were made accessible after the death of Tupac Amaru. In the rocky cliffs nearby are the remains of the mines begun in Ocampo's day. The present air of desolation and absence of population is probably due to the decay of that industry. The site was "where the Spaniards who first discovered this land found the flocks and herds," and modern Vilcabamba is on grassy slopes, well suited for "flocks and herds." On the steeper slopes potatoes are still raised, although the valley itself is given up today almost entirely to pasture lands. We saw horses, cattle, and sheep in abundance where the Incas must have pastured their llamas and alpacas.

The fact that we saw no llamas or alpacas in the upland pastures, but only domestic animals of European origin, would also seem to indicate that for some reason or other this region had actually been abandoned by the Indians themselves. It is difficult to believe that if the Indians had inhabited these valleys continuously from Inca times to the present we should not have found at least a few of the indigenous American camels here.

Captain Ocampo, in his "Description of the Province of St. Francis of Victory of Vilcapampa," says: "To this city of Vilcapampa, when it was first peopled, after 1572, there came the monks of our Lady of Mercy and founded a convent. They were given land for building and for sowing. They built a living house and a church where they said mass."

We found that the ancient church was in very bad repair and we were told that mass was seldom said here now.

When Don Pedro Duque of Santa Ana was helping us to identify places mentioned in Calancha and Ocampo, the reference to "Vilcabamba Viejo" or Old Vilcapampa, was supposed by two of his informants to point to a place called Conservidayoc. Don Pedro told us that in 1902 Lopez Torres, who had traveled much in the *montaña* looking for rubber trees, reported the discovery there of the ruins of an Inca city. All of Don Pedro's friends assured us that Conservidayoc was a terrible place to reach. "No one now living has been there." It was "inhabited by savage Indians who would not let strangers enter their villages."

When we reached Paltaybamba, Señor Pancorbo's manager confirmed what we had heard. He said further that an individual named Saavedra lived at Conservidayoc and undoubtedly knew all about the ruins, but was very averse to receiving visitors. Saavedra's house was "extremely difficult to find." "No one had been there recently and returned alive." Opinions differed as to how far away it was. Señor Pancorbo himself, although he admitted that he had heard there were Inca ruins near Saavedra's station, begged us to desist from the attempt. He said Saavedra was "a very powerful man having many Indians under his control and living in grand state, with fifty servants, not at all desirous of being visited by anybody." The Indians were "of the Campa tribe, very wild and extremely savage. They use poisoned arrows and are very hostile to strangers."

By this time our curiosity was thoroughly aroused. We were familiar with the current stories regarding the habits of savage tribes who lived in the *montaña* and whose services were in great demand as rubber gatherers. We had even heard that Indians did not particularly like to work for Señor Pancorbo, who was an energetic, ambitious man, anxious to achieve many things, results which required more laborers than could easily be obtained. We could readily believe there might possibly be Indians at Conservidayoc who had escaped from his rubber estate of San Miguel. Undoubtedly, Señor Pancorbo's own life would have been at the mercy of their poisoned arrows. All over the Amazon Basin tribes visited with impunity by the explorers of the nineteenth century had now become so savage and revengeful as to lead them to kill all white men at sight.

Professor Foote and I considered the matter in all its aspects. We finally came to the conclusion that in view of the specific reports regarding the presence of Inca ruins at Conservidayoc we could not afford to follow the advice of the friendly planter. We

Bronze Axes, Chisels, and a Champi or Crow Bar of Bronze found at Machu Picchu

Every Inca town was provided with a supply of fresh water brought to fountains like the one here depicted where the women whose business it was—and still is—to make chicha—the native beer, favorite drink of the Incas, could fill their jars easily. The Indian girls in the picture are wearing shawls, fastened with shawl-pins just as their ancestors have done for centuries: We found many bronze shawl-pins at Machu Picchu.

The customary dress of the mountain Indians who like bright colors and warm clothes. His face gives a good idea of what the builders of Machu Picchu looked like. His language is Quichua which was carried over a good part of the Andes by the Incas and which is spoken by more American aborigines than any other native tongue today.

A fine type of Quichua woman, undoubtedly a descendant of one of the distant relatives of the Chosen Women of the Sun. She looks capable of having been a mamacuna *herself had she lived four hundred years ago.*

A young Quichua girl of the type selected by the Incas to go to the national boarding schools where the Chosen Women of the Sun were trained to weave fine textiles and make choice chicha for the refreshment of Inca nobles and priests.

Cap. III. Entra el Padre fray Diego Ortiz a Vilcabanba, i dales el Inga tormento en agua a los dos Religiosos, i tientalos con Indias vestidas con ábito de frayles.

AGuardando dejamos al Padre fray Diego Ortiz i al Padre fray Iuan del Cãto la licencia del Prelado para entrar en las montañas, vino licencia para que solo el Padre fray Diego Ortiz entrase en esta ocasion, i aconpañase al Padre fray Marcos, remitiendo para quando creciese mas aquel Cristianismo el añadir obreros, que aunque avisava el Padre fray Marcos que ya el Inga era apostata disimulado, i que las cosas de la fe en aquellas montañas no ivan con los crecimientos que prometian los principios, no resfriò el ardor de nuestros Iuan i Diego, antes encendiò las ansias, i reforcò los brios; pero sucediò en estos dos Religiosos lo que en los Apostoles Iuan i Diego, porque los nonbres correspondiesen a los fines, que solicitando anbos su martirio muriò Diego dentro de poco tienpo martirizado por el Rey Erodes, i a S. Iuã Evangelista no le quiso Cristo dejar que muriese a manos de tiranos, sino que muriese su muerte natural de mas de noventa años: asi sucede a estos dos Religiosos Iuan i Diego ermanos en la profesion, i ermanados en el deseo, pues quiere que entre fray Diego a morir, i que fray Iuan del Canto se quede, muera de viejo, que como veremos muriò de mas de ciento i diez años, tan siervo de Dios, como adelante nos dirà su vida: llorò mas de quarenta años el aver desmerecido la corona de martir. Puede pensarse que fue en la acepta-

Con toda priesa vino el Padre fr. Diego dosde Guarancalla, ò a recoger las cosas de la Iglesia, ò a tratar que no se fuese el Padre fray Marcos asta aguardar otro Religioso que estuviese en su lugar, i disponer con prudencia las cosas dòle en Puquiura, consultaron lo conveniente, i asentaron el sufrir i padecer por predicar, i aviendo ido los dos a ver al Inga, les dijo: Yo os quiero llevar a Vilcabanba, pues ninguno de los dos a visto aquel pueblo, ireys conmigo, que quiero festejaros. Salieron otro dia en conpañia del Inga, que llevò poco aconpañamiento de sus capitanes, i caziques, i sienpre los Reyes Ingas caminavan en andas. Llegaron a un parage llamado Ungacacha, i alli puso en egecucion la maldad que avia concertado, i fue que llenasen los caminos de agua, inundando la canpiña cõ arrojarle el rio, porque los Padres deseavan, i lo avian tratado de yr a Vilcabanba a predicar, porque era el mayor pueblo, i en que estava la Vniversidad de la Idolatria, i los catedraticos echizeros maestros de las abominaciones. Pero el Inga por espantarlos, i que no pretendiesen vivir, ò predicar en Vilcabanba, sino irse de la Provincia consultò este echo sacrilego i diabolico. Amaneciò, i a poco trecho bajando a un llano pensaron los dos Religiosos que era laguna, i el Inga les dijo: Por el medio desta agua avemos de pasar todos. O cruel apostata! el iva en andas, i los dos Sacerdotes a pie i descalços! Entraron los dos ministros Evangelicos en el agua, i como si pisaran alcatifas ivan gozosos, porque en odio de la ley Evangelica recibian tales baldones i tales tormentos de agua; davales la cintura elandoles al vientre, no estando vsados a mojar el pie: aqui caian resvalado, i no avia quien los ayudase a levantar, el uno al otro se davan las manos mientras los sacrilegos davan gritos de risa, azian

The modern town of Ollantaytambo, built by the Spaniards on the ruins of an Inca fortress whose terraces may be seen on the hillside above the town. We had our headquarters here for some time as the climate is pleasant and the town is located near the principal entrance to the Cordillera Vilcabamba.

Parts of pages 800 and 803 of Calancha's Chronicle of the Augustinian Order in Peru. *Note the words in the right-hand column:* "porque los Padres deseavan, i lo avian tratado de yr a Vilcabamba a predicar, porque era el mayor pueblo, i en que estava la Universidad de la Idolotaria, i los catedraticos echizeros maestros de las abominaciones." *I.e., "Because the Fathers desired and had entreated him to let them go to Vilcapampa to preach, because it was the principal city, and in it was the University of Idolatry, and the professors of sorcery, masters of the abominations." Since Machu Picchu meets these conditions, we know it was the original city of Vilcapampa, principal residence of the Inca Emperors.*

The pass between Mts. Soray, 19,400 feet, and Salcantay, 20,550 feet, is at an elevation of 15,200 feet. Before the new road was built down the Urubamba valley, this was one of the two "gateways" to the province of Vilcabamba. It was used by the Count de Sartiges in 1834 but is considered very dangerous and is only open during a few weeks in the "dry season." Our route lay to the left of the large glacier. We were fortunate in that very little snow had fallen for some time and the blue ice of the glacier was not covered. It is easy to understand why the conquistadors did not follow Manco to Vitcos.

The Urubamba valley road, blasted out of precipices by the Peruvian government about 1895 and which here runs in sight of the granite cliffs that surround Machu Picchu, enabled us to discover a part of the Inca empire which the Spaniards never saw and which was inaccessible to the explorers of the mid-nineteenth century like Raimondi and Paz Soldan and Wiener.

Ñusta Ispanna or Yurak Rumi, the great white rock over a spring of water described by Father Calancha as being near a Temple of the Sun which was near Vitcos. It was my discovery of this ancient shrine in 1911 that enabled us to identify the ruins of Rosaspata on the neighboring hillside as the site of Vitcos where Manco lived and where he was killed by Spanish refugees whom he had befriended. This rock was a very ancient mochadero *of the* montaña, *the place where the priests of the Sun God practiced the sacred ceremony of extending their hands to the sun and throwing kisses to it.* Mucha *is the Quichua word for a kiss.*

Our guide, the Gobernador Mogrovejo, standing in one of the few doorways left intact of the palace of Manco and his sons at Vitcos, now called Rosaspata. It is made of granite ashlars. Captain Ocampo who was a contemporary of Titu Cusi says the doors of this palace were of nicely cut "marble." There is no marble in this part of the Andes but that sounded better to Spanish ears than to say "white granite."

The houses of the West City seem to have been built at a later period than the massive walls of the ancient terraces on which they rest. In the foreground is the top of the Beautiful Wall adjoining a two-story-and-a-half "priest's house." Between the very regular niches are finely cut blocks or stone-pegs, carefully cut out of the ashlars themselves. In temple walls the stone-pegs are rectangular and ceremonial. In dwelling houses they are usually rounded so as not to chafe the ropes. Probably the huge aryballi or chica jars were suspended from them.

The Aobamba valley is extremely difficult of access. Its jungles are dense. It was one of the obstacles that kept the Spaniards from discovering Machu Picchu.

The Urubamba river, winding through a granite canyon, almost surrounding Huayna Picchu, as it looks from the top of Machu Picchu mountain. The picture was taken before we had done much clearing of the ruins, so they only show faintly in the saddle of the ridge. A recent visitor wrote that he was "thunderstruck" to find that the "tourist world . . . can harbor such an eighth wonder in a location that is itself as wonderful as anything in Switzerland or Norway, a marvel that can be reached without hardship."

A portion of the west wall of the Principal Temple showing the exquisite care with which the white granite ashlars were cut, fitted together, and gracefully graded in size so as to give the impression of strength at the base and lightness at the top. No architect ever designed a more graceful wall. The patience that was required to construct a thing of beauty like this wall and the artistic skill behind it are the more amazing when one remembers that the Incas had no iron tools and no instruments of precision—only stone and bronze.

The ruins of the Lost City lie on top of the ridge above steep cliffs.

must at least make an effort to reach them, meanwhile taking every precaution to avoid arousing the enmity of the powerful Saavedra and his savage retainers.

On the day following our arrival at the Spanish town of Vilcabamba, the *Gobernador*, Condore, taking counsel with his chief assistant, had summoned the wisest Indians living in the vicinity, including a very picturesque old fellow whose name, Quispi Cusi, was strongly reminiscent of the days of Titu Cusi. It was explained to him that this was a very solemn occasion and that an official inquiry was in progress. He took off his hat—but not his knitted cap—and endeavored to the best of his ability to answer our questions about the surrounding country. He said that the Inca Tupac Amaru once lived at Rosaspata. He had never heard of Vitcos or Vilcapampa Viejo, but he admitted that there were ruins in the *montaña* near Conservidayoc. Apparently, however, neither he nor any one in the village, had actually seen the ruins or visited their immediate vicinity. They all agreed that Saavedra's place was "at least four days' hard journey on foot in the *montaña* beyond Pampaconas." No village of that name appeared on any map of Peru, although it is frequently mentioned in the documents of the sixteenth century. Rodriguez de Figueroa, says that he met Titu Cusi at Banbaconas. He says further that the Inca came there from somewhere down in the *montaña* and presented him with a macaw and two hampers of peanuts, products of a warm region.

We had brought with us the large sheets of Raimondi's invaluable map which covered this locality. We also had the new map of South Peru and North Bolivia which had just been published by the Royal Geographical Society and gave a summary of all available information. The Indians said that Conservidayoc lay in a westerly direction from Vilcabamba, yet on Raimondi's map all of the rivers which rise in the mountains west of the town are short affluents of the Apurimac and flow southwest. We wondered whether the stories about ruins at Conservidayoc would turn out to be as barren of foundation as those we had heard from the trustworthy foreman at Huadquiña. One of our informants said the Inca city was called Espiritu Pampa, or the "Pampa of Ghosts." Would the ruins turn out to be "ghosts"? Would they vanish on the arrival of white men with cameras and measuring tapes?

Although no one at Vilcabamba had seen the ruins, they said that at Pampaconas, there were Indians who had actually been to Conservidayoc. Accordingly we decided to go there immediately.

After the usual delays, caused in part by the difficulty of catching our mules, which had taken advantage of our historical investigations to stray far up the mountain pastures, we finally set out from the boundaries of known topography headed for "Conservidayoc," a vague place surrounded with mystery, a land of hostile savages, albeit said to possess the ruins of an Inca town.

Our first day's journey was to Pampaconas. Here and in its vicinity the *gobernador* told us he could procure guides and the half-dozen carriers whose services we would need on the jungle trail where mules could not be used. As the Indians were averse to penetrating the wilds of Conservidayoc and were also likely to be extremely alarmed at the sight of men in uniform, the two *gendarmes* who were now accompanying us were instructed to delay their departure for a few hours and not to reach Pampaconas with our pack train until dusk. The *gobernador* said that if the Indians of Pampaconas caught sight of any brass buttons coming over the hills they would hide so effectively that it would be impossible to secure any carriers. Apparently this was due in part to that love of freedom which had led them to abandon the more comfortable towns for a frontier village where landlords could not call on them for forced labor. Consequently, before the arrival of any such striking manifestations of official authority as our *gendarmes*, the *gobernador* and his friend Mogrovejo proposed to put in the day craftily commandeering the services of a half dozen sturdy Indians. Their methods will be described presently.

Leaving modern Vilcabamba, we crossed the flat, marshy bottom of an old glaciated valley, in which one of our mules got thoroughly mired while searching for the succulent grasses which cover the treacherous bog. Fording the Vilcabamba River, which here is only a tiny brook, we climbed out of the valley and turned westward.

At the top of the pass we turned to look back and saw a long chain of snow-capped mountains towering above and behind the town of Vilcabamba. We searched in vain for them on our maps. Raimondi, followed by the Royal Geographical Society, did not leave room enough for such a range to exist between the rivers Apurimac and Urubamba. According to the latest maps of this region, published in the preceding year, we ought now to have been swimming in "the Great Speaker," near its junction with the river Pampas. Actually we were on top of a lofty mountain pass surrounded by high peaks and glaciers. The mystery was finally solved by Albert H. Bumstead, Chief Topographer of our expedition, when he determined the Apurimac and the Urubamba to be thirty miles farther apart at this point than any one had supposed. Our surveys opened an unexplored region, *1500 square miles in extent*, whose very existence had not been guessed before 1911. It proved to be one of the largest undescribed glaciated areas in South America. Yet it is less than a hundred miles from Cuzco, the chief city in the Peruvian Andes, and the site of a university for more than three centuries. That this region could have so long defied investigation and exploration shows better than anything else how wisely Manco had selected his refuge.

Looking west, we saw in front of us a great wilderness of deep green valleys and forest-clad slopes. We supposed from our maps that we were now looking down into the basin of the Apurimac. As a matter of fact, we were on the rim of the valley of the hitherto uncharted Pampaconas, a branch of the Cosireni, one of the affluents of the Urubamba. Instead of being the Apurimac Basin, what we saw was another unexplored region which drained into the Urubamba!

The "road" was now so bad that only with the greatest difficulty could we coax our surefooted mules to follow it. Once we had to dismount, as the path led down the long, steep, rocky stairway of ancient Inca origin. At last, rounding a hill, we came in sight of a lonesome little hut perched on a shoulder of the mountain. In front of it, seated in the sun on mats, were two women shelling corn. As soon as they saw the *Gobernador* approaching, they stopped their work and began to prepare lunch. It was about eleven o'clock and they did not need to be told that Señor Condore and his friends had not had anything but a cup of coffee since the night before. In order to meet the emergency of unexpected guests they killed four or five of the squealing guinea pigs that are usually to be found scurrying about the mud floor of the huts of mountain Indians. Before long the savory odor of roast *cuy*, well basted, and cooked to a turn on primitive spits, whetted our appetites.

I am willing to admit that this was the first time that I had ever knowingly tasted their delicate flesh. Had I not been very hungry, I might never have known how delicious a roast guinea pig can be. The meat is not unlike squab.

After this delicious lunch, Condore and Mogrovejo divided the extensive rolling countryside between them and each rode quietly from one lonesome farm to another, looking for men to engage as bearers. When they were so fortunate as to find the man of the house at home or working in his little bit of cultivated ground they greeted him pleasantly. When he came forward to shake hands, in the usual Indian manner, a silver dollar was unsuspectingly slipped into the palm of his right hand and he was informed that he had accepted pay for services which he must now render. It seemed very hard but this was the only way in which it was possible to secure carriers.

During Inca time the Indians never received pay for their labor. As has been said, a paternal government saw to it that they were properly fed and clothed and either given abundant opportunity to provide for their own necessities or else permitted to draw on official stores. In colonial days a less paternal government took advantage of the ancient system and enforced it without taking pains to see that it should not cause suffering. Then, for generations, thoughtless landlords, backed by local authority, forced the Indians to work without suitably recompensing them at the end of their labors or even pretending to carry out promises and wage agreements. The peons learned that it was unwise to perform any labor without first having received a considerable portion of their pay. When once they accepted money, however, their own custom and the law of the land provided that they must carry out their obligations. Failure to do so meant legal punishment.

Consequently when an unfortunate Pampaconas Indian found he had a dollar in his hand, he bemoaned his fate, but realized that service was inevitable. In vain did he plead that he was "busy," that his "crops needed attention," that his "family could not spare him," that "he lacked food for a journey." Condore and Mogrovejo were accustomed to all varieties of excuses. They succeeded in "engaging" half a dozen carriers. Before dark we reached the village of Pampaconas, a few small huts scattered over grassy hillsides, at an elevation of 10,000 feet.

In the notes of one of the military advisers of the Viceroy Francisco de Toledo is a reference to Pampaconas as a "high, cold place." This is correct. Nevertheless, I doubt if the present village is the Pampaconas mentioned in the documents of Garcia's day as being "an important town of the Incas." There are no ruins hereabouts. The huts of Pampaconas were newly built of stone and mud, and thatched with grass. They were occupied by a group of sturdy mountain Indians, who enjoyed unusual freedom from official or other interference and a good place in which to raise sheep and cultivate potatoes, on the very edge of the dense forest.

We found that there was some excitement in the village because on the previous night a jaguar, or possibly a cougar, had come out of the forest, attacked, killed, and dragged off one of the village ponies. We were really in new country.

We were conducted to the dwelling of a stocky, well-built Indian named Guzman, the most reliable man in the village, who had been selected to be the head of the party of carriers that was to accompany us to Conservidayoc. Guzman had some Spanish blood in his veins, although he did not boast of it. We carried on a most interesting conversation with him. He had been to Conservidayoc and had himself actually seen Inca ruins at Espiritu Pampa. At last the mythical "Pampa of Ghosts" began to take on, in our minds, an aspect of reality, even though we were careful to remind ourselves that another very trustworthy man had said he had seen ruins "finer than Ollantaytambo" near Huadquiña. Guzman did not seem to dread Conservidayoc as much as the other Indians, only one of whom had ever been there. To cheer them up we purchased a fat sheep. Guzman immediately butchered it in preparation for the journey.

Toward noon of the next day, all the Indian carriers but one having arrived, we started for Conservidayoc. We were told that it would be possible to use the mules for this day's journey. San Fernando, our first stop, was "seven leagues" away, far down in the densely wooded Pampaconas Valley. Leaving the village we climbed up the mountain, back of Guzman's hut, and followed a faint trail by a dangerous route along the crest of the ridge. The rains had not improved the path. Our saddle mules were of little use. We had to go nearly all the way on foot. Owing to cold rain and mist we could see but little of the deep canyon which opened below us, and into which we now began to descend four thousand feet through the clouds by a very steep, zigzag path, to a hot tropical valley. Below the clouds we found ourselves near a small abandoned clearing. Passing this and fording little streams, we went along a very narrow path, across steep slopes, on which maize had been planted. Finally we came to the end of the mule trail, another little clearing with two extremely primitive little shanties, mere shelters not deserving to be called huts; and this was San Fernando! It was with great difficulty we found and cleared a place for our tent, although its floor was only seven feet square.

At 8:30 P.M. August 13, 1911, while lying on the ground in

our tent, we noticed an earthquake. It was felt also by the Indians in the nearby shelter, who from force of habit rushed out of their frail structure and made a great disturbance, crying out that there was a *temblor*. Even had their little thatched roof fallen upon them, as it might have done during the stormy night which followed, they were in no danger; but, being accustomed to the stone walls and red tiled roofs of mountain villages where earthquakes sometimes do very serious harm, they were greatly excited. The motion seemed to me to be like a slight shuffle from west to east, lasting three or four seconds, a gentle rocking back and forth, with eight or ten vibrations. Several weeks later, near Huadquiña, we happened to stop at the Colpani telegraph office. The operator said he had felt two shocks on August 13th—one at five o'clock, which had shaken the books off his table and knocked over a box of insulators standing along a wall which ran north and south. He said the shock which we felt was the lighter of the two.

After a rainy night we set out again.

Our carriers were good for about fifty pounds apiece. Half an hour's walk brought us to Vista Alegre, another little clearing on an alluvial fan in the bend of the river. Opposite us rose abruptly a heavily forested mountain, whose summit was lost in the clouds a mile above. To circumvent this mountain the river had been flowing in a westerly direction; now it gradually turned to the northward. Again we were mystified, for, by Raimondi's map, it should have gone southward.

We now entered a dense jungle, where the narrow path became more and more difficult for the bearers. Crawling over rocks, under branches, along slippery little cliffs, on steps which had been cut in earth or rock, over a trail which not even a dog could follow unassisted, slowly we made our way down the valley. Owing to the heat, the humidity, and the frequent showers, it was mid-afternoon before we reached another little clearing called Pacaypata. Here, on a hillside nearly a thousand feet above the river, our men decided to spend the night in a tiny little shelter six feet long and five feet wide. Professor Foote and I had to dig a shelf out of the steep hillside with a hatchet in order to pitch our tent.

The next morning, not being detained by the vagaries of a mule train, we made an early start. As we followed the faint little trail across the gulches tributary to the river Pampaconas, we had to negotiate several unusually steep ascents and descents. Twice we had to cross the rapids of the river on primitive bridges which consisted only of a few logs lashed together and resting on slippery boulders. The carriers suffered from the heat. They found it more and more difficult to carry their loads.

By one o'clock we found ourselves on a small plain (ele. 4500 ft.) in dense woods surrounded by tree ferns, vines, and tangled thickets, through which it was impossible to see for more than a few feet. Here Guzman told us we must stop and rest a while, as we were now in the territory of *los salvajes,* the savage Indians who acknowledged only the rule of Saavedra and resented all intrusion. Guzman did not seem to be particularly afraid, but said that we ought to send ahead one of our carriers, to warn the savages that we were coming on a friendly mission and were not in search of rubber gatherers; otherwise they might attack us, or run away and disappear into the jungle. He said we should never be able to find the ruins without their help. The carrier who was selected to go ahead did not relish his task at all. Leaving his pack behind, he proceeded very quietly and cautiously along the trail and was lost to view almost immediately. There followed an exciting half-hour while we waited, wondering what attitude the savages would take toward us, and trying to picture to ourselves the mighty potentate, Saavedra, who had been described as sitting in the midst of savage luxury, "surrounded by fifty servants," and directing his myrmidons to checkmate our progress.

Suddenly we were startled by a crackling of twigs and the sound of a man running. We were instinctively holding our rifles a little higher in readiness for whatever might befall—when there burst out of the woods a pleasant-faced young Peruvian *mestizo,* quite conventionally clad, who had come in haste from Saavedra, his father, to extend to us a most cordial welcome! It seemed scarcely credible, but a glance at his face showed that there was no ambush in store for us. It was with a sigh of relief that we realized there was to be no shower of poisoned arrows from the impenetrable thickets. Gathering up our loads, we continued along the jungle trail, through woods which gradually became higher, deeper and darker, until presently we saw sunlight ahead, and, to our intense astonishment, the bright green of waving sugar cane. A few moments of walking through cane fields found us at a large comfortable hut, welcomed very simply and modestly by Saavedra himself. A more pleasant and peaceable little man it was never my good fortune to meet! We looked furtively around for his fifty savage servants, but all we saw was his good-natured Indian wife, three or four children, and a wild-eyed maid-of-all-work, evidently the only savage present. We asked our host what was the name of his estate. He said some called it "Jesus Maria" because that is what they exclaimed when they saw it. He himself had given it the hybrid name of Conservidayoc because it was a life saver for him. The word means "a spot where one may be preserved from harm."

It is difficult to describe our feelings as we accepted Saavedra's invitation to make ourselves at home, and sat down to an abundant meal of boiled chicken, rice, and sweet cassava (manioc). Saavedra gave us to understand that we were not only welcome to anything he had, but that he would do everything possible to enable us to see the ruins. They were, he said, at Espiritu Pampa, some distance farther down the valley, to be reached only by a hard trail passable for barefooted savages, but scarcely available for us unless we chose to go a good part of the distance on hands and knees.

Saavedra's plantation, being rich in humus, had produced more sugar cane than he could grind. In addition to this, he had bananas, coffee trees, sweet potatoes, tobacco, and peanuts. Instead of being "a very powerful chief having many Indians under his control"—a kind of Poo-Bah—Saavedra was merely a pioneer. In the utter wilderness, far from any neighbors, surrounded by dense forests and a few savages, he had established his home. He was not an Indian potentate, but only a frontiersman, soft-spoken and energetic, an ingenious carpenter and mechanic, a modest Peruvian of the best type.

Near the sugar mill were some very interesting large jars un-questionably Inca, which Saavedra was using in the process of boiling the juice and making crude sugar. He said he had found them in the jungle not far away. Four of them were of the familiar Aryballus type. Another was of a closely related form, having a wide mouth, pointed base, single incised, conventionalized animal-head nubbin attached to the shoulder, and band-shaped handles attached vertically below the median line. Although capable of holding more than ten gallons, this huge pot could be carried on the back and shoulders by means of a rope passing through the handles and around the nubbin. Saavedra said that he found near his house several bottle-shaped cists lined with stones, with a flat stone on top—evidently ancient graves. The bones had entirely disappeared. The cover of one of the graves had been pierced; the hole was covered with a thin sheet of beaten silver. He had also found a few stone implements and two or three bronze Inca axes. The bronzes and the pottery eloquently told us, beyond the peradventure of a doubt, that Incas had once lived down here in this damp jungle.

We finally left Conservidayoc by the trail which Saavedra's son and our Indians had been clearing. We emerged from the thickets near a promontory where there was a fine view down the valley and particularly of a heavily wooded alluvial fan just below us, the Indian village of Espiritu Pampa, or "Pampa of the Ghosts." In it were two or three small clearings and the little oval huts of savages.

On top of the promontory was the ruin of a small, rectangular building of rough stone, probably an Inca watch-tower. Our trail now followed an ancient stone stairway, about four feet in width and nearly a third of a mile long. It was built of uncut stones.

Possibly it was the work of Titu Cusi's soldiers whose chief duty it was to watch from the top of the promontory. We arrived at the principal clearing just as a heavy thunder shower began. The huts were empty. We hesitated to enter the home of a savage without an invitation, but the terrific downpour overcame our scruples, if not our nervousness. The hut had a steeply pitched roof. Its sides were made of small logs driven endwise into the ground and fastened together with vines. A small fire had been burning on the ground. Near the embers we saw two black ollas of Inca origin, hundreds of years old.

In the little clearing, cassava, *coca*, and sweet potatoes were growing in haphazard fashion among charred and fallen tree trunks. Nearby were the ruins of eighteen or twenty circular houses arranged in an irregular group. We wondered if this could be the "Inca City" which Lopez Torres had reported. It seems likely that they represent the dwellings of the fierce Antis whom Rodriguez de Figueroa saw with Titu Cusi.

While we were wondering whether the Inca themselves ever lived here, there suddenly appeared the naked figure of a sturdy young savage, armed with a stout bow and long arrows, and wearing a bamboo fillet. He had been hunting and showed us a bird he had shot. Soon afterwards there came two adult savages we had met at Saavedra's, accompanied by a cross-eyed friend, all wearing long tunics. They offered to guide us to other ruins. It was very difficult for us to follow their rapid pace. Half an hour's scramble through the jungle brought us to a natural terrace on the banks of a little tributary of the Pampaconas. They called it Eromboni Pampa. Here we found several artificial terraces and the rough foundations of a rectangular building 192 feet long. The walls were only a foot high. There was very little building material in sight. Apparently the structure had never been completed. Nearby was a typical Inca fountain with three spouts. Two hundred yards beyond the water-carrier's rendezvous, hidden behind a curtain of hanging vines and thickets so dense we could not see more than a few feet in any direction, the savages showed us the ruins of a group of Inca stone houses whose walls were still stand-ing in fine condition. The walls were of rough stone laid in adobe. Like some of the Inca buildings at Ollantaytambo, the lintels of the doors were made of three or four narrow uncut blocks. Below a stone-faced terrace was a partly enclosed fountain with a stone spout and a stone-lined basin. The shapes of the houses, their general arrangement, the niches, stone roof-pegs and lintels, all pointed to Inca builders. In the buildings we picked up several fragments of Inca pottery.

The next day, led by Saavedra's energetic young son, the savages and our carriers continued to clear away as much as pos-sible of the tangled growth at Eromboni Pampa near the best ruins. In this process, to the intense surprise not only of ourselves, but also of the savages, they uncovered, just below the little foun-tain where we had stood the day before, the well-preserved ruins of two Inca buildings of very superior construction, well fitted with stone-pegs and niches, symmetrically arranged. These houses stood by themselves on a little terrace. In them were fragments of characteristic pottery.

Nothing gives a better idea of the density of the jungle than the fact that the savages themselves had often been within five feet of these fine walls without being aware of their existence.

Encouraged by this important discovery of the best Inca ruins found in the valley, we continued the search, but all that any one was able to find was a carefully built stone bridge. Saavedra's son questioned the savages carefully. They said they knew of no other ruins.

There appears to me every reason to believe that the ruins here are those of one of the favorite residences of Titu Cusi. It may have been the place from which he journeyed to meet Rodri-guez in 1565.

The houses are of late Inca pattern, not of a kind which would have required a long period to build. The unfinished buildings may have been under construction during the latter part of the reign of Titu Cusi.

Who built the best buildings of Eromboni Pampa? Was this the "Vilcabamba Viejo" of Father Calancha, that "University of Idolatry where lived the teachers who were wizards and masters of abomination," the place to which Friar Marcos and Friar Diego went with so much suffering? Was there formerly on this trail a place called Ungacacha where the monks had to wade, and amused Titu Cusi by the way they handled their monastic robes in the water? They called it a "three days' journey over rough country." Calancha speaks of Puquiura as being "two long days' journey from Vilcabamba." It was "rough country" all right, but it took us five days to go from Espiritu Pampa to Puquiura. It did not seem to be reasonable to suppose that the priest and Virgins of the Sun (the personnel of the "University of Idolatry") who fled from cold Cuzco with Manco and were established by him somewhere in the fastnesses of Vilcapampa would have cared to live in this hot valley. The difference in climate is as great as that between Scotland and Egypt. They would not have found in Espiritu Pampa the food which they liked. Furthermore, they could have found the seclusion and safety which they craved just as well in several other parts of the province, together with a cool, bracing climate and food stuffs more nearly resembling those to which they were accustomed. Finally Calancha says "Vilcabamba the Old" was "the largest city" in the province, a term hardly applicable to anything here.

On the other hand there seemed to be no doubt that Eromboni Pampa and the Pampaconas Valley met the requirements of the place called Vilcabamba by the companions of Captain Garcia. They spoke of it as the town and valley to which Tupac Amaru, the last Inca, escaped after his forces lost the "young fortress" of Vitcos.

In 1572, when Captain Garcia took up the pursuit of Tupac Amaru the Inca fled "inland toward the valley of Simaponte . . . to the country of the Manaries Indians, a warlike tribe and his friends, where *balsas* and canoes were posted to save him and enable him to escape." There is now no valley in this vicinity called Simaponte. The Manaries live on the banks of the lower Urubamba. In order to reach their country Tupac Amaru probably went down the Pampaconas. From the "Pampa of the Ghosts" to canoe navigation would have been but a short journey. Evidently his friends who helped him to escape were canoemen. Captain Garcia gives an account of the pursuit of Tupac Amaru in which he says that, not deterred by the dangers of the jungle or the river, he, Garcia, constructed five rafts on which he put some of his soldiers and, accompanying them himself, went down the rapids, escaping death many times by swimming, until he arrived at a place called Momori, only to find that the Inca, learning of his approach, had gone farther into the woods. Nothing daunted, Garcia followed him, although he and his men now had to go on foot and barefooted with hardly anything to eat, most of their provisions having been lost in the river, until they finally caught Tupac and his friends; a tragic ending to a terrible chase, hard on the white man and fatal for the Incas.

Whether Tupac Amaru partook of such a delicacy as monkey meat, which the Amazonian Indians relish, but which is not eaten by the highlanders, may be doubted. Garcilasso speaks of Tupac Amaru's preferring to entrust himself to the hands of the Spaniards "rather than to perish of famine." His Indian allies lived well in a region where monkeys abound. It is doubtful whether they would ever have permitted Captain Garcia to capture the Inca had they been able to furnish Tupac with such food as he was accustomed to.

At all events, our investigation seemed to point to the probability of this valley having been an important part of the domain of the last Incas. It would have been pleasant to go further, but the carriers were anxious to return to Pampaconas. Although they did not have to eat monkey meat, they were afraid of the savages and nervous as to what use the latter might make of their powerful bows and long arrows.

At Conservidayoc Saavedra kindly took the trouble to make some sugar for us. He poured the syrup in oblong molds cut in a big log of hard wood. In some of the molds his son placed handfuls of nicely roasted peanuts. The result was an emergency ration which we greatly enjoyed on our return journey.

At San Fernando we met the pack mules. The next day, in the midst of continuing torrential downpours, we climbed out of the hot valley to the cold heights of Pampaconas. We were soaked with perspiration and drenched with rain. Snow had been falling near the village. Our teeth chattered like castanets. Professor Foote immediately commandeered Mrs. Guzman's fire and filled our tea kettle. It may be doubted whether a more wretched, cold, wet, and bedraggled party ever arrived at Guzman's hut; certainly nothing ever tasted better than that steaming hot sweet tea.

The Aobamba

We knew that the Incas had taken refuge in the Cordillera Vilcabamba and we thought we had found and identified most of the sites mentioned in the Chronicles but it was necessary to cover the region as exhaustively as possible in order to make assurance doubly sure. So I asked one of my young engineers to make an archaelogical and topographical reconnaissance of the hitherto unexplored Aobamba Valley. Assistant Topographer Heald undertook to approach this problem from the mouth of the valley at the junction of the Aobamba and Urubamba rivers. He met with almost insuperable difficulties.

Although the work looked easy as far as we could see from the mouth of the valley, he found that four miles from the mouth, up the winding stream, the jungle was almost impassable. There was no trail. The foliage was so dense that observations were impossible. During a hard afternoon's work with four or five men he succeeded in advancing only one mile.

There was little of archaeological interest in the portion of the valley which Mr. Heald succeeded in reaching. Quite unexpectedly, however, I got into the upper reaches of the valley about ten days later, and found some interesting ruins. It happened in this wise:

Don Tomas Alvistur of Huadquiña, an enthusiastic amateur archaeologist, took a considerable amount of interest in our work and was quite delighted when he discovered that some of his Indians knew of three localities where there were Inca ruins, so they said, that had not previously been visited by white men.

Don Tomas invited me to accompany him on a visit to these three groups of ruins, but when the time came to go he found that "business engagements" made it impossible for him to do more than accompany me part of the way to the first group. He went to the trouble, however, of securing three Indian guides and carriers and gave them orders to carry my kit whenever the pack-mule could not be used, and to guide me safely to the three ruins and home again.

The end of the first day found us on top of a ridge between the valleys of the Aobamba and the Salcantay, about 5,000 feet above the estate of Huadquiña where we had started. Here we did discover a number of ruins and two or three modern huts.

The Indians said that the place was called Llacta Pata. But this is a descriptive term as "llacta" means "town" and "pata" means "a height." We found evidence that some Inca chieftain had built his home here and had included in the plan ten or a dozen buildings. They were made of rough stones laid in clay with the usual symmetrical arrangement of doors and niches. It may very well have been built by one of Manco's captains. It was on a strategic spot.

The next morning we crossed a high pass and descended rapidly into a steep-walled valley, containing one of the upper tributaries of the Aobamba. The lower slopes were covered with a dense forest. About 2 o'clock in the afternoon we reached the valley bottom at a point where several smaller tributaries unite to form the principal west branch of the Aobamba. The place was called Palcay.

Here we found two or three huts, one of them located in a very interesting ruined stronghold to which the Indians again gave the Quichua name for town, Llacta. As the location of the stronghold in the bottom of a valley was not easily defensible, a wall about 12 feet in height surrounded the quadrangular group of houses. The characteristics of the buildings were distinctly Inca.

The chateau, if so it might be called, was about 145 feet square and divided by two narrow cross streets into four equal quarters. Two of these quarters had been completed, and consisted of five houses arranged around a courtyard in a symmetrical fashion. The third quarter was almost complete, while the fourth quarter had only the beginnings of two or three houses. Each one of the four quarters had a single entrance gate on its north side. The gnats were very bad, which made the work of measuring and mapping the ruins extremely annoying.

The most remarkable feature of this Inca stronghold is that the streets run north and south, east and west, on the exact cardinal points. These ruins are in the Southern Hemisphere, so the North Star is not visible, yet one street follows the meridian exactly. How was it done?

The next day we found ourselves near the ruins of a village. Judging by its primitive appearance it could not have been a place of much importance and it is impossible to say whether it had been occupied since the Spanish conquest or not. The guide either did not give it a name or we were unable to understand what he said.

After proceeding with great difficulty over snowcovered mountain trails, we came down into a new valley just at dusk and found that we were in one of the upper branches of the Chamana River, a tributary of the Urubamba, where we discovered several groups of Inca ruins, not shown on any map. These ruins may have been in the minds of the Indians who had reported to Don Tomas Alvistur at Huadquiña that they could show us "three" which had "never been visited by white men."

Near them the Incas, desiring to save as much of the upland valley floor as possible for agricultural purposes, had straightened the bed of a meandering stream and inclosed it in a stone-lined channel, making it practically straight for nearly three-quarters of a mile.

This journey actually produced excellent results in the discovery of hitherto undescribed ruins and gave further evidence of the Inca occupancy of all available terrain in the Cordillera Vilcabamba. Yet, we still had not identified Vilcapampa—the "principal city" of Manco and his sons.

Part 3
Machu Picchu

1.

The Discovery

IT WILL BE REMEM-
bered that it was in July 1911, that I began the search for the last
Inca capital. Accompanied by a dear friend, Professor Harry
Ward Foote, of Yale University, who was our Naturalist, and my
classmate Dr. Wm. G. Erving, the Surgeon of the Expedition,
I had entered the marvelous canyon of the Urubamba below the
Inca fortress of Salapunco near Torontoy.

Here the river escapes from the cold plateau by tearing its way
through gigantic mountains of granite. The road runs through a
land of matchless charm. It has the majestic grandeur of the
Canadian Rockies, as well as the startling beauty of the Nuuanu
Pali near Honolulu, and the enchanting vistas of the Koolau Ditch
Trail on Maui, in my native land. In the variety of its charms and
the power of its spell, I know of no place in the world which can
compare with it. Not only has it great snow peaks looming above
the clouds more than two miles overhead; gigantic precipices of
many-colored granite rising sheer for thousands of feet above the
foaming, glistening, roaring rapids, it has also, in striking contrast,
orchids and tree ferns, the delectable beauty of luxuriant vegetation, and the mysterious witchery of the jungle. One is drawn
irresistibly onward by ever-recurring surprises through a deep,
winding gorge, turning and twisting past overhanging cliffs of
incredible height.

Above all, there is the fascination of finding here and there

159

under swaying vines, or perched on top of a beetling crag, the rugged masonry of a bygone race; and of trying to understand the bewildering romance of the ancient builders who, ages ago, sought refuge in a region which appears to have been expressely designed by nature as a sanctuary for the oppressed, a place where they might fearlessly and patiently give expression to their passion for walls of enduring beauty. Space forbids any attempt to describe in detail the constantly changing panorama, the rank tropical foliage, the countless terraces, the towering cliffs, the glaciers peeping out between the clouds.

You will remember that after passing Maquina where the sugar machinery had been abandoned because it could not be carried across the face of a great granite precipice, we had entered a little open plain called Mandor Pampa. Except where the rapids roared past it, gigantic precipices hemmed it in on all sides.

We passed an ill-kept, grass-thatched hut, turned off the road through a tiny clearing, and made our camp at the edge of the river on a sandy beach. Opposite us, beyond the huge granite bowlders which interfered with the progress of the surging stream, the steep mountain was clothed with thick jungle. Since we were near the road yet protected from the curiosity of passers-by, it seemed to be an ideal spot for a camp. Our actions, however, aroused the suspicions of the owner of the hut, Melchor Arteaga, who leased the lands of Mandor Pampa. He was anxious to know why we did not stay at his "tavern" like other respectable travelers. Fortunately the Prefect of Cuzco, our old friend J. J. Nuñez, had given us an armed escort who spoke Quichua. Our *gendarme*, Sergeant Carrasco, was able to reassure the inn keeper. They had quite a long conversation. When Arteaga learned that we were interested in the architectural remains of the Incas, and were looking for the palace of the last Inca, he said there were some very good ruins in this vicinity—in fact, some excellent ones on top of the opposite mountain, called Huayna Picchu, and also on a ridge called Machu Picchu!

The morning of July 24th dawned in a cold drizzle. Arteaga

shivered and seemed inclined to stay in his hut. I offered to pay him well if he would show me the ruins. He demurred and said it was too hard a climb for such a wet day. But when he found that I was willing to pay him a *sol* (a Peruvian silver dollar, fifty cents, gold), three or four times the ordinary daily wage in this vicinity, he finally agreed to go. When asked just where the ruins were, he pointed straight up to the top of the mountain. No one supposed that they would be particularly interesting. And no one cared to go with me. The Naturalist said there were "more butter-flies near the river!" and he was reasonably certain he could col-lect some new varieties. The Surgeon said he had to wash his clothes and mend them. Anyhow it was my job to investigate all reports of ruins and try to find the Inca capital.

So, accompanied only by Sergeant Carrasco I left camp at ten o'clock. Arteaga took us some distance upstream. On the road we passed a snake which had only just been killed. He said the region was the favorite haunt of "vipers." We later learned the lance-headed or yellow viper, commonly known as the fer-de-lance, a very venomous serpent, capable of making considerable springs when in pursuit of its prey, is common hereabouts.

After a walk of three quarters of an hour Arteaga left the main road and plunged down through the jungle to the bank of the river. Here there was a primitive bridge which crossed the roaring rapids at its narrowest part, where the stream was forced to flow between two great bowlders. The "bridge" was made of half a dozen very slender logs, some of which were not long enough to span the distance between the bowlders, but had been spliced and lashed together with vines!

Arteaga and the Sergeant took off their shoes and crept gingerly across, using their somewhat prehensile toes to keep from slipping. It was obvious that no one could live for an instant in the icy cold rapids, but would immediately be dashed to pieces against the rocks. I am frank to confess that I got down on my hands and knees and crawled across, six inches at a time. Even after we reached the other side I could not help wondering what would happen to the "bridge" if a particularly heavy shower should fall in the valley above. A light rain had fallen during the night and the river had risen so that the bridge was already threatened by the foaming rapids. It would not take much more to wash it away entirely. If this should happen during the day it might be very awkward. As a matter of fact, it did happen a few days later and when the next visitors attempted to cross the river at this point they found only one slender log remaining.

Leaving the stream, we now struggled up the bank through dense jungle, and in a few minutes reached the bottom of a very precipitous slope. For an hour and twenty minutes we had a hard climb. A good part of the distance we went on all fours, sometimes holding on by our fingernails. Here and there, a primitive ladder made from the roughly notched trunk of a small tree was placed in such a way as to help one over what might otherwise have proved to be an impassable cliff. In another place the slope was covered with slippery grass where it was hard to find either hand-holds or footholds. Arteaga groaned and said that there were lots of snakes here. Sergeant Carrasco said nothing but was glad he had good military shoes. The humidity was great. We were in the belt of maximum precipitation in Eastern Peru. The heat was excessive; and I was not in training! There were no ruins or *andenes* of any kind in sight. I began to think my companions had chosen the better part.

Shortly after noon, just as we were completely exhausted, we reached a little grass-covered hut 2,000 feet above the river where several good-natured Indians, pleasantly surprised at our unexpected arrival, welcomed us with dripping gourds full of cool, delicious water. Then they set before us a few cooked sweet potatoes. It seems that two Indian farmers, Richarte and Alvarez, had recently chosen this eagles' nest for their home. They said they had found plenty of terraces here on which to grow their crops. Laughingly they admitted they enjoyed being free from undesirable visitors, officials looking for army "volunteers" or collecting taxes.

Richarte told us that they had been living here four years. It seems probable that, owing to its inaccessibility, the canyon had been unoccupied for several centuries, but with the completion of the new government road, settlers began once more to occupy this region. In time somebody clambered up the precipices and found on these slopes at an elevation of 9,000 feet above the sea, an abundance of rich soil conveniently situated on artificial terraces, in a fine climate. Here the Indians had finally cleared off and burned over a few terraces and planted crops of maize, sweet and white potatoes, sugar cane, beans, peppers, tree tomatoes, and gooseberries.

They said there were two paths to the outside world. Of one we had already had a taste; the other was "even more difficult," a perilous path down the face of a rocky precipice on the other side of the ridge. It was their only means of egress in the wet season when the primitive bridge over which we had come could not be maintained. I was not surprised to learn that they went away from home "only about once a month."

Through Sergeant Carrasco I learned that the ruins were "a little further along." In this country one never can tell whether such a report is worthy of credence. "He may have been lying" is a good footnote to affix to all hearsay evidence. Accordingly, I was not unduly excited, nor in a great hurry to move. The heat was still great, the water from the Indians' spring was cool and delicious, and the rustic wooden bench, hospitably covered immediately after my arrival with a soft woolen poncho, seemed most comfortable. Furthermore, the view was simply enchanting. Tremendous green precipices fell away to the white rapids of the Urubamba below. Immediately in front, on the north side of the valley, was a great granite cliff rising 2,000 feet sheer. To the left was the solitary peak of Huayna Picchu, surrounded by seemingly inaccessible precipices. On all sides were rocky cliffs. Beyond them cloud-capped snow-covered mountains rose thousands of feet above us.

We continued to enjoy the wonderful view of the canyon,

but all the ruins we could see from our cool shelter were a few terraces.

Without the slightest expectation of finding anything more interesting than the ruins of two or three stone houses such as we had encountered at various places on the road between Ollantaytambo and Torontoy, I finally left the cool shade of the pleasant little hut and climbed farther up the ridge and around a slight promontory. Melchor Arteaga had "been there once before," so he decided to rest and gossip with Richarte and Alvarez. They sent a small boy with me as a "guide." The Sergeant was in duty bound to follow, but I think he may have been a little curious to see what there was to see.

Hardly had we left the hut and rounded the promontory than we were confronted with an unexpected sight, a great flight of beautifully constructed stone-faced terraces, perhaps a hundred of them, each hundreds of feet long and ten feet high. They had been recently rescued from the jungle by the Indians. A veritable forest of large trees which had been growing on them for centuries had been chopped down and partly burned to make a clearing for agricultural purposes. The task was too great for the two Indians so the tree trunks had been allowed to lie as they fell and only the smaller branches removed. But the ancient soil, carefully put in place by the Incas, was still capable of producing rich crops of maize and potatoes.

However, there was nothing to be excited about. Similar flights of well-made terraces are to be seen in the upper Urubamba Valley at Pisac and Ollantaytambo, as well as opposite Torontoy. So we patiently followed the little guide along one of the widest terraces where there had once been a small conduit and made our way into an untouched forest beyond. Suddenly I found myself confronted with the walls of ruined houses built of the finest quality of Inca stone work. It was hard to see them for they were partly covered with trees and moss, the growth of centuries, but in the dense shadow, hiding in bamboo thickets and tangled vines, appeared here and there walls of white granite ashlars carefully cut and exquisitely fitted together. We scrambled along through the dense undergrowth, climbing over terrace walls and in bamboo thickets where our guide found it easier going than I did. Suddenly without any warning, under a huge overhanging ledge the boy showed me a cave beautifully lined with the finest cut stone. It had evidently been a Royal Mausoleum. On top of this particular ledge was a semi-circular building whose outer wall, gently sloping and slightly curved bore a striking resemblance to the famous Temple of the Sun in Cuzco. This might also be a Temple of the Sun. It followed the natural curvature of the rock and was keyed to it by one of the finest examples of masonry I had ever seen. Furthermore it was tied into another beautiful wall, made of very carefully matched ashlars of pure white granite, especially selected for its fine grain. Clearly, it was the work of a master artist. The interior surface of the wall was broken by niches and square stone-pegs. The exterior surface was perfectly simple and unadorned. The lower courses, of particularly large ashlars, gave it a look of solidity. The upper courses, diminishing in size toward the top, lent grace and delicacy to the structure. The flowing lines, the symmetrical arrangement of the ashlars, and the gradual gradation of the courses, combined to produce a wonderful effect, softer and more pleasing than that of the marble temples of the Old World. Owing to the absence of mortar, there were no ugly spaces between the rocks. They might have grown together. On account of the beauty of the white granite this structure surpassed in attractiveness the best Inca walls in Cuzco which had caused visitors to marvel for four centuries. It seemed like an unbelievable dream. Dimly, I began to realize that this wall and its adjoining semicircular temple over the cave were as fine as the finest stonework in the world.

It fairly took my breath away. What could this place be? Why had no one given us any idea of it? Even Melchor Arteaga was only moderately interested and had no appreciation of the importance of the ruins which Richarte and Alvarez had adopted for their little farm. Perhaps after all this was an isolated small place which had escaped notice because it was inaccesible.

Then the little boy urged us to climb up a steep hill over what seemed to be a flight of stone steps. Surprise followed surprise in bewildering succession. We came to a great stairway of large granite blocks. Then we walked along a path to a clearing where the Indians had planted a small vegetable garden. Suddenly we found ourselves standing in front of the ruins of two of the finest and most interesting structures in ancient America. Made of beautiful white granite, the walls contained blocks of Cyclopean size, higher than a man. The sight held me spellbound.

Each building had only three walls and was entirely open on one side. The principal temple had walls twelve feet high which were lined with exquisitely made niches, five, high up at each end, and seven on the back. There were seven courses of ashlars in the end walls. Under the seven rear niches was a rectangular block fourteen feet long, possibly a sacrificial altar, but more probably a throne for the mummies of departed Incas, brought out to be worshipped. The building did not look as though it ever had a roof. The top course of beautifully smooth ashlars was not intended to be covered, so the sun could be welcomed here by priests and mummies. I could scarcely believe my senses as I examined the larger blocks in the lower course and estimated that they must weigh from ten to fifteen tons each. Would anyone believe what I had found? Fortunately, in this land where accuracy in reporting what one has seen is not a prevailing characteristic of travelers, I had a good camera and the sun was shining.

The principal temple faces the south where there is a small plaza or courtyard. On the east side of the plaza was another amazing structure, the ruins of a temple containing three great windows looking out over the canyon to the rising sun. Like its neighbor, it is unique among Inca ruins. Nothing just like them in design and execution has ever been found. Its three conspicuously large windows, obviously too large to serve any useful purpose, were most beautifully made with the greatest care and solidity. This was clearly a ceremonial edifice of peculiar signifi-cance. Nowhere else in Peru, so far as I know, is there a similar structure conspicuous for being "a masonry wall with three windows." It will be remembered that Salcamayhua, the Peruvian who wrote an account of the antiquities of Peru in 1620 said that the first Inca, Manco the Great, ordered "works to be executed at the place of his birth, consisting of a masonry wall with three windows." Was that what I had found? If it was, then this was not the capital of the last Inca but the birthplace of the first. It did not occur to me that it might be both. To be sure the region was one which could fit in with the requirements of Tampu Tocco, the place of refuge of the civilized folk who fled from the southern barbarian tribes after the battle of La Raya and brought with them the body of their king Pachacutec who was slain by an arrow. He might have been buried in the stone-lined cave under the semi-circular temple.

Could this be "the principal city" of Manco and his sons, that Vilcapampa where was the "University of Idolatry" which Friar Marcos and Friar Diego had tried to reach. It behooved us to find out as much about it as we could.

2.

Exploration of Machu Picchu and Huayna Picchu

IN VIEW OF THE probable importance of the ancient Inca city which we had found on top of the ridge between the peaks of Machu Picchu and Huayna Picchu, our first task was to make a map of the ruins. On account of the forest and the dense undergrowth this proved to be a difficult task, but it was finally accomplished by Herman Tucker and his volunteer assistant, Paul Lanius. After the map was completed everyone was amazed at the remarkable extent of the area which had once been the site of an important city. In 1912 it was determined to organize under the auspices of of Yale University and the National Geographic Society an Expedition with the object of exploring it as thoroughly as possible.

The task was not an easy one, even though the President of Peru, Augusto B. Leguia, gave us the full support of his government and the Prefect of Cuzco was instructed to aid us in every possible way. Had it not been for this cooperation we should not have been able to secure the services of enough Indian workmen to clear the ruins.

Our first problem was to open a feasible route for the transportation of supplies going in and specimens coming out because everything would have to be carried on men's backs. Our food boxes weighed sixty pounds. Each was designed to provide all the supplies needed for two men for eight days. When filled with potsherds, they would weigh more.

The trail up which I had been guided by Melchor Arteaga was on the east side of the ridge, starting at a frail little bridge formed of half a dozen logs lashed together with vines, which had been washed away soon after my visit. Besides, as I have said, for a good part of the distance the climbing was difficult. It would have been impossible for an Indian bearer to carry more than a very small load.

The path on the west side of the ridge, which began at the San Miguel bridge was the one most frequently used by the Quichua Indians, Richarte and Alvarez, who lived near the ruins.

Tucker and Lanius had been obliged to use the west trail and had reported that it was perilous, winding along the face of rocky precipices and in two or three places crossing in front of sheer rock cliffs on fragile, rustic ladders. In fact, it was so difficult and so dangerous as to make it impassable for our Indian carriers. By electing to improve it we could avoid the necessity of building a bridge over the Urubamba, but its use would involve an additional climb of five hundred feet for every load that had to be carried up to camp. Moreover, the foot of this trail lay four miles farther down the rapids, four miles farther from our base at Cuzco. Consequently it was decided to try to build a bridge of our own and construct a new trail on the east side of the ridge. Fortunately I was able to intrust this work to Kenneth C. Heald, one of the topographers of the Expedition, whose Colorado training as a mining engineer and whose determination to surmount all obstacles made him invaluable to our undertaking.

The width of the Urubamba River at its narrowest point, the most feasible place for building the new footbridge, was about eighty feet. The roaring rapids, impossible to ford even in the dry season, are here divided into four parts by huge bowlders. For material Mr. Heald had to depend on the tropical forest which grows along the banks of the river. This of itself added another problem, for although there are many kinds of trees in the bottom of the canyon, all the species are covered with moss and lichen, so that it is difficult to determine their character. The quality of the timber varies greatly; some of the species produce hard, durable wood of great density and fine texture; other, quick-growing species produce wood of inferior quality, soft and brittle. Mr. Heald was finally able to select several fine, straight, hardwood varieties growing close to the east bank of the stream near the spot where he planned to construct his bridge. For workmen he had ten dull, unwilling Quichuas who had been forced to accompany him by the *gobernador* of a nearby town. Mr. Heald's only real assistant was an excellent *gendarme*, Tomas Cobinas, an energetic young *mestizo* who had been assigned to us by the prefect and who could be counted on to see to it that the Indians kept steadily at work.

The cutting of the logs for the first section of the bridge and the placing of them in position over an eight foot reach was simple enough. To cross the next forty feet of the icy white rapids proved more difficult. In the absence of derricks or any heavy tackle, Heald's first plan was to lay a log in the stream parallel to the bank above the bridge, fasten the lower end and let the current swing the upper end around until it lodged on the central bowlder. On trying this, however, the timber proved to be of such dense hardwood that it sank immediately and was lost in the rapids. Mr. Heald then very ingeniously contrived a primitive cantilever device with which he finally succeeded in crossing the torrent.

He then built an excellent rustic bridge which served its purpose admirably until the end of our work at Machu Picchu. Recently the Peruvian Government has built a new bridge here over which mules can pass and serve to carry tourists up to the ruins from the end of the narrow gauge railway which brings them down from Cuzco. An automobile road is about finished.

The construction of our first trail was retarded by dense tropical jungle, by the steepness of the slope, and finally by the

Deep in the jungles of the Pampaconas river we discovered Inca ruins near a place now called Espiritu Pampa. Resting on top of the Inca's bridge is the author wearing his useful hunting coat, designed to carry everything.

The "Lost City of the Incas," favorite residence of the last Emperors, site of temples and palaces built of white granite in the most inaccessible part of the grand canyon of the Urubamba; a holy sanctuary to which only nobles, priests, and the Virgins of the Sun were admitted. It was once called Vilcapampa but is known today as Machu Picchu. Behind it is the peak of Huayna Picchu flanked by precipices which rise 2500 feet from the foaming rapids in the horseshoe bend of the Urubamba river.

The Inca sanctuary of Vilcapampa, which we now call Machu Picchu, was protected from undesirable visitors by a dry moat and a high wall. Here on top of the narrow ridge was the entrance, the City Gate. Only Inca nobles, priests and priestesses, and the novitiates or Chosen Women of the Sun were permitted within the sacred precincts of the sanctuary.

The inside of the City Gate. Over the massive lintel is an eye-bonder which projects so as to be able to support a hanging gate or vertical bar. In the corner of the largest block in the left gate-post a hole had been cut to permit the insertion of a small perpendicular stone-pin which we call a bar-hold because it could be used to fasten the end of a horizontal bar back of the door. A corresponding bar-hold is on the right side of the gate. The bar-holds in this case are set into saucer-shaped depressions cut into the ashlars above and below. (Following page).

There are more than a hundred stairways in the ruins of Machu Picchu, but the finest of all is this megalithic flight leading from the Sacred Plaza to the top of Intihuatana Hill. On ceremonial occasions and great festivals connected with the worship of the Sun God, a gay procession of Inca nobles, priests, and Virgins of the Sun must have used this fine granite stairway in marching to the top of the hill to witness the worship of their favorite deity. The Chosen Women then saw the finest products of their handlooms displayed to advantage. (Preceding page).

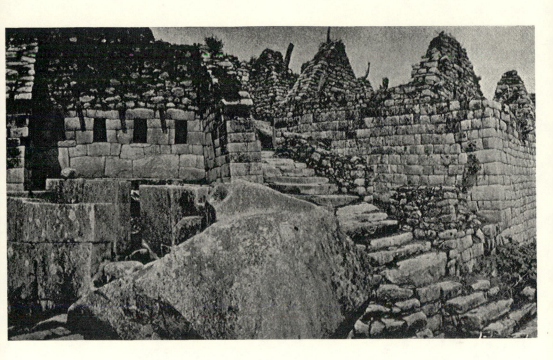

The Heart of the City of Vilcapampa. At the left are well built dwellings, probably for the Priests of the Sun. The semi-circular temple over the great ledge was probably the center of Sun worship. Under it is a carefully constructed mausoleum. In the center is a building that may have been used for the manufacture of chicha *for the Inca. It overlooks a very fine fountain, the highest of a long series that adjoin the Stairway of the Fountains. Beyond the stairway is a magnificent compound, probably the residence of the Inca Emperor himself, the "King's Group."*

Each of the three large niches in this stone temple had bar-holds cut into the middle ashlars. The niches also were furnished with very small niches which could have held votive offerings if, as we suppose, the large niches were intended for mummy bundles of distinguished persons.

The interior of one of the better houses in the East City has stone mortars, useful in the process of grinding corn or frozen potatoes, carved out of the ledge on which the house rests. In between the niches, just above the head of one of my Indian helpers, may be seen a roughly cylindrical block of stone bonded into the wall. It was customary in most Inca houses to have one of these stone-pegs placed between each pair of niches. They served as useful hooks while the niches served as cupboards. Probably the pointed chicha jars, sometimes called aryballi, were hung from these stone-pegs.

The Intihuatana of the Inca builders of Machu Picchu—the place where the High Priest of the Sun God succeeded in tying him up on the occasion of the winter solstice when it seemed likely to the unfortunate Indians that the Sun who made life bearable in the high Andes was leaving them. The priests of the Sun God, students of astronomy, knew that on the day of the solstice the sun would start coming back again from his annual pilgrimage to the northern hemisphere, so it would then be safe to claim that they had tied him to the Intihuatana stone. Learning the importance of this stone pillar in the religion of the Incas, the Spanish conquistadors were accustomed to break it off whenever they found one. As they never reached Machu Picchu, the pillar still stands as it was left by the ancient worshippers.

A portion of the Sacred Plaza with the Principal Temple on the left and the Memorial Temple of Three Windows on the right. The former had no roof. The latter had a roof which was partly supported by great beams which rested on the column in the center.

The northeast corner of a perfect gem of a house which adjoins
the Principal Temple and which was built with the utmost skill
and a marvelous sense of symmetry and proportion. It is possible
that the bench was intended to receive the mummy bundles of
noble ancestors.

The wives of our Indian workers, Richarte and Alvarez, standing
in front of one of the great polygonal blocks of white granite
used in the north wall of the Memorial Temple of the Three
Windows. The cavity in the upper left-hand corner was intended
to receive the end of a great beam or plate which supported the
roof on the side opposite the three windows.

The Semicircular Temple, the Beautiful Wall, and a part of the West City. In the distance are some of the hundreds of terraces which were built to provide the denizens of the city with such food as potatoes, corn, beans and quinoa, tomatoes and sweet potatoes. A small conduit brought the water supply along the terraces and back of the temple to the Stairway of the Fountains which begins at this point. Our tents may be seen on one of the terraces near a group of buildings which seem to have been built for workmen or guards who were not allowed to enter the sacred city. In the Semicircular Temple may be seen the problematical window from which the golden image of the Sun God may have been suspended.

slowness and extreme caution of the Indians, who dreaded to take the risk of meeting a viper unexpectedly. Their fears were justified. During the next ten days eight venomous reptiles were killed, including several specimens of the deadly bushmaster. Fortunately none of the men was bitten.

Mr. Heald had several narrow escapes, but from other causes. On the second day, while reconnoitering the steep slopes above the workmen and out of their sight, he suddenly discovered that they had started a fire in the bamboo scrub. In less than a minute it had gained great headway and was roaring up the mountain side faster than anyone could possibly climb. Retreat by the route he had come was impossible. The flames leaped fifteen and twenty feet into the air. There was nothing to do but make a strenuous effort to get around the raging fire before it should spread sideways. Tearing blindly through the dense thicket, he fell head-long over a small cliff. Fortunately he landed in a mass of bamboo, which broke the force of his fall and saved his life.

A few days later he had an even more exciting experience. I had asked him to see whether he could get to the top of the needle-like peak called Huayna Picchu and investigate the story that there were "magnificent ruins" upon its summit. Melchor Arteaga, the Quichua who originally took me up to the ruins at Machu Picchu, had said there were other ruins "equally good," though more inaccessible, on Huayna Picchu. He finally admitted that they might be slightly inferior but repeatedly declared that they were of "great importance." The peak rises twenty-five hundred feet sharply above the Urubamba River, which surrounds it on three sides. On its south side is the ridge on which the ruins of Machu Picchu are located. On its east side is a precipice nearly sheer from the top of the needle to the bank of the stream. On the north side, below the upper precipices of the needle, are slopes now forest-covered but bearing marks of ancient agricultural terraces. The presence of these terraces, some of which had been cultivated recently by Arteaga, made it seem reasonable that there might be important ruins on the slopes of Huayna Picchu, which, owing to the density of the great forest which covered the slopes, had hitherto escaped attention. Arteaga, however, insisted that there were beautiful ruins on top of the very peak itself. But when Mr. Heald tried to employ him as a guide, he refused to go —possibly having a dim realization of some of the lies he had told. Nothing daunted, Heald, having found the place where Arteaga had built a rustic bridge to enable him to reach his clearings, started out with four Indians and Tomas Cobinas, his trusty *gendarme*.

Crossing the river on four shaky poles which resembled the bridge I had once used, he found even the lower slopes to be so vertical that it frequently was necessary to cut steps. He was greatly hindered by the bamboo vines and high coarse grasses which had sprung up in former clearings and also on the higher and steeper slopes following the fires set in past years by Melchor and other exponents of that primitive system of agriculture known to agronomists as *milpa*, clearing by fire. Progress was very slow. Finally the Indians gave out, weary with climbing and cutting their way through the bamboo jungle. Leaving the *gendarme* behind to see that the Indians should continue cutting a trail as fast as strength permitted, Mr. Heald determined to conquer the mountain alone and by a rapid reconnaissance ascertain how much of a path it would be advisable to make. His report is so graphic that I give it in his own words:

"I pushed on up the hill, clearing my way with the machete, or down on all fours, following a bear trail (of which there were many), stopping occasionally to open my shirt at the throat and cool off, as it was terribly hot. The brush through which I made my way was in great part *mesquite* terribly tough and with heavy, strong thorns. If a branch was not cut through at one blow it was pretty sure to come whipping back and drive half a dozen spikes into hands, arms and body. Luckily I had had enough practice to learn how to strike with a heavy shoulder blow and for the most part made clean strokes, but I didn't get away untouched by any means. Finally, about 3 P.M., I had almost gained the top of the lowest part of the ridge, which runs along like the back-plates of some spined dinosaur. The trees had given way to grass or bare rock, the face of the rock being practically vertical. A cliff some two hundred feet high stood in my way. By going out on the edge of the ridge I could look almost straight down to the river, which looked more like a trout brook than a river at that distance, though its roar in the rapids came up distinctly. I was just climbing out on top of the lowest "back-plate" when the grass and soil under my feet let go and I dropped. For about twenty feet there was a slope of about seventy degrees and then a jump of about two hundred feet, after which it would be a bump and repeat (2000 feet) down to the river. As I shot down the sloping surface I reached with my right hand and grasped a *mesquite* bush that was growing in a crack about five feet above the jump-off. I was going so fast that it jerked my arm up and, as my body was turning, pulled me from my side to my face; also, the jerk broke the ligaments holding the outer end of clavicle and scapula together. The strength left the arm with the tearing loose of the ligaments, but I had checked enough to give me a chance to get hold of a branch with my left hand. After hanging for a moment or two, so as to look everything over and be sure that I did nothing wrong, I started to work back up. The hardest part was to get my feet on the trunk of the little tree to which I was holding on. The fact that I was wearing moccasins instead of boots helped a great deal here, as they would take hold of the rock. It was distressingly slow work, but after about half an hour I had gotten back to comparatively safe footing. As my right arm was almost useless, I at once made my way down, getting back to camp about 5:30, taking the workmen with me as I went. On this trip I saw no sign of Inca work, except one small ruined wall. . . ."

Five days later, although he had had no chance to consult a doctor, Mr. Heald judged that his arm was in sufficiently good shape so that he could continue the work, and he very pluckily made another attempt to reach the top of Huayna Picchu. This likewise ended in failure; but on the following day he returned to the attack, followed his old trail for some seventeen hundred feet and, guided this time by Arteaga, eventually reached the top. His men were obliged to cut steps in the steep slope for a part of the distance until they came to an Inca stairway which led them practically to the top which consisted of a jumbled mass of granite bowlders. There were no houses, though there were several flights of stone steps and three little caves. Probably it was once used as a signal station. And this was what Arteaga had told us was "equally as good" as the ruins of Machu Picchu! To-day it is possible for energetic climbers to get to the top of Huayna Picchu without serious difficulty, enjoy the magnificent view and see the primitive ruins of the watch tower, as has been done by one of our American Ambassadors and his wife.

A day or two after Mr. Heald had completed the trail from his new bridge to the top of the ridge, Dr. George F. Eaton, osteologist of the Peabody Museum of Yale University, and Elwood C. Erdis, a civil engineer who was to supervise the clearing of the ruins and the search for artifacts, arrived and we began our investigations.

One of my fellow delegates on the mission to the Pan American Scientific Congress in Chile was Dr. William H. Holmes, then Director of the National Museum. It was due to his hearty praise of the distinguished English archaeologist, A. P. Maudslay, Esq., for clearing the jungle from some of the most important sites in the Maya country that I was led to undertake the discouraging task of chopping down the entire hardwood forest which stood on the city terraces and on top of some of the buildings at Machu Picchu. We not only cut down all the trees and bushes, we removed and burned all the debris, and even cleaned the moss off the walls of the ancient buildings and the carved rocks. We made a determined effort to uncover everything that had been hidden by Nature in the course of the centuries and did our best to restore the beauties of the Inca's favorite residence. We wanted to learn all we could from everything that was left of the great sanctuary. We were anxious to secure photographs which would give some idea of the remarkable art and architecture of the white granite structures, even though this meant an enormous amount of painstaking labor.

The tropical forest had held undisputed sway for a very long time. During the course of our clearing we found massive trees, two feet thick, perched on the gable ends of small, beautifully constructed houses. It was not the least difficult part of our work to cut down and clear away such trees without seriously injuring the old walls.

We were fortunate to have as our chief aide Lieutenant Sotomayor, an officer of the Peruvian *gendarmerie*. His knowledge of the Quichua tongue was of the greatest assistance to us in dealing with the Indians, most of whom spoke no Spanish. A few of our workmen had come with us voluntarily from Cuzco, where they had been employed in excavations which we had made in that vicinity. On the other hand, so loath were the local Quichuas to leave their own villages and undertake profitable employment elsewhere, that it was impossible to secure enough voluntary labor even though we paid more than the neighboring planters and worked our men shorter hours. We were obliged, therefore, to depend on the chief village officials, the *gobernadors*, each of whom, acting under the orders of the Prefect, supplied us from time to time with ten or a dozen men for a fortnight.

We found it necessary to conform to the ways of the country and provide each workman, the first thing in the morning, with a handful of dried green *coca* leaves. This was enough for four quids. The quid of *coca* leaves, carefully and deliberately made by chewing the leaves one at a time, usually was allowed to remain in the mouth for two hours. Making the quid occupied the first ten minutes of the "working day," a ten minute recess in the middle of the morning, the first period of the afternoon "working" time, and a recess about three o'clock. The employer who fails to provide his Quichua workmen with the daily ration of *coca* leaves is like to find it impossible to secure voluntary laborers and very hard to get cheerful efforts from his conscripts.

We gave the Indians small presents on pay day, Saturday. These consisted of beads, mirrors, or other trinkets which had been carefully selected from one of Mr. Woolworth's emporiums in New Haven. Mirrors were particularly in demand and seemed to give the greatest satisfaction. Nevertheless only a few volunteers returned to work week after week. A small handful worked regularly, but others would absent themselves for several weeks to attend to the duties of their own little farms and then return for a fortnight of labor with us. The great majority, however, worked only when the *gobernador* forced them to come. Sometimes we had forty or more; sometimes we had only a dozen.

The Indians made little huts for themselves near the spring close to the houses occupied by Richarte and Alvarez. We pitched our tents on one of the large terraces not very far from the city wall and commanding a magnificent view of the Urubamba canyon.

Lieutenant Sotomayor took personal charge of the Indians who were engaged in cutting down the forest, removing and burning the rubbish. No one could have been more efficient or persistent. So rapidly did the jungle grow, however, that we had to cut the bushes and bamboo scrub three times in the course of four months. The final cutting, made in ten days by a gang of thirty or forty Indians moving rapidly with sharp machetes, immediately preceded and accompanied the intensive photographic work at the end of the season. A few of the five hundred pictures I took then are included in this volume. They are all on file in the libraries of Yale University, the National Geographic Society and the Hispanic Society of America.

The extensive clearing which we were able to accomplish at that time and the subsequent exploration of the region, as well as the clearing carried on in recent years by various archeological parties enable us now to be sure that this was indeed the largest city in the province besides being an important Inca sanctuary.

3.

Vilcapampa the Old

THE RUINS OF WHAT WE now believe was the lost city of Vilcapampa the Old, perched on top of a narrow ridge lying below the peak of Machu Picchu, are called the ruins of Machu Picchu because when we found them no one knew what else to call them. And that name has been accepted and will continue to be used even though no one now disputes that this was the site of ancient Vilcapampa.

The sanctuary was lost for centuries because this ridge is in the most inaccessible corner of the most inaccessible section of the central Andes. No part of the highlands of Peru is better defended by natural bulwarks—a stupendous canyon whose rock is granite, and whose precipices are frequently a thousand feet sheer, presenting difficulties which daunt the most ambitious modern mountain climbers. Yet, here, in a remote part of the canyon, on this narrow ridge flanked by tremendous precipices, a highly civilized people, artistic, inventive, well organized, and capable of sustained endeavor, at some time in the distant past built themselves a sanctuary for the worship of the sun.

Since they had no iron or steel tools—only stone hammers and little bronze crowbars—its construction must have cost generations if not centuries of effort. To prevent their enemies or undesirable visitors from reaching their shrines and temples, they relied, first,

177

on the rapids of the Urubamba, which are dangerous even in the dry season and absolutely impassable during at least half of the year. On three sides this was their outer line of defense. On the fourth side the massif of Machu Picchu is accessible from the plateau only by a narrow razor-like ridge less than forty feet across and flanked by precipices, where they constructed a strong little fort—a veritable Thermopylae. No one could reach the sacred precincts unless the Inca so decreed, as Friar Marcos and Friar Diego found to their cost.

Not only was the Sanctuary protected against the pollution of casual visitors it was admirably adapted for military purposes as a citadel.

FORTIFICATIONS

While the lower slopes of Huayna Picchu are relatively easy of access in the dry season, the mass of Huayna Picchu is separated from the ruins by another razor-like ridge impassable on the east side and having only a footpath for sure-footed Indians on the west side. This trail passes for more than a hundred yards along a horizontal cleft in an overhanging precipice of sheer granite. Two men could defend it against an army and it is the only route by which Machu Picchu may be reached from Huayna Picchu.

So much for the northern approach. The east and west side of the ridge are sufficiently precipitous for fifteen hundred feet to be well-nigh unassailable. Rocks could easily have been rolled down upon invaders in the manner referred to by the conquistadors as a favorite method of Inca soldiers. If a path was maintained on each side, as is the case today, these paths, in turn, could easily have been defended by a handful of men. Wherever breaks in the precipices would give a foothold to intruders they were walled up and the natural defense strengthened.

On the southern side rise the precipitous cliffs of Machu Picchu Mountain. In ancient times they were flanked by two Inca roads. The road on the west side of the peak ran along another horizontal cleft or fault in the very face of a magnificent precipice. It can still be seen but rock slides have destroyed it. On the opposite side of the mountain the Inca road climbed the abrupt declivity by means of a stone stairway and circumvented the mountains by a trail which only goats could have followed with ease. Both of these roads led to the little ridge on which was the aforementioned Thermopylae, and which alone gave access to Machu Picchu Mountain from the plateau and the southern rim of the canyon. Both of them could have been readily defended in various places.

In accordance with their well-known practice, we found on top of both neighboring peaks on Machu Picchu and Huayna Picchu the ruins of Inca signal stations from which it was possible for messages to be sent and received across the mountains. The arrival of unwelcome visitors or even the distant approach of an enemy could have been seen and instantly communicated to the city. That on top of Machu Picchu was necessarily the more important. No pains were spared to make it safe and convenient. Its construction required great skill and extraordinary courage. It is located on top of one of the most stupendous precipices in the Andes. If any of the workmen who built the retaining wall on the very edge of the signal station slipped he must have fallen three thousand feet before striking any portion of the cliff broad enough to stop his body. I do not mind admitting that when I took pictures from it I not only lay flat on my stomach, I had two trusty Indians hang on to my legs. It really was a dizzy height. But imagine building a wall on it!

The Sanctuary of Vilcapampa was regarded as so sacred that in addition to the outer defenses and the reinforced precipices which protected the city against enemies, two walls were built to keep out visitors or workmen who had been allowed to pass the mountain Thermopylae. On the south side of the city are an outer wall and an inner wall. The outer runs along the ends of a magnificent tier of agricultural terraces. Nearby are half a dozen buildings which may have been intended as barracks for the soldiers whose duty it was to protect the city on the only side where it could be reached by the ancient roads, and was comparatively vulnerable. There was still an inner line of defense. At the narrowest part of the ridge, just before one reaches the city from the south, a fosse or dry moat was dug, its sides faced with stone. Above it the wall of the city proper extends across the top of the ridge and down each side until it reaches precipitous cliffs which make the wall no longer necessary.

On the very top of the ridge the wall was pierced by a large gateway built of massive stone blocks. The gate itself, probably a screen of heavy logs lashed together, could be fastened at the top to a large ring-stone or eye-bonder firmly embedded above the lintel and underneath six or eight feet of masonry. At the sides, the door could be fastened by a large crossbar whose ends were tied to powerful stone bar-holds, stone cylinders, firmly anchored in holes left in the doorposts for that purpose. Such a door might, of course, have been smashed in by an attacking force using a large log as a battering ram. To avoid the likelihood of this the engineer who constructed the fortifications brought forward a salient from the wall at right angles to the doorway. By this means the defenders standing on top of the salient could have rained down a lateral fire of rocks and bowlders on the force attempting to batter down the gate.

The walls of the city were high enough so that they could not be scaled with ease. In fact, an attacking force which had been so fortunate as to overcome all the natural defenses of this powerful stronghold and had circumvented the defenders of the several Thermopylae-like passes would have found themselves in a very bad situation when rushing along the terraces toward the inner fortifications. At the end of the terraces they would have found it necessary to jump down into the dry moat and scale its farther side as well as the city wall, all the time subjected to a shower of stones from the slings of the defenders. It is difficult to imagine that any attacking force could possibly have been large enough to overcome a vigorous defense even if the city were held by only a few score determined soldiers. Of course the walls served equally well in peace time to keep intruders from entering the sacred precincts of the Sanctuary. In the *accla-huasi* or Houses of the Chosen Women of the Sun, no men were permitted to enter except the Emperor, his sons, the Inca nobles and the priests.

The City Gate shows evidences of being repaired. The top of the narrow ridge is at this point occupied by a large granite bowlder, which was worked into the fortifications, or, rather, the walls were strengthened by its being used as a member. As a result, the outer gatepost of the massive entrance rests on an artificial terrace. This terrace has settled a few inches, due to erosion in the steep hillside. Consequently the wall has been thrown out of the perpendicular and has started to destroy the fine old gateway. It will not be long before the great lintel will fall and carry with it the repaired part of the wall which is superimposed above it. One clearly gets the feeling, in looking at the entrance to the citadel, that it was rather hastily repaired at a period long subsequent to its original construction, probably by Manco II.

STAIRWAYS

Space was limited and the houses were crowded closely together, but an extensive system of narrow streets and rock-hewn stairways made intercommunication within the walls of the city comparatively easy. In fact perhaps the most conspicuous feature of Machu Picchu is the quantity of the stairways, there being over one hundred, large and small, within its limits. Some of them, to be sure, have but three or four steps while others have as many as a hundred and fifty. In several cases the entire flight of six, eight or even ten, steps was cut out of a single bowlder. The stairways which connect the various agricultural terraces follow the natural declivity of the hill even where it is so steep as to make them seem more like a ladder than a flight of stairs. In several places a little garden plot was tucked into a terrace less than eight feet square behind and above a dwelling house. In order to make little garden terraces like these accessible the Incas constructed fantastic stairways scarcely wide enough to permit the passage of a boy. Within the city, however, and particularly in the narrow streets or alleyways, the stairs were constructed on a comfortable grade.

The stairway or flight of steps as an ornamental or ceremonial motif in Inca architecture does not seem to occur here, although it might well have originated in this locality. In the ruins of a monolithic gateway at Tiahuanaco, Bolivia, in a curiously carved rock at Concacha, near Abancay, Peru, and on the famous carved rock called Kkenko, near Cuzco, are little flights of stairs which were carved for ceremonial or ornamental purposes and which serve no useful object so far as one can see. The stairways of Machu Picchu, on the other hand, with possibly one exception, all appear to be available for reaching locations otherwise difficult of access. While they are more numerous than was absolutely necessary, none of them appears useless, even today. The longest stairway, which may properly be described as the main thoroughfare of the city, commences at the top of the ridge at the terrace by which the highway enters the walls, and, roughly dividing the city into two parts, runs all the way down to the impassable cliffs on the northeastern slope.

The central thoroughfare in the heart of the city consisted in part of this granite stairway of one hundred and fifty steps and was the site of the principal waterworks.

WATER SUPPLY

As usual, the Incas took great pains to do everything possible to provide adequate water.

There are several springs on the side of Machu Picchu Mountain, within a mile of the heart of the city. The little *azequia* or conduit which brought the water from the springs may still be followed along the mountain side for a considerable distance. It has been partly destroyed by landslides but may be seen where it runs along one of the principal agricultural terraces, crosses the dry moat on a slender stone aqueduct, passes under the city wall in a narrow groove less than six inches wide, and is carried along one of the terraces to the first of the series of fountains or little stone basins which are located near the principal stairway. The first four are south of the stairway. Near the fourth the stairway is divided into two flights. At this point there begins a series of twelve. The *azequia* runs south from the last fountain and empties into the moat.

The basins of the Stairway of the Fountains are usually cut out of a single block of granite placed on a level with the floor of the little enclosure into which the women came to fill their narrow-necked jars. Frequently one or two little niches were constructed in the side walls of the enclosure as a shelf for a cup or possibly for the stoppers of the bottles, made of fiber or twisted bunches of grass. Sometimes a small lip was cut in the stone at the end of the conduit so as to form a little spout, thus enabling the water to fall clear of the back wall of the fountain. In other cases the water would usually pass through the narrow orifice with sufficient force to reach the opening of the jar without the necessity of the carrier dipping the water from the basin. In times of water scarcity, however, we may be sure that the latter method was followed, and that the reason for the sixteen basins was not only in order to permit many jars to be filled at once but to keep the all too precious fluid from escaping. The *azequia* is narrower than any I have seen anywhere else, being generally less than four inches in width.

The little stone basins are about thirty inches long by eighteen inches wide and from five to six inches in depth. In some places both the basin and the entire floor of the fountain enclosure are made of a single slab of granite. Sometimes holes were drilled in one corner of the basin to permit the water to flow through carefully cut underground conduits to the next basin below. In case of necessity these holes could easily have been plugged up to permit the basin to fill. The conduits run sometimes under the stairway and sometimes at its side. It is perhaps worth noting that the modern Peruvians call these fountains *baños*, baths, but it does not seen to me likely that they were used for this purpose. On account of the rarefied air, the cold, and the rapid radiation, even Anglo-Saxons do not bathe frequently in the Peruvian highlands and the mountain Indians of today never bathe. It is hardly to be supposed, therefore, that the builders of Machu Picchu used these basins for such a purpose. On the other hand, the Incas were fond of making easy the work of the water carriers and providing them with nicely constructed fountains.

Possibly one reason for abandoning Machu Picchu as a place of residence was the difficulty of securing sufficient water. In the dry season the little springs barely furnished enough water for cooking and drinking purposes for the forty or fifty Indian workers and ourselves. In the earliest times, when the side of the mountain was forested, the springs undoubtedly did better; but with the deforestation which followed continued occupation and the resultant landslides and increased erosion of the surface soil, the springs must at times have given so little water as to force the city dwellers to bring the water in great jars on their backs for considerable distances.

It is significant that the sherds found near the City Gate represent forty-one containers of liquid refreshment as compared with only four cooking pots, nine drinking ladles, and not a single food dish. Evidently the dispensers of *chicha* were stationed here. The results are the more striking when compared with the finds in the southeastern quarter, where almost as many food dishes were found as jugs.

GARDEN PLOTS

The largest flat space within the city limits lies in a swale at the widest part of the ridge. This was carefully graded and terraced, and at the time of our visit had recently been cultivated by Richarte and his friends. In fact, one would have to go a good many miles in the canyon of the Urubamba to find an equally large "pampa" at an elevation of not less than seven thousand nor more than ten thousand feet. In other words, this little pampa offered an unusual opportunity to a people accustomed to raising such crops as flourished in Yucay and Ollantaytambo. The fact that it was possible for them also to cover the adjacent hillside with artificial terraces which would increase the potentiality of the region as a food producer was doubtless as important a factor in the selection of this site as the ease with which it could be made into a powerful citadel or a very sacred sanctuary. One of the most carefully constructed stairways leads directly from the chief temples to the little pampa itself. It may have been the pampa where the *huilca* tree grew—the *huilca-pampa*.

There is only one city gate. The northern, or Huayna Picchu side was not defended by a transverse wall but by high, narrow terraces built on little ledges which would otherwise give a foot-hold on the precipices. Near these terraces there is a broad saddle connecting Machu Picchu with a conical hill that is part of a ridge leading to the precipitous heights of Huayna Picchu. South of the saddle, which was once covered with a dense forest, is a rude amphitheater. It had been terraced and there are five or six different levels, recently used for the small plantations of the Indians. This might very well have been the special garden plot for raising food for the rulers. On the surface of the ground, among the cornstalks, pumpkin vines, and onion patches, we found occasional pieces of pottery.

CLAN GROUPS

Looking out on the amphitheater on the east side are twenty houses. Four of them appear to have contained windows. Two of these are marked by having three windows each, the third appears to contain only one, while the fourth is so much in ruins that it is difficult to say whether it has two or three. The houses on this east side of the amphitheater are nearly all made of stone laid in clay and only roughly finished. In the northeast corner there are two terraces with a marked difference from the others, the stones are much larger and more irregular. Most of the houses are built of rather small stones of a nearly uniform size.

The terraces are built sometimes of large stones and sometimes of small. None of this construction would have taken long to build. It might well have been done by Manco's forces after he had moved the religious capital of his realm from Cuzco to this ancient temple of the Sun. On the east side of the ancient city there are few, if any, temples, but many well built dwelling houses and clan groups.

Only one group of houses, that near the south end, appears to have been built with special care; in this the stones are fitted together without clay and the walls are in a beautiful state of preservation. A large group of houses here has three entrances, so we called it the Three-Door Group. In our excavations we found a rubbish pile in front of it, which, with what we collected inside, yielded pieces of one hundred and fifteen pots. It must have been occupied a long time.

Each of the compounds differs from the others either in the arrangement of its buildings or in some distinctive feature of its architecture. One of them is characterized by very unusual niches. In one of its houses there are two niches large enough to permit an Indian to stand in them, and in the back wall of each niche is a small window at the height of an Indian's face. The shrine of this group was built on a picturesque crag, the side walls of the temple being keyed into the sloping surface of the rock in a very extraordinary manner. It was done with such skill as to have prevented slipping for centuries. Into the top of the rock the usual stone platform was cut. Above it were three niches each large enough to receive a huddled-up Peruvian mummy. It was the custom in mummifying a body to draw the knees up to the chin so as to make the mummy take up as little room as possible. Mummies had multifarious wrappings and look not unlike small barrels, the final wrapping in some cases consisting of yards and yards of braided rope. Each of these three niches was large enough to receive such a bundle and was provided with a stone bar-hold so the mummy could be tied in, or taboo sticks could have been fastened in front of each niche to ward off any interference with the mummy. Each niche in turn had three little niches, one on the back wall and one on each of the side walls. The little niches were probably for the reception of offerings, articles presumed to be of value and interest to the departed. A long stone platform carved into the solid rock immediately below the niches was probably intended to receive offerings of food and drink; or the mummies may have been placed there to dry in the sun. It is said that the Incas did not use preservatives as did the Egyptians but relied on the power of the tropical sun to dry the flesh after the removal of the viscera. So the mummies had to be sun dried frequently.

Another clan group was characterized by particularly ingenious stone-cutting. Here the bar-holds of the principal gateway were themselves cut out of the heart of solid granite ashlars. The top of the bar-hold was set into a saucer-shaped depression in a member of the next course above, but the base of the bar-hold formed a part of the ashlar in which it was cut. Access to the bar-hold was gained by cutting a square hole in the center of the face of the ashlar. Surely it was not only an ingenious but a patient and devoted stone cutter who would have taken the trouble to make such a neat contrivance for securing artistic permanency in the bar-holds of his compound. He probably used bronze chisels to carve the deep hole in the ashlar.

Excavations in the principal house of this group yielded pieces of eight pots and brought to light the tops of two granite bowlders which originally projected above the level of the floor. These bowlders had been carved into useful permanent and unbreakable mortars or grinding stones where maize could be ground, and frozen potatoes crushed under the smooth-faced mullers or rocking stones which have been in use throughout the central Andes since time immemorial. Near the mortars we actually found one of the ancient mullers which had been rocked here centuries ago. The wife of the chief of this group must have enjoyed a sense of superiority over her neighbors who, in making their corn meal, had no such permanent conveniences built into their kitchens. This group also contains several stone benches. One house had a stone couch, built in a corner, as though someone here preferred not to be always sleeping and sitting on the ground.

In this group is the only example in the city of a large gabled building divided into two sections by a party wall rising to the peak, pierced with three windows. This type, so rare here, is common enough at Choqquequirau and Ollantaytambo. It was probably a very late development in the art of building. On the rougher, interior walls of some houses of this compound we found some surfaces still covered with reddish clay. It was one of these houses which had been selected a few years ago by Richarte or one of his friends as a good structure to be repaired and roofed for use, but was abandoned, as being too far from water.

One of the stairways in this group is fantastically wedged in between two huge granite rocks which are so close together that it would have been impossible for a fat man to use it at all. In another flight, not only the steps of the stairway but also the balustrades were cut out of a single ledge. Considering the fact that the only tools obtainable for a job of this kind were cobblestones or pebbles of diorite which could be obtained in the bed of the roaring rapids two thousand feet below, it must have taken somebody a long, long while and a good deal of effort to carve these steps out of the living rock. At any rate, the stone cutter had the satisfaction of knowing that his work would achieve something as near immortality as anything made by the hands of man.

The walls of the buildings of a neighboring group are of very roughly squared stones laid in clay in irregular courses, yet the terrace on which they were built is faced with unusually large ashlars nicely joined, presumably the work of an earlier period. Before the more recent wall was constructed a small conduit was cut into the top of one of the fine old blocks of the retaining wall so as permit the courtyard of this compound to be properly drained.

On the west side of the city are by all odds the finest and most interesting structures. Beginning with the northwest corner, after ascending a series of terraces one comes to a sightly spot on top of a hill which commands a magnificent view in all directions, including not only the city itself and the cultivated terraces but also the Grand Canyon of the Urubamba. I know of no place in Peru that has a more inspiring prospect. Many of the mountains are covered by dense tropical vegetation from top to bottom; other are bare except for scant pasture; while still others consist of sheer granite precipices. On clear days snow-capped peaks may be seen both east and west, the finest being those of Salcantay and Soray, which are conspicuous from the lower Cuzco Valley.

On top of this little hill, from which the bridge of San Miguel may be seen two thousand feet below, there was built a beautiful little temple near a fine *intihuatana* or sundial stone, "the place to which the sun was tied," such as formed an important part of all temples of the Sun. Remains of similar stones may be seen in Cuzco, Pisac, and Ollantaytambo. The top of a bowlder was partly cut away leaving near the center a square upright pillar. The height of the pillar is a trifle over half a yard, thus making it the highest *intihuatana* stone found in Peru. The top of the stone shows evidence of a fracture but there is no indication that this was broken off in recent years. Squier reported an *intihuatana* in Ollantaytambo of about the same height as having been destroyed by the Spaniards. It seems to be a generally accepted fact that the Spanish priests took pains to knock off the top of the *intihuatana* stones wherever they were found. The fact that this one is intact adds further evidence to the failure of the ecclesiastical forces of the Viceroy Toledo to reach this site or even learn of its whereabouts.

Near this interesting and mysterious rock are the ruins of two attractive houses built, like the rest, of white granite blocks squared as nicely as could be done without the use of instruments of precision unknown to the builders, fitted absolutely together without clay, and bearing the marks of extreme attention to detail. Both of these small houses are marked by one curious feature. As originally planned they had handsome, though narrow, end doors;

then the doors were filled up to two-thirds of the original height, leaving only windows. The best preserved house contains two fine niches and two windows. Both of the houses appear to have been originally a story and a half high with gable ends. They also have a peculiar feature common to a number of houses here in Machu Picchu in that, while the main portion of the wall is of stone laid without mortar, the gables above are of much rougher blocks, not carefully fitted together but laid in clay and possibly plastered over.

The south end of this hilltop has been rounded and roughly faced with stones, one of the larger of which has been curiously carved so as to leave a lug with a vertical hole pierced through it. This may have been intended for a pole displaying a banner. The terraces below and around the hilltop are of rough stone faced nearly flat and laid in clay. On the south side thirteen terraces go down to the edge of the precipice. The hill itself is partly composed of huge, irregular blocks of granite. In many places where these overhang they have been propped up with stone walls, leading one to suppose that there might be graves within. Earlier excavators had been led to the same conclusion and, so far as I could judge, had encountered the same results, namely that there was nothing behind the walls but earth and that the walls had been built chiefly to give a finished appearance to the rude bowlders. Our excavations on this hill yielded very poor results. Probably it was used only for the most solemn services connected with tying the Sun to the Intihuatana. Tradition ascribes the reciting of poetical orisons to this worship.

THE SACRED PLAZA

Leaving the hilltop and going in a southerly direction, one descends several flights of stone stairs and approaches a little flattened space which we have termed, for want of a better name, the Sacred Plaza, because on two sides of it are the largest temples. Before reaching it one passes on the left a very singular bowlder shaped more or less like a giant clam. Leading to the top are seven stairs cut in the soft disintegrating granite, and from the top one can get a charming view. Stones have also been fitted into the top of the bowlder so as to form a little platform on which three or four persons could stand and salute the rising sun.

North of this bowlder and below it are the walls of a little house, about ten by fifteen feet in diameter, built in the best workmanship of the finest Inca style, that is to say, with carefully cut, selected white granite blocks, many of them apparently rectangular. Some of the large ones are remarkably polygonal, but all are keyed together without cement. The lower course is of particularly large, fine ashlars about four feet in length and two feet in height; the upper tiers are smaller but all quite symmetrical. On the left of the door as one enters this house is a single gigantic block cut so as to form the entire lower half of that part of the front wall. Not only were the lower portions of two of the niches with which this house is lined cut out of this stone but in a spirit of almost freakish ingenuity or playfulness the builders carved part of the corner of the room itself in this extraordinary block, so that it even forms a very small part of one of the end walls. In the palace of the Inca Rocca in Cuzco is a stone made famous by early Spanish writers because it had fourteen angles. Visitors always look at it. This stone has thirty-two angles!

The little building has another unsual feature—a long stone bench or couch extending the entire length of the house opposite the door. It is made of beautifully cut ashlars.

This house adjoins the Principal Temple which has already been described. When I first saw it I was inclined to believe that it was the High Priest's house but further study leads me to think it was a royal mausoleum and that the bench or couch was intended for the mummies of Inca emperors. It is certain that no pains were spared to make this little structure a gem of masonry. The building is lined with niches so nearly alike that the eye can scarcely detect any difference in shape or size. In the selection of the ashlars, in the finish of the blocks, in the proportions of the room and in the artistic care with which it was built, it belongs

at the top. Other ancient buildings may equal it in beauty, but I
know of none which surpasses it. It gives abundant evidence that
here at Machu Picchu was one of the finest sanctuaries ever built
by the Incas, or any other pre-historic Americans.!

The Sanctuary of the Sun in Cuzco in addition to containing
the high altar and its appurtenances, held the mummies of the dead
emperors of the Inca line. According to Juan de Betanzos who
lived in Cuzco in 1550, just after the Conquest of Peru, the
mummies were seated on benches of wood beautifully carved.
He says that the Inca Pachacutec arranged the dead emperors
there in the presence of the image of the sun, but also "caused
to be made, many bundles, as many as there had been Lords who
had succeeded Manco Ccapac down to his father, Inca Viracocha."

It is quite possible, it seems to me, that some of the mummies
that were represented in the Temple of the Sun in Cuzco by
"bundles" may have been really preserved at Machu Picchu.

The High Priest was nearly always an uncle or a brother of
the reigning emperor. Under him were two classes of priests, those
who performed the most solemn rites being always Incas by blood,
and those who officiated in the less important ceremonies being
Incas-by-privilege, that is members of the families of powerful
nobles whom the Inca desired to honor.

It is significant that this little gem of a building is at the foot
of the stairway going up to the *intihuatana* and actually adjoining
the principal temple. The state religion of the Incas, worship of
the Sun, was linked with the destinies and the administration of
the empire in the closest intimacy.

The priests of the sun, were, of course, most highly favored
and it is not surprising to find the beautiful stone stairway which
leads to the *intihuatana* the most carefully constructed of any at
Machu Picchu. The steps are about four feet wide, yet each of
them was made of a single block of granite. There is a low parapet
on each side of this stairway. North of the royal mausoleum or
high priest's house, runs a walk, and a balustrade overlooking the

beautiful valley and the river two thousand feet immediately below.

Keyed into the "priest's house" and evidently built at the same time—for one of the lower stones forms a part of both edifices—is the Principal Temple, which had held me spellbound when I first saw that unique building.

Its entire east wall appears to have settled nearly a foot, carrying with it a part of the north wall. It is not strange that this settling should have taken place, for the wall appears to have only a dirt foundation. So perfectly keyed together was it, however, that it has settled as a mass without disturbing the arrangement of the stones except at the corner.

Perhaps the most marked peculiarity of this temple is that the ends of both the east and west sides are not perpendicular; nor do they have the customary inward slope characteristic of nearly all ancient Peruvian structures. As a matter of fact, they form an obtuse angle. The lower half of the angle is in each case the edge of the single Cyclopean member of the lowest course in the end walls, which slope inward toward the bottom. The upper half of the angle is formed of the six remaining courses, and slopes inward toward the top. The point of the angle contains a hole cut into the Cyclopean block of the lowest course, evidently intended to permit the admission of a large wooden beam which probably extended across the open front to the point of the angle in the front of the opposite end.

My first impression was that such a log would have been used to support the roof of the structure, but the perfect finish of the topmost course leads me to believe that this building never had a roof but that these holes supported the ends of a log which in turn supported a screen or curtain of the finest ancient cloth, a superlatively beautiful textile. It could be removed when it was not needed. Such a device would have permitted the interior of this temple to have been constantly exposed to the sun while at the same time it was screened off from the view of anyone in the

Sacred Plaza. If it were the place in which the mummies of the departed ancestors were brought for purposes of worship the presence of a roof would have been undesirable and would have interfered with the ceremony of giving the mummies a comfortable sun bath.

No pains were spared to make this unique structure conform to all that was best and most solid in the architecture of the Incas. Its builders had a remarkable sense of symmetry. They matched niche for niche and almost matched block for block. No building in Peru gives a finer impression of the high stage of art and architecture reached by the ancient people of the Andes. While there is no carving anywhere in the temple the sides of the largest Cyclopean block were cut in such a manner as to give the pleasing effect of three tiers of stones, more or less carrying out the lines of the regular courses of ashlars. The large altar stone at the back has two projecting lugs at the base. They are not alike, are not symmetrically placed and may be merely projections left to assist the builders in prying the huge block into its proper place. It must weigh at least ten tons.

On the west side of the plaza is a semicircular bastion about ten feet in diameter and eight feet high. It overlooks the valley of the Urubamba and is the highest of a flight of fine terraces which extend down to the edge of the cliffs. The bastion is made of large granite blocks cut to form a nearly perfect semicircle. This type of remarkable stone-cutting is another evidence of the very great age of the Inca civilization. Architects tell me that such skill in building a graceful circular tower is not arrived at easily or early in the history of this art.

On the south side of the plaza is a large rectangular building, of typical late Inca construction, built of small, roughly finished stones laid in adobe, having two doors, and no windows. Its inner walls were lined with symmetrically placed niches, the whole forming obviously an important residence but one which would have required only a few weeks or months to construct. It is quite possible that this was built after the flight of Manco from Cuzco, at the time when this ancient sanctuary had to be enlarged to receive the priests and other attendants of the last Inca and the Chosen Women who sought refuge here in the days of Pizarro.

On the opposite and eastern end of the plaza are the ruins of the most significant building of all, the Temple of the Three Windows.

The walls of this temple, like those of the Principal Temple, are on three sides only, the fourth side being left open to the Sacred Plaza with the exception of a unique monolithic pillar intended to support the front roof-plate of the building, a device not found in any other building in the city. The building had a gable roof, the stones in the end of the gable being larger than customary but nevertheless laid in clay instead of fitted together. As in the Principal Temple, Cyclopean blocks were employed in the lower course and the ends of the side walls form an obtuse angle instead of being perpendicular. Similarly, the point of each angle contains a cavity, evidently intended here to permit the admission of the end of a roof-plate. The top of the monolithic pillar, located halfway between these two cavities was notched.

In order to build this structure the architect was obliged to construct a foundation for the eastern wall down to the level of the next terrace. To do this, he used four large stones and built a wall which rises eleven feet from the terrace to the level of a window sill. The sill of each window forms part of a Cyclopean polygonal block. The walls of the temple are of massive blocks, some of them quite irregular, but all of them of well-selected white granite, beautifully worked. The granite could have been quarried in the immediate vicinity.

Group of the Temple of the Sun

The highest of the fountains is in a remarkable group which should be called the Group of the Temple of the Sun itself as its principle building bears a striking resemblance to the well known Temple of the Sun in Cuzco.

This was the first really fine building seen on my original visit.

At that time I could not see all of the wall adjoining the semi-circular temple. After we had scrubbed the wall clean we discovered that the most experienced master mason of his time had here constructed the most beautiful wall in America, built in the form of a try-square, and connecting the temple with what may have been a priest's house.

The effect is softer and more pleasing, if less splendid, than that of the marble temples of the Old World. Here we have an example of the remarkable ability of the Inca architects. Since this wall was obviously built with the utmost care by an artist who desired it to be a permanent object of beauty, it was necessary that there should be no cracks in it, that the seams between the closely fitting ashlars should never open. Yet at the south end of the wall was the priest's dwelling, a two-story-and-a-half house, its second floor opening onto the terrace which supported the Beautiful Wall, its lower floor opening onto the next terrace below. In the course of time such a house, whose attic was entirely above the level of the Beautiful Wall, would tend to lean away from the wall, and the seams would open. Consequently the stone mason ingeniously keyed the ashlars together at the point where the greatest strain would occur, by altering the pattern from one which is virtually rectangular to one containing hookstones, thus making a series of keys which would prevent the ashlars from slipping and keep the house from leaning away from the ornamental wall. The result was successful. Although this is a land where earthquakes are not uncommon and the builders used neither cement nor metal clamp, each ashlar still fits smugly into its neighbors and there is no place where a pin could be inserted between the stones. They fit together and hold as tightly as a glass stopper fits into a glass bottle. Friction and an absolutely perfect fit does the trick. Some of them are shown on the jacket.

The uppermost part of the great rock on which the semi-circular building rests is carved into seats or stone platforms. It was probably an altar on which were placed offerings, or a place of sacrifice for burnt offerings.

When subject to great heat the surface of granite bowlders flakes off in shells around the point where the greatest heat strikes the stone. An examination of the top of this rock which occupies most of the space within the Semicircular Temple shows that at some time or other a really extraordinary amount of heat must have been applied. Total absence of ashes or pieces of charcoal indicate that this took place a very long time ago, probably long before the advent of the first modern Indians. It is difficult to account for all the flaking which has taken place unless it was caused by repeated fires or by one in which the fuel was often replenished, and it is impossible to believe that the damage was done by burning an ordinary thatched roof. Were it not that the upper courses of the Temple seem to indicate the former presence of a roof one might suppose that this had been verily a place of burnt offerings.

In this temple are three windows. Two of them look out over the valley; each is about two feet in height. They are decorated with four nubbins, one at each end of lintel and sill. These may have been supports on which were hung the gold ornaments associated with Sun Temples. There are no others like them.

The third window in the Semicircular Temple is larger than the others and offers much food for thought and speculation. It is what archaeologists commonly call "problematical." Its beautiful monolithic lintel was cracked by the heat of the fires which took place long previous to our visit, and part of it has fallen, further evidence that it was no small conflagration that so ravaged the temple. The sill of this window is most unusual, broken as it is by two flights of steps, facing each other. These steps contain a little habyrinth of holes and very small passages or channels less than an inch in diameter which lead to cavities cut out of the blocks in the interior of the wall. The openings of these channels vary in size; some are two inches in diameter. Other similar holes lead nowhere, and some of the passages have less conspicuous openings. In the Cuzco Temple of the Sun, now the Dominican Monastery, I noticed holes similar to these. They are in a portion of the wall which cannot be further examined. It is quite possible that the holes were intended to facilitate the exhibition of gold plaques or sun ornaments which according to the early writers were displayed in the Temple of the Sun.

We are told by Sarmiento, the conquistador, in his History of the Incas, that he was told by the wise natives whom he consulted with regard to their traditions, that "as Pachacuti Yupanqui was curious about the things of antiquity and wished to perpetuate his name, the Inca went personally to the hill of Tampu-tocco or Paccari-tampu, names for the same thing, and entered the cave whence it is held for certain that Manco Ccapac and his brethren came when they marched to Cuzco for the first time. . . . After he had made a thorough inspection, he venerated the locality and showed his feelings by festivals and sacrifices. He placed doors of gold on the window Ccapac-tocco, and ordered that from that time forward the locality should be venerated by all, making it a prayer place and *huaca*, whither to pray for oracles and to sacrifice. Having done this the Inca returned to Cuzco."

There is no evidence that Sarmiento ever went to Paccari-tampu. We did, but we could find no ruins there that answer to the requirements of this highly venerated place. On the other hand the window where the gold doors were placed might easily have been this ceremonial window in the semi-circular temple at Machu Picchu.

This is one of the reasons why I believe that the "Lost City of the Incas" was originally called Tampu Tocco, as will be set forth in a later chapter.

In view of the similarities between the semi-circular temple and the famous Temple of the Sun in Cuzco, it is interesting to note here that the great golden image of the Sun which had been one of the chief ornaments of the temple in Cuzco was probably kept here at Machu Picchu after Manco escaped from Cuzco. It was in the possession of his son, Tupac Amaru, the last Inca Emperor, who lived here during his young manhood and was captured from him by the Viceroy Toledo who sent it to Philip II with the suggestion that the King send it to the Pope. The chances are that that golden image was once displayed here and may have been hung from the "problematical" window. When Tupac Amaru had to flee down into the *montaña*, he took it with him along with other valuable gold ornaments, which Francisco de Toledo was only too pleased to seize and send to King Philip as being of that "noteworthy quality" desired by his monarch.

There are two gateways to the compound which includes the Temple of the Sun. The inner one is a beautiful specimen of stonework and seems to have had a stone roof. Its bar-holds are integral parts of the stone blocks of the gateway, being cut into the surface of the ashlars. This group is further distinguished by containing the only house in the city consisting of two and a half stories. Its gable end is of rough stones laid in adobe. This is characteristic of every structure that was undoubtedly roofed. No matter how fine the walls of a house, that portion of the wall which would come immediately under the eaves and the gable ends is never nicely fitted together but always laid in adobe. This may have been to facilitate fastening the rafters to the wall, or it may have been due to the fact that originally houses did not have gable ends. They may have been added by later tenants. I do not remember seeing a single Inca gable in the city of Cuzco, although they are common in Ollantaytambo and other places.

Our excavations in this group yielded practically nothing, but on the terraces just below, the old rubbish piles contained pieces of more than two hundred jars. A few had been thrown over into the dry moat. Not a house in the three groups contained a thing; evidently the former owners were good housekeepers and insisted on broken pots being taken away to the rubbish piles.

THE KING'S GROUP

Across the great stairway from the semi-circular Temple of the Sun is a compound which I have called the King's Group because of the extremely solid character of the walls which enclose it, and also because it seems as though no one but a king could have insisted on having the lintels of his doorways made of solid blocks of granite each weighing about three tons. In the other compounds the houses almost invariably have duolithic lintels, not too heavy to be lifted into place by two men. But in this group the owner had sufficient manpower to overcome the mechanical difficulties involved in placing a monolithic three-ton lintel on top of his doorposts and fitting it accurately to them. Even had he possessed cranes, pulleys, and steam winches, he would have found it no easy task. Since he had none of these things, he must have built up a solid inclined plane side by side with the wall as it rose so that the workmen could raise the heavy lintels with levers. What a prodigious amount of patient effort had to be employed! Altogether the artistic workmanship is superb and must be seen to be appreciated. My photographs do not do it justice.

The door of the King's compound is close to the highest of the fountains so that his retainers would never have any difficulty in filling their jars with fresh water. There are no windows in these royal houses. There were none of the dreaded "night drafts which cause illness." We can easily imagine that the houses were fitted with luxurious rugs of vicuña wool as well as the finest blankets and robes that the most skillful of the Chosen Women could weave for the Inca's personal use.

The gables of the houses in this group are also unusually steep. Even heavy tropical downpours would not leak through such steep roofs. No buildings in Machu Picchu except the temple opposite have such fine walls as these.

I believe that this group of houses was once occupied by Titu Cusi and his mother and brother. They certainly lived in comparative luxury. Tupac Amaru was probably living here when he learned of the fatal illness of Titu Cusi and of his own accession to the throne of his ancestors. It should be called the Palace of the Emperor.

4.

Results
of Excavations
at Machu Picchu

OUR FIRST TASK WAS
to see whether excavation in the principal structures would lead
to the unearthing of potsherds or artifacts which might throw
light on the former inhabitants. Our workmen, who fully believed
in the "buried treasure" theory, started with a will. Tests made
with a crowbar in the Principal Temple enclosure resulted in such
resounding hollow sounds as to give them assurance that there
were secret caves beneath the floor of the ancient temple. Amid
the granite bowlders under the carefully constructed floor our
excavation was carried to a depth of eight or nine feet, but all
this back-breaking work ended only in disappointment. Although
we penetrated many crevices and holes between the bowlders,
there was nothing to be found; not even a bone or a potsherd.

Digging inside the Temple of the Three Windows had similar
negative results. Later we carefully replaced and regraded the
floor of the temple. But digging on the outside and below the
three windows resulted in the discovery of an extraordinary
quantity of decorated potsherds, pieces of vases and jars. Most of
them lay from two to four feet under the surface of the ground.
For centuries it must have been the custom to throw earthenware

out of the windows of this temple. It is extremely doubtful if this building was ever used as a dwelling, since its windows were too large to permit of its being occupied by a people unaccustomed to sleeping in the fresh air and anxious to avoid all drafts. Were these pots, then, offerings to the gods? I cannot say. It certainly does not seem likely that this great mass of sherds on the terrace under the three ceremonial windows was formed entirely by throwing perfectly good pots out of the windows. Possibly these bushels of sherds represent pottery broken in the course of religious ceremonies or in the drunken orgies which followed.

At the end of a week of hard and continuous labor we had not succeeded in finding anything except these sherds—no whole pots, no pieces of bronze, not a single ornament or utensil, not even a stray skull or human bone. It began to look as though our efforts to learn any more of the life of the builders of Machu Picchu than could be gained by a study of their architecture and small fragments of earthenware would be a failure. We then began to look for burial caves such as I had first seen at Choqquequirau. The Indians who lived here had been instructed by their *Patron*, Señor Don Mariano Ferro, the owner of the land, to assist us. They were undoubtedly thoroughly familiar with the whole mountain side and we asked them to hunt for burial caves. They went off for two days but their search yielded no results whatever. Could it be possible there were no graves at all? Remembering the success of the pecuniary rewards which we had offered the *gobernador* at Lucma, I offered a Peruvian silver dollar to anyone who could report the whereabouts of a cave containing a skull and who would leave the cave exactly as he found it, allowing us to see the skull actually in position.

The next day all of our workmen were released from excavations in a feverish hunt for burial caves. At the end of the day the half-dozen worthies who had followed us from Cuzco came slowly in, one by one, sadder and no wiser, their hopes of the coveted bonus destroyed. They had been tattered and torn by the thickets and jungles and baffled by the precipitous cliffs of Machu

Picchu. One of them had split his big toe with a machete while hewing his way through the jungle. The thorny scrub and the ever aggravating bamboo vines had not only torn their clothes to shreds but had cruelly scratched their almost naked bodies. Unfamiliar with the region, they had found nothing. On the other hand Richarte and his friends were more fortunate. It was not for nothing that they had been cultivating the ancient terraces. Furthermore, they had undoubtedly engaged in treasure hunting between crops. At any rate, they responded nobly to the proposed bonus and came back late in the day with smiling faces and sparkling eyes, none the worse for wear, and cheerfully announced that they had just discovered *eight* burial caves, and desired eight dollars! At the prevailing rate of wages on the sugar plantations this was more than the three of them could earn in a week.

These were two of the Indians who had found "nothing" on the two preceding days. It was perfectly natural that they should not have been too eager to show us the sources of the pottery which from time to time they had sold to passing travelers. Furthermore, a certain amount of bad luck might happen to their crops should they desecrate the bones of the ancient people buried in the vicinity. No possible amount of agricultural good luck, however, could compete with such a bonus as we had offered. Consequently they now exerted their utmost efforts and the results far exceeded our expectations.

The day after Richarte and his friends had reported the discovery of "eight burial caves," Dr. Eaton and I followed them across the ruins of the city and plunged down the wooded slope on the eastern side of the ridge until we reached a moss covered ledge under which was a small cave to which our guides proudly pointed.

Sure enough here were the bones of a woman, about thirty-five years old, a representative of the middle coast region of Peru, and possibly one of those attractive types who were commanded by Inca Titu Cusi to attempt the seducing of the Augustinian Fathers who wished to enter the city of Vilcapampa the Old.

Judging by the position of the bones, she had been buried in the usual contracted position, the knees drawn up under the chin. With her were buried the remains of her cooking pots and food vessels.

The second cave yielded fragments of two small adult skulls but no pottery or bronze. In the third cave, my joy knew no bounds when I was able to lay hands for the first time at Machu Picchu on a perfect piece of Inca pottery. It was an excellent specimen of a two-handled dish, nicely decorated. This cave was divided into two parts by a stone wall. The outer section contained the skeleton of a woman about thirty-five years of age, the skull being of the oblong type usually found in the mountain regions.

Encouraged by what we had found in the first three caves the work was continued until our ambitious Indian guides had covered every accessible—and many seemingly inaccessible—parts of Huayna Picchu and Machu Picchu Mountains and the ridge between. As the burial caves occurred generally on very steep rocky slopes, more or less covered with dense tropical jungle, the work of visiting and excavating them was extremely arduous. The work of the collectors, like that of the road builders, was several times interrupted by poisonous snakes. Nevertheless Richarte and Alvarez were unsparing in their patient continuous searches. Practically every square rod of the ridge was explored; the last caves opened being very near the Urubamba River. In some of the caves only the most fragmentary skeletal remains were found; only the larger bones and a skull or two. Other caves contained not only nearly complete skeletons, but Inca type pottery in more or less perfect state of preservation.

More than fifty caves were opened under Dr. Eaton's personal direction and fully as many more were located and explored by his Indian helpers. The caves proved a veritable buried treasure for Richarte and Alvarez. Although the graves did not actually contain objects of gold, they did give forth a quantity of skeletal remains and artifacts which brought prosperity to the cheerful little Indians, who now secured in a week as much silver as they had formerly earned in the course of two months.

Some caves were divided into two or more compartments by thin partitions of irregular rock walls. Projecting ledges, over-hanging bowlders, and other rock shelters were taken advantage of in the effort to secure a relatively dry, safe place for the reception of the mummy bundles. The front of the cave was sometimes, though rarely, closed by a roughly built wall of rocks and earth. When this wall was in good condition the bones of the skeletons were generally found lying on the surface of the cave floor, or in the shallow humus, just as they had fallen when the mummy wrappings decayed. Near the bones were often found artifacts, usually pottery, more rarely bone implements, weavers' pointed tools made by grinding llama bones. Sometimes there were pieces of bronze. When the wall was in poor condition so that treasure hunters or wild beasts, bears or members of the cat family, could have entered, the bones and potsherds were likely to be found strewn about the cave or even outside the protecting wall. Some-times the bodies had been actually buried underground, and then the front of the cave would be merely marked by a low wall or rough terrace. In a very few instances bodies were interred in crudely fashioned "bottle-shaped graves."

The region near the first caves we opened I shall refer to as Cemetery No. 1. It lay halfway down the mountain side, north-east of the city, on the edge of a precipice eight hundred feet above the river. Under the bowlders and ledges of this region the remains of about fifty individuals were found. Nearly all of them were determined by our osteologist, Dr. Eaton, to be female, only four being clearly male. This was a very exciting and significant discovery. Apparently the last residents of Machu Picchu were Chosen Women, the "Virgins of the Sun" associated with sanc-tuaries where the Sun was worshipped.

A thousand feet south of the first cave, in a region east of the city, and from two to six hundred feet below the end of the principal stairway, we found another group of burial caves. This we called "Cemetery No. 2." It lies near the end of the outer city wall; in fact, one of the caves was only about a hundred yards from the lowest house. There was some evidence of earlier burials having been disturbed to provide room for the later ones. Here the remains of some fifty individuals were found. Only five or six appear to have been male. None were rugged individuals. Evidence began to accumulate that here had been a "University of Idolatry." Here the Chosen Women had been taught to weave beautiful textiles and made chicha for the Incas.

One day we located the burial place of the High Priestess or *Mama-cuna*, the Lady Superior of the convent, the person chiefly responsible for the training of the Chosen Women. It was a very sightly location on a rock-sheltered terrace on the slopes of Machu Picchu Mountain, about a thousand feet above the highest part of the ruins. The terrace was about forty feet long above some agricultural terraces and connected with the highest by two flights of steps. It was almost completely overhung by an immense bowlder which looked like a peaked crag of the grey granite mountain. The flat-faced projecting portion of the bowlder was at least fifty feet high. The terrace was constructed largely of rock and gravel. Sheltered from the fierce noonday heat of the sun, it offered an ideal resting place for the Mother Superior.

Close to her bones we found her small personal belongings, her pottery and the skeleton of her dog, a collie-like type bred by the Incas.

The lady's possessions included two large bronze shawl-pins, bronze tweezers, two sewing needles made from plant spines, and a dainty and minute bronze curette with an ornamental head in the design of a flying bird.

Besides some small fragments of fabrics of wool and vegetable fiber, there were two beautifully made jugs with human faces modeled and painted on the necks, a most unusual pattern. She also had a fine cooking pot or beaker-shaped *olla*, carefully made and decorated with a snake in bas relief.

The most interesting object buried with this distinguished lady was a concave bronze mirror. Now a concave mirror is not only more difficult to make than a flat mirror, but is far less convenient toilet article. However, we know that on certain ceremonial occasions the *Mama-Cuna,* or Mother Superior of the Virgins of the Sun is reported to have ignited a tuft of cotton wool by concentrating the sun's rays with a concave bronze mirror. Whether this can actually be done I do not know, but as Dr. Eaton once said: "Even if the Priestess failed to ignite the tuft of cotton by the reflected rays of the Sun-God, the holy mystery might have been made to seem very real to the assembled devotees, through a little legerdemain." Anyhow, it was not difficult to believe that the lady with the choice pottery, the collie dog, the toilet set and the handsome concave mirror was one who had progressed far in the service of the Temple of the Sun. Pathological examination of the skeleton of this delicately formed woman shows that unfortunately she suffered from syphilis.

At any rate she was given a very beautiful resting place under the stunning great rock and beneath a carefully constructed ceremonial terrace from which a magnificent view of the sacred city as well as the wonderful canyon and the snow capped peaks could be obtained.

In view of the richness of the material buried with this lady and her evident importance—no other grave contained anything like as fine garniture—and in view of our good fortune in finding this grave undisturbed although located in the most striking cemetery at Machu Picchu, it is worth noting, particularly for the benefit of our Peruvian critics, that not a single article of gold was found here (or anywhere else). Gold must indeed have been extremely scarce if none could have been spared for such a *grande dame* as was here interred. Perhaps whatever gold she may have possessed had been confiscated and sent to form part of the ransom of the unfortunate Atahualpa, whose failure to fill a room full of gold for Pizarro cost him his life! On the other hand, since the Viceroy Toledo did secure some rich booty when he captured the last of the Incas, young Tupac Amaru probably took all the gold ornaments and vessels with him when he fled.

Not far from the rock-sheltered terrace another place of burial was found under an overhanging crag or bowlder which projected from the mountainside for about thirty feet. It was explored under the direction of Dr. Eaton who found a fragment of a female skull with the lower jaw showing slight Aymara deformation. A *chicha* jug, with a grotesque fat man modeled in relief on the neck was found buried close to the skull. Alvarez, one of his Indians, while excavating at random, lightly drove the point of a small combination pick and mattock through the loop of the jug handle, and drew forth the piece uninjured. The rascal then insisted on going through the whole performance again, just to show how skilful and careful he was. He may thank the great and small Gods of the Mountains that his encore was successful.

Among the various skeletons which were found beneath the surface of this large cave was a fragment of a large and heavy male skull, with fragmentary skeleton. The very decayed condition of these remains suggests a burial considerably older than some of the others. The skull undoubtedly belonged to a large male of the coastal type, and the long bones were of corresponding proportion. Close to this skull, and presumably placed with it, was a bronze crowbar, a *champi,* one of the best we found. Its owner may have been one of the principal stone masons who built the city, long before the days of Manco II and his sons.

Llama bones were found in profusion beneath the floor of the caves, around and above the interments, the skeletal material of these useful beasts being almost as plentiful as the human remains. Nearly every skeletal part of the animal was represented. However, it should be noted that, with the exception of the toes and the knee caps, no entire llama bones were to be seen.

The long bones of the llama may have been split in order that the marrow could be eaten by the friends of the deceased. In some places it is known to have been the practice of the persons who had charge of the mummies to consume the offerings of food made to the dead during the annual festivals.

In a cave from which pottery on the surface might easily have been removed was the undisturbed grave of a young woman. With the bones were found the young woman's two shawl-pins. She must have been a person of consequence, for these were of silver. Near the grave was a large flat rocking muller of rare shape, used for grinding corn. Since one of the chief occupations of the Chosen Women was the making of *chicha* for the Inca and his nobles and priests, and the making of it required the crushing of the sprouted corn after it had been boiled, this was probably used in the sanctuary.

On the northern slopes of Machu Picchu Mountain, above the ruins, we found a large cave, thirty feet long and fifteen feet wide, which, although containing a walled-up grave, seems to have been used as a primitive dwelling or rock shelter. There was no protecting wall in front of it, but the sides and back had been nicely finished off with neatly laid stone walls. These walls may have been intended to act as partial insurance that the huge bowlder, a portion of whose flat under surface formed the roof of the shelter, would not settle down on the occupants. Since no human bones were found except those in a walled-up grave at one end, it seems quite likely that this fine dry cave should have once been occupied as a shelter for workmen engaged in neighboring quarries, or carriers who had occasion to use the old Inca road not far away. It was by this road, as we learned later, that the inhabitants normally came down to the city from the plateau behind the mountain where there were a large number of agricultural terraces and several Inca towns in ancient times.

In one cave, with the skeleton of a young woman, we found quite a collection of bones of various animals including a llama, an agouti, a small deer and a Peruvian hare. While these are all edible animals, particularly the agouti, a cavy the size of a rabbit which I learned years ago in Venezuela to prize as a tasty morsel, it seemed a bit strange that this young lady should have been provided with so many "baked meats." Possibly however these little bones had been carefully collected by her and she had intended to carve them into tools. We found in her grave a very well-made specimen of the kind of pointed instrument used by Peruvian weavers in beating up or striking into place the weft threads in the fabric. There was also a small knife-like instrument of bone. Since the Chosen Women were taught useful arts and needed weaver's tools, their fashioning may have been her special hobby.

In a small chamber at the rear of another large natural cave with the skeleton of a woman about fifty years of age was a plant-spine needle, a child's jaw-bone, an imperfect beaker-shaped *olla* or cooking pot, and a deep plate with a broken handle, also several fragments of llama bones, representing food for the dead. In another grave, apparently undisturbed, a small adult female was buried beneath a mass of earth and stones, with a broken *olla*. In an adjoining cave was the skeleton of a woman about fifty years of age accompanied by a heavy bronze shawl-pin, and a beaker-shaped *olla*. It is interesting to note that in many of the caves where women had been buried we found their blackened cooking pots. They were usually placed on top of the ground, presumably next to the mummy bundle. Frequently there were no other dishes.

In one cave two persons of importance, both small adult women, were buried at a depth of nearly five feet. Over their bones, but well concealed beneath the earth and cobbles of the floor was a complete set of Cuzco style dishes and jars suitable for ladies. They included two beaker-shaped cooking *ollas*, two two-handled food dishes, two deep plates, two pelike-shaped jugs; and two containers for liquid refreshment. Evidently the owners were important ladies. Not far from here another grave was found to contain the bones of a woman who also may have been a favorite of the Inca. She was buried with a bronze knife, a bronze shawl-pin, and two silver pins of similar size and shape. Among the well-to-do Indian women of Peru and Bolivia today, silver shawl-pins are often the most valuable of their personal belongings.

A single undisturbed stone-lined grave or cyst was found to contain the bones of a woman and four oblong stone pendants, probably pieces of a necklace. Necklaces of durable material do not seem to have been common.

In another locality a large bowlder covered the remains of three women and a child of six years. With the bones was a perfect specimen of a drinking ladle and the nearly complete remains of three beaker-shaped *ollas*, four two-handled dishes, a two-handled bowl, and a fragment of a large *amphora*.

One locality one mile southeast from the city, in a saddle of Machu Picchu Mountain contained the bones of a man and a woman, both of small stature. Their property consisted of two two-handled dishes, a diota-shaped *olla*, a deep plate, a wooden deep plate, a wooden spindle-whorl, a stone counter, two small bone awls, and seven "polishing stones." A few llama bones and the lower jaw of an agouti represented the funeral "baked meats." If they used the *olla* for cooking, the dishes for serving their stews, the two plates for drinking, we have their entire kitchen furniture. The woman, like all Indian women in the Andes today, had her spinning and weaving to do. The man was a stone mason but possibly he was fond of wood-working. He did some hunting. They were temperate folk. They had no jugs. They were poor. They had nothing of metal, no silver or bronze. They may have been llama drivers. They were buried not far from the old Inca stone-paced road which led around the slopes of the mountain to the open country and the llama pastures beyond.

Late in the season I was conducted by Richarte along a narrow and dangerous trail under the cliffs, on the west side of Huayna Picchu, to a very large cave, nearly ninety feet in length and partly lined with walls of cut stone. It could have been used as a shelter for a considerable number of people. It might have been used as a burial cave. On account of its accessibility from the lower slope of Huayna Picchu, which can easily be approached at low water, it had probably long been known to Melchor Arteaga and other Indian treasure hunters of the neighborhood.

Nevertheless, it was new to Richarte and he was greatly excited by its discovery, thinking that it was going to yield him a rich return in the way of bonuses and prizes. Greatly to his disappointment, although a grave or two were found near by, the cave contained nothing at all, not even a bone. It had probably been used as a rock shelter by workmen engaged in cultivating the fields of Huayna Picchu rather than as a burial cave.

A certain proportion of the burial caves showed evidences of having been visited before, even as long ago as the days when the city was still occupied. The object of these visitors was to make room for later burials and they ruthlessly swept the earlier occupants into a corner. Other visitors were probably the treasure seekers of the generation past. Señor Lizarraga, for instance, is known to have sold a pot or two which he said came from Machu Picchu, but the difficulty of the climb up to the ruins and the low price of pots probably dissuaded him from making any serious effort to locate graves. Richarte and his friends had small inducement to disturb any graves until the days of our arrival and the opportunity of securing liberal gratuities. They could not have sold more than one or two *ollas* without being detected by their landlord, who would have immediately claimed anything of this kind. The most frequent visitors to the caves on the mountainside were undoubtedly animal prowlers searching for food and shelter, and especially the spectacled bears, which are still common in this vicinity.

A cave two hundred feet from the City Gate contained the well-preserved skeletons of two men, one about twenty years of age, the other a small man approaching middle age. These men were not builders, no hammer-stones or crowbars being buried with them. The younger man had an elaborately carved grey talk necklace ornament of unique design, a number of bone beads, and pieces of what appears to be a bead made of fused green glass! The older man had a few ornaments, small stone tokens and bronze necklace pendants. Also he had a jug, the only jug, by the way, that was not found associated with women's bones. His bones were free from decay. The muscles of his left thigh still adhere to the bone. There were even a few pieces of cloth and cord made from brown llama wool. Evidently this was one of the most recent of all burials. It is curious and significant that these two men should have female ornaments as well as a woman's jug. Their unusual place of burial, their feminine adornments, the absence of masculine possessions, the extraordinary presence of a mass of desiccated muscle tissue on the older man's thigh, the little jug, all point to something peculiar about these two. Why were they buried in this unusual place? Were they unwelcome visitors who came to the outskirts of the sacred city and were buried near the gate without being admitted to the society of the Virgins of the Sun? And what about that bead of fused green glass? Where did the young man get that? It is probably of European origin. To be sure, it is only a little thing, but it would seem to say that the young man came here after the Spaniards had reached Cuzco. Were these men spies, sent by the Spaniards to try and locate the refuge of the Virgins of the Sun who had escaped from the holy city? Did they bring presents for the sacred women, necklaces, and a jug and a precious glass bead, the like of which none of them had ever seen before? Who can tell? It seems to be an insoluble puzzle.

It will be remembered that our excavations in the fortress of Vitcos, the last Inca capital, resulted in the finding of a number of iron articles of European manufacture, including a buckle, a pair of scissors, several saddle ornaments, and three jews' harps, mementos of the days of the Spanish Conquest. Had Machu Picchu been known to the conquerors or been occupied by Inca soldiers who had opportunities, as did the followers of the last Inca Manco, to waylay Spanish travelers, we might expect to find similar foreign artifacts here. It is all the more striking and significant, therefore, to note that after the most thorough and painstaking search in the one hundred caves or graves which contained objects of interest, as well as in the many other caves which yielded only negative results, only two others contained objects which could be surely assigned to the post-Columbian era. Furthermore, in no case was the object one that might not perfectly well have been brought to the caves long after the burials had taken place and Machu Picchu had been abandoned as a place of residence. In a cave halfway down the mountainside, east of the hut of Richarte, at a considerable distance from the city and the principal cemeteries, was found a piece of rusty iron, little more than a thin rust flake about 3 cm. long and 1 cm. wide. It looks as if it might be the shard of a knife blade. There is no reason why it may not be from the knife of a treasure hunter, particularly in view of the fact that no objects of bronze or pottery of marketable value were found in this cave. The presence of several artistic little carved stone chips of animals in silhouette makes it seem likely that other attractive articles were once here. On the other hand, it may have belonged to one of the occupants of the neighboring grave. The knife blade, if such it was, may have been used to carve the little stone tokens. In the only burial cave near this one was found a well-preserved example of typical coast pottery, a stirrup-shaped spherical bottle, totally unlike anything of Inca workmanship; also more carved animals. The contents of these caves as well as their location would seem to dissociate their occupants from those who were buried in one of the regular cemetery areas. On the other hand, the use of the local chloritic schist as the medium for perpetuating the appearance of certain animals would seem to identify the individuals as permanent residents rather than as transients.

The only other cave containing anything of post-Columbian origin was about five hundred yards from the camp in a southerly direction and a little above the level of the Rock-Sheltered Terrace. It lies fairly near, if not actually in, Cemetery No. 3, where many of the chief people of Machu Picchu were buried. This cave contained two peach stones and a beef bone, "a fragment from the shaft of a bovine tibia," as Dr. Eaton describes it. In view of the complete absence of beef bones in any other cave I am inclined to assume that the peach stones and the bone were the remains of some visitor's lunch. Machu Picchu was reported to exist as an interesting archaeological site as early as the unsuccessful attempt of Wiener to find it in 1875. We know that Lizarraga had been treasure hunting on these forest-clad slopes at least ten years before our visit to the cave. It is also significant that neither at this cave nor at another whose location is recorded in the same general terms and which was probably close to it, did our workmen find any pottery, bronzes, or other artifacts of commercial value. It seems possible that their absence may be attached to the successful treasure hunter who brought the peach stones and the beef bone. Except for the bead of fused green glass, none of the burial caves near the city or in Cemeteries Nos. 1 and 2 contained any evidence that the persons buried there had had any contact with the Spanish conquerors. It seems reasonable to conclude, therefore, that the last occupants of the city perished without having been visited by any Europeans.

A careful count of the skeletal material found in the various caves and graves seems to show the remains of one hundred and seventy-three individuals, of whom perhaps one hundred and fifty were women, an extraordinary percentage unless this was a sanctuary whose inhabitants were the Chosen Women of the Sun. In view of the size and importance of the city and the very large number of persons who must have been employed as agricultural laborers, hewers of wood and drawers of water, in and around the sanctuary, it is possible that only persons of high rank or priests or the Chosen Women themselves were permitted to be buried in the caves near the city. It is doubtful whether any except members of the family of the Inca and the attendants in the great sanctuary were even permitted to enter the city gate. That appears to have been the ancient custom. This would account for the absence of the bones of husky workers.

In the graves we found pieces of about three hundred and fifty dishes and jars. The cemetery containing the largest number of pots per person is the one nearest to and most accessible from the ruins of the city. About twice as many were found here. The reason for this would seem to lie in the possibility that many of these potsherds represented the garniture of burials which had taken place so long ago that all of the bone material had disintegrated. This hypothesis is borne out by the fact that in the rocky region south and southwest of the Sacred Plaza, probably an ancient burial ground from which nearly all the skeletal material had disappeared, a very large number of potsherds were found, from which we have been able to identify five hundred and twenty-one different pots, including specimens of every one of the principal types known to Machu Picchu. Although nearly all the burial caves contained pieces of pottery only one of them yielded a fragment of a three-legged brazier. Probably the people whose bones were found in the caves did not use the braziers, the metal workers being undoubtedly men.

The art of trepanning seems to have been rather widely practiced in ancient Peru. Consequently there is considerable food for reflection in the fact that none of the burial caves opened on the sides of Machu Picchu and Huayna Picchu contained a single "trepanned" skull. Yet practically all the large burial caves which we opened in the valley within a distance of thirty miles contained a number of "trepanned" skulls. Evidently the warriors whose wounds required this treatment did not live at Machu Picchu. It should be noted, however, that many of the so-called "trepanned skulls" are claimed by competent surgeons to show more evidence of disease than of surgery. The bones of the men who built Machu Picchu have disappeared. Some may have been buried elsewhere. Of those who died in this immediate vicinity probably all vestige has been lost.

Patient and systematic excavation was carried on in the city. With few exceptions the interior of the houses yielded little or no results; but certain localities gave us quantities of valuable material. The most fruitful digging was on the ridge south of the little plaza on which stood the Temple of the Three Windows between it and the City Gate. This region is dotted with a considerable number of very large rocks. Possibly it was the quarry from which some of the building stone was taken but where blocks too large for the purpose of the stone masons and too difficult to be broken up into desired size without the use of blasting materials were left in place. The result of the quarrying left a small area which was not worth terracing; stone quarries naturally do not make good gardens.

A few rods northwest from the top of the main stairway, Erdis discovered a huge bowlder or ledge on the top of which several figures of snakes had been carved. We called it Snake Rock. It may have been the center of the original cemetery long before the last occupation. Under the rock he found a cave which contained fragments of a skull and jaw bone but none of the larger bones of the skeleton. That the burial here included persons or a person of importance is shown by the artifacts found under the rock. Among them are two bronze mirrors with pierced square handles, two bronze knives, a very fine unusually long bronze shawl-pin, a drinking cup, two disks of green chloritic schist, half a dozen chips or counters of the same material, a broken knife of chalcedony and a piece of red paint, not to mention numerous pebbles and potsherds. Why small pebbles were brought up from the river bed and put in the grave with such valuable bronzes is a puzzle. However, as we have seen, Father Cobo, the Jesuit, saw guinea pigs cooked by the Aymara in Bolivia with "smooth pebbles from the river, of the kind called *calapurca*, the Aymara word for belly-stones, so called because placed in the belly of the cuy." It is amusing to imagine that one of the persons of importance who was buried here under the great Snake Rock was an Aymara damsel, one of the Chosen Women of the Sun, who had been brought all the way from the country around Lake Titicaca to minister to the happiness of the Inca and had brought with her the knowledge that guinea pigs cooked with *calapurca* were particularly toothsome!

Not far from the Snake Rock was unearthed an artistic little bronze knife with a fisherboy and his catch, a unique design, which was regarded by Dr. W. H. Holmes as one of the finest examples of the ancient art of working in bronze, ever found in America. Unquestionably it is a remarkable example of a mature creative art which took delight in expressing well-known scenes in an artistic manner. It is now in the Yale Museum.

Near the "Snake Rock" are the very irregular foundations of houses or huts unlike in design anything else in the city, and underneath some of the large bowlders are small caves which at one time might have served as shelters.

In the process of his patient digging within the limits of the city Mr. Erdis made the discovery that in the vicinity of these bowlders, artifacts were likely to be found two or three feet underground. In this part of the city, quite a number of little bronzes, two stone dishes, and some artifacts were found which did not occur in any of the digging in other parts of the city nor in the excavations in burial caves on the slopes of the ridge. It would seem to be obvious that this part of the site represented a much earlier occupancy than most of the ruins.

Very little skeletal material was found within the city, though a female skull was discovered under a bowlder about 250 feet south of the Principal Temple. We did find, near the Sacred Plaza, several caves which had probably contained mummies at one time or another, and a stone-lined bottle-shaped grave, but all were empty. It is impossible to say whether they were despoiled by the first treasure seekers who visited the city in the nineteenth century or whether they were emptied long before that. I incline to the latter view because of the extreme unlikelihood of treasure seekers caring to remove every single bone, and the fact that in this humid sub-tropical climate mummies and mummy wrappings would not last long enough to make them commercially valuable, as they are when found in the cemeteries of the arid Peruvian coastal desert.

For four months Mr. Erdis and his carefully selected Indian assistants excavated and prospected within the walls and on the terraces of Machu Picchu. The zeal of the Indian assistants was kept at high pitch by a sliding scale of bounties and gratuities. No part of the city was neglected in their efforts to find significant traces of the past. One might have supposed that the pieces of broken pottery would be fairly well distributed among the different houses, or at least among the different quarters of the city, but such was not the case. Digging inside the walls of the houses rarely gave any results, whereas certain fairly well-defined rubbish piles yielded good results. Some quarters of the city had almost nothing, others had an extraordinary amount.

The northeast quarter, containing a larger number of dwellings than any other quarter of the city, had relatively little, sherds of only one hundred and sixty-one pots being found in the excavations here. As these houses are quite like those found at Choqquequirau and Qquente it seems fair to say they were among the last to be built and were "late Inca."

The northwest quarter includes the Principal Temple, the Sacred Plaza, and the Temple of the Three Windows. It contained a surprisingly small amount of material. There was practically nothing on Intihuatana Hill and nothing in the buildings on the plaza, a fact which was most disappointing. It should not be forgotten, however, that this group of buildings adjoins the so-called Snake Rock Cemetery, most prolific of all localities.

The southeast quarter of the city was at a considerably lower level than any other and contained rather poorly built houses, so one would not expect to find much there. Yet we did find remains of some seventy-five pots. The southwest quarter of the city, from the City Gate to the Stairway of the Fountains, contains the finest dwellings, the Royal Mausoleum and the real center of the city life, the main thoroughfare and the water supply. So it was not strange to find this quarter plentifully supplied with thousands of sherds. They represent some five hundred and fifty-eight examples of Inca pottery. More than fifty jars were found near the City Gate in a rubbish pile on the north side of the main street. Pieces of more than one hundred jars were found near the very best compound where the Inca himself may have lived.

On top of the ridge Mr. Erdis and his faithful workers found quantities of curiously shaped little stones of a type of which very few specimens have ever found their way into any museum. They vary greatly in size. Some of them are in the shape of poker chips, others are carved into fantastic shapes. Although their use is problematical they seem to me to be counters or record stones.

Many of them are made of a green micaceous or chloritic slaty schist, a small quantity of which exists at the foot of one of the precipices on Machu Picchu Mountain. These "record stones" form one of our most interesting finds. They include one hundred and fifty-six stone disks, of which only three were found in caves containing skeletal material, and they may therefore have belonged to an earlier culture than that represented by the majority of the burials. On the other hand it may be said that they belonged to some occupation in which the Chosen Women were not allowed to participate. There are more small disks than large ones, half of them being about an inch in diameter. One might say that the large portion of small ones was due to the necessity of providing digits, the lesser number of medium-sized ones to the smaller necessity of providing counters for 10's and so on up. In the language of the poker table, "they needed more white chips than blue ones;" yet there is nothing to determine where the line could be drawn since all are of the same color and there are no actual designs on their surfaces.

Possibly the largest two disks, which seem out of all proportion to the others, may have been intended as covers for *chicha* jars. Indeed, eight or ten of the larger disks could easily have been so used. It seems to me probable, however, that the relative infrequency of large disks was due to their having been used as counters. We may suppose the large counters signified a large number.

The two largest disks are rough hewn, partially ground and polished. Most of the large disks, in fact, are roughly made, but a few are nicely rounded, ground, and polished to a fairly consistent thickness. Only one was incised, the largest of the regular series measuring about five and a half inches in diameter. It has a single cross incised on one side in the center of the disk, the bars of the cross being about two inches in length.

Four of the disks were perforated and the edges of one disk were notched with four small incisions. A careful examination of the smaller disks or counters shows that practically all were carefully ground and polished, a large number being nicely rounded. Nearly all still show the scratches made in the grinding and polishing. A few were ground so thin as to be translucent.

A group of exceedingly well-made smaller disks, sixteen in all, besides a discoidal stone pendant of similar size, was found in one hole near the Snake Rock. All of them are carefully ground and polished and all bear in addition to the marks of grinding and polishing, suspicious scratches, yet even here there is no certainty that they bore tally marks.

While there are suspicious scratches on perhaps a dozen of the disks and occasional markings that resemble tallying, there seems to be no regular rule about them. Since the green micaceous schist is soft and easily scratched, it was quite suitable for being marked with tallies if it was so desired, and the tally could easily have been erased later by a slight amount of grinding and polishing. If that had taken place, however, I believe that we should be in no doubt about the marking, and that more of them would have been found to contain clear tally marks such as actually do exist on the baked-clay cubes to be described later.

In addition to the disks of green micaceous schist there are one or two of sandstone or other rock. Two or three flat discoidal pebbles of similar material were found in connection with the disks.

Forty-two oblong stone counters of green schist were found. Nearly all bear marks of having been ground and polished but none appears to have been engraved, although a number have irregular scratches of a suspicious character which might, however, have been made accidentally in the course of manufacture. Most of them came from the Snake Rock Region and the upper part of the city.

The collection also includes nineteen triangular "chips," found generally in places where other types of record stones occurred. None came from the burial caves. Besides the disks, oblongs and triangles, there are a number of very irregular chips some of which are incised, others carved into highly problematical shapes impossible of classification. Some of the triangles and oblongs are pierced with holes as though for use as pendants or amulets.

In one grave four little green stone chips were found, each one carved to represent a denizen of the jungle. Possibly they were buried with their owner and designer, who, in carving them as silhouettes of a peccary, an ant eater, an otter, and a parrot, may have wished to record a visit to the forests of the lower Urubamba. Two chips were found representing in miniature an Australian boomerang. One has the outlines of a pipe, another of the head and shoulders of an animal, still another of a small flat reel or spool on which thread could be wound. Several are carved in the shape common to bronze knives and axes but in miniature. These might well have been used as offerings to the god of metallurgy, in the hope that the bronze castings would be successful.

Most of these little green chips appear to be record stones. Probably they belonged to an earlier culture than that of the Incas. They have been found in Ecuador, although they are almost wholly unknown in such European and American collections of Peruvian antiquities as I have seen. At Machu Picchu they came mainly from excavations in the city and occurred in greatest profusion in the vicinity of Snake Rock, which was possibly the most ancient cemetery.

Similar record stones were found by Professor Saville and by Dr. Dorsey on the Island of La Plata, off the coast of Ecuador. An eminent Peruvian archaeologist, Señor Gonzales de la Rosa, believes that the predecessors of the Incas kept their accounts by means of record stones. The Incas themselves used *quipus*, knotted strings of different colors arranged in decimal series. Velasco, the author of a History of the Kingdom of Quito, quotes from an ancient Spanish missionary chronicle, the work of Friar Marco de

Niza, a work that is not known to exist at present. The Friar says that the Caras, or ancient rulers of Ecuador, "used a kind of writing more imperfect than that of the Peruvian *quipus*." They kept their records by means of "little stones of distinct sizes, colors and angular form" arranged in containers of wood, stone or clay. "With the different combination of these they perpetuated their doings and formed their count of all." By means of these crude archives they kept a record of their kings. That the system seems to have been unsatisfactory and imperfect is shown in Velasco's statement that some interpreted the deposits to mean that eighteen rulers covered a period of seven hundred years while others interpreted the succession as covering only five hundred years.

In treating of the burial customs of the pre-Inca rulers of Quito, Velasco says that above the mummy of each ruler was a little niche, inside of which "were the small stones of various shapes and colors which denoted his age, the years and the month of his reign." Professor Saville notes that little stones of distinct sizes, colors, and angular shapes used for the purpose of keeping historical and other records are to be found in various places on the western coast of Ecuador not far from the southern frontier of Colombia. The Caras were eventually conquered by the Incas and forced to adopt their customs, including the use of *quipus*, or records strings.

The finding at Machu Picchu of similar record stones made of the local green micaceous or chloritic schist might indicate that at some time in its history Machu Picchu was inhabited by people who had not yet learned to use string records. Or else these were brought from Ecuador by the Incas, which is possible. No record stones have been found elsewhere in this region, and were it not for Professor Saville's discoveries we would have been at a loss as to how to regard these little green chips. Under the circumstances it seems proper to suggest that the high niches in the Principal Temple might have been intended to receive collections of record stones and were purposely placed out of reach so as to obviate the likelihood of their being disturbed. That none were found in these niches need not necessarily destroy this hypothesis. In the first place, when the time came for the use of record stones to be abandoned in favor of *quipus* they all might have been removed by order of the high priest and buried near the Sacred Plaza. In the second place, when the Principal Temple was no longer used for worship the priests may have carried away or hidden the record stones which were in its high niches. In the third place, it must be remembered that the Principal Temple was stripped of any ornaments or objects of interest which it contained long before my first visit. It would have been one of the first things to be found by Indian treasure seekers working their way along the top of the ridge and it is to be presumed that they long since would have carried away anything of interest which it contained. Finally, it is interesting to note that our careful searches and excavations in other groups of Inca ruins in this region, including Choqquequirau, Rosaspata, and Patallacta, have not yielded any similar stones, tokens or counters. Had only a few "record stones" been found here it might easily be supposed that they were brought from Ecuador after the conquest of that region in the last century of the Inca Empire. As most were made of local green schist, it seems likely that they were made here by some of the Incas.

In an excavation near the city gate, twenty-nine obsidian pebbles, slightly larger than ordinary marbles, were found. One more was dug up a few feet away but none was found anywhere else. The late Professor Pirsson, of the Sheffield Scientific School, was kind enough to examine them for me, said that similar obsidian pebbles are found in all parts of the world, citing especially Honduras, Arizona, and central Europe. The finding of these rounded chunks of volcanic glass in some localities where there has been no recent volcanic action has led to the suggestion that they might be extra-terrestrial, possibly a "meteoric shower." Whatever their origin, their location near the gateway of the city would seem to indicate that they might have been used as record stones, possibly to keep tally on those who brought alpaca wool for the Chosen Women.

We also found a few tokens or counters of baked clay. They are extremely rare in collections of Peruvian antiquities. There were likewise a few pentagonal clay disks made of rounded potsherds, marked on five sides so as to be used as counters up to five.

Also of potter's clay were ear-plugs, flute-like whistles, paint dishes, and dice-like counters. They are incised with straight lines and crosses clearly intended to represent a numerical tally. Very little is known about these last, and although they are fairly common at Machu Picchu, few, if any, have found their way into the larger museums of the world. Like the stone disks, they do not seem to have been used by the Incas but probably by an earlier people previous to the invention of the *quipu*.

There is a story in Montesinos that before the invention of *quipus*, or knotted mnemonic strings, there was another method of keeping accounts. Since the tradition in Montesinos relates to an event centuries old at the time of his investigations, it is barely possible that the old method of writing which is referred to in the tradition means the use of record stones and incised terra-cotta cubes such as have been found at Machu Picchu. It is possible that the use of counters was carried to a greater degree at Machu Picchu than elsewhere in Peru but that the invention of the *quipu* and the ease with which it could be adapted to a decimal system prevented the spread of the use of stone counters. Whether one prefers to regard the story in Montesinos as a somewhat embroidered account of an actual event or as a reference to the abandonment of the use of record stones and the commencement of the use of the *quipu* is not important. The interesting fact remains that at Machu Picchu we have evidence of a different system of notation from that employed by the Incas at the time of the Spanish Conquest.

Besides the record stones, artifacts found at Machu Picchu included beads in the shape of disks, perforated bars, possibly used as spreaders, pendants, points for needles or shuttles, whorl bobs for spinning, polishing stones, scrapers, knives, pestles, mortars and grinding stones. There are two pestles made in the shape of cylinders, seven or eight inches long and two or three inches in diameter, very beautifully cut and polished. Some of the mortars are merely circular or oblong depressions in roughly squared rectangular blocks. Two or three grinding stones possibly intended for ceremonial purposes, were cut out of broad, thin slabs looking strikingly like old fashioned gravestones, two feet long and a foot and a half wide. Near them were found equally long thin slabs with a curved edge, the ceremonial rocking stone mullers.

In the excavation on the ridge near the Snake Rock and the Temple of the Three Windows, Mr. Erdis found pieces of a beautifully decorated rectangular dish, originally carved out of a single piece of schist. Its shape and its design were so unusual, he dug up every foot of ground to a depth of about two feet over a fairly large area. By examining every pebble he finally was successful in finding nearly all the pieces of this beautiful dish, which is probably pre-Inca and of very great age. It is about eight inches long by five inches wide and two and a half inches high. He also found another smaller dish of similar design.

A number of crude stone dishes and bowls were found, one nearly circular and about twelve inches in diameter and five inches in depth. Pieces of two or three handsomely made circular stone dishes showing evidence of having been carefully cut and polished were found. Such dishes are eagerly sought by Peruvian collectors of antiquities, so it is not surprising that we found no good examples. Relatively few objects of stone occurred in any of the burial caves.

Five primitive obsidian knives were found in one of the oldest parts of the city near a ledge marked with incised serpents. We also found a stone flake knife of chalcedony very like a couple which I picked up in some pre-Inca ruins near Lake Parinacochas.

We found a hundred specimens of Inca bronze including axes,

chisels, clubs, shawl-pins and knives. In the city were many pieces of little braziers which had been used in their manufacture. Rough usage had destroyed most of them so that it was only possible to restore one brazier with any degree of accuracy. None were found in any of the graves. They seem not to have been used by the women who were buried there.

Hundreds of hammer-stones were found, indicating the great importance and frequent use of this primitive paleolithic implement which enabled the Incas to accomplish such incredible feats. They consist usually of hard, compact pebbles or cobblestones of diorite or other firmly consolidated rock material. Sometimes slight depressions permitted the thumb and finger to hold them securely, but in most instances there is only the chipped point of the pebble to show that it was used as a hammer-stone.

One cobblestone, eight inches long and four inches wide, bears evidence of having been used by its ingenious owner for three different purposes. This original three-in-one tool has a small depression carved in its side which could serve as a mortar for grinding pigments; its ends are both abraded by it having been used as a hammer-stone; and one side is smoothly rounded so that it could be used as a rocking-stone pestle or muller.

Among the articles of wood is the charred fragment of a dish which possibly was an inch and a half deep and six inches in diameter; a nicely made crochet needle over five inches long, the handle slightly flattened, incised on the edges and decorated with a feather pattern; a needle five inches long made from a large stout thorn, its base flattened and perforated; another needle about four inches long with a small metallic ring fastened to the base. No examples were found of that painted woodenware frequently seen in collections of Cuzco antiquities which seem to represent an art practiced during the early days of the Spanish Conquest under the influence of European design.

Four bone articles were found: a whorl-bob made possibly from the end of a femur, and three pointed tools, still used in the hand looms of Peru to beat up the thread of the woof. Two of them are perforated; one has a nicely decorated handle consisting of two birds facing each other.

Our knowledge of the textiles made and worn at Machu Picchu must rest mostly on the beautiful specimens already referred to which have been found in the tombs of the Peruvian coastal desert. However, we know from Rodriguez, an eye witness, that Titu Cusi who lived here, and some of his nobles were sumptuously dressed. In this moist climate—we had frequent showers even in the dry season—it is not to be supposed that articles of cloth would last very long. A few very small fragments of nicely woven woolen textiles were found in some of the burial caves where they were most thoroughly protected against the weather. They were so decayed, however, as to make it impossible to determine the size or nature of the original garments.

One terra-cotta ear-plug was found, its outer surface covered with small holes in which possibly little colored feathers had once been placed. We know that the Inca nobles were distinguished by the large size of their ear ornaments, to receive which the lobe of the ear had to be punctured and stretched. This was such a conspicuous feature of the nobles that the conquistadors called them *orejones*, "big ears."

The Incas were fond of bright colors and of using the feathers of forest birds as ornaments and as part of their costume. We found many birds in this vicinity. In fact the Urubamba Valley acts as a highway or migratory route for birds between the highlands and the low country.

The collection of mammals gathered by my Peruvian expeditions consists of over nine hundred specimens, belonging to eighty species. The bird collection numbers seven hundred specimens, but contains a far greater number of species than the mammal collection. We found approximately four hundred species of birds; many of which are represented by only a single specimen. In addition to the mammals and birds we brought home specimens of some twenty different species of snakes, ten lizards and a variety of fishes. All of these animals must have been known to the Incas and most of them were probably used in one way or another by the people of Machu Picchu.

Practically all of our natural history specimens were deposited in the Smithsonian Institution. The archeological material is mostly in the Yale University Museum, except that which was excavated in 1914-1915, which was all returned to the Peruvian Government.

5.

The Search for
Inca Roads Leading
to Machu Picchu

AFTER THE CLEARING
of the ruins was fairly under way, the next object which demanded
attention was the location of ancient highways connecting the
city with the surrounding country. We were able to locate a paved
road running south from the City Gate along the terraces and the
back of the ridge toward Machu Picchu Mountain. Due to a
rock-fall in front of one of the great precipices on the mountain,
this road had been partially destroyed. On the other side of the
rock-fall we were able to find it again and to follow a carefully
made granite stairway to the top of the ridge east of the mountain.
At that point it divided, the left-hand fork leading to seemingly
impassable cliffs on the south side of the mountain, the right-hand
fork following the top of the ridge to the summit. There we
found, as has been said, the ruins of an Inca house which would
accommodate a dozen soldiers, and a carefully terraced signal
station or lookout on the very top of the peak 4,000 feet directly
above the San Miguel bridge over the Urubamba River.

We heard from one of the Indians that there were ruins in a
region of high mountains and impassable jungles south of Machu
Picchu Mountain. It was tantalizing to think of the possibilities

of exploration in a country which in ancient days must have been so closely connected with the hidden city. The mystery of the deep valleys which lie in the quadrant north to northeast of Mount Salcantay had long demanded attention. Separated from Ollantay-tambo and Amaybamba by the Grand Canyon of the Urubamba, protected from Cuzco by the gigantic barrier of Salcantay, isolated from Vitcos by deep valleys and inhospitable high wind-swept bleak regions called *punas*, it seems to have been unknown to the Spanish conquerors and unsuspected by their historians. Garcilasso Inca de la Vega, from whom Prescott drew so much of his fascinating *Conquest of Peru*, makes no reference to places which can with any certainty be located in the Machu Picchu quadrant. Cobo and Balboa in their detailed accounts of Inca con-quests take the story right around this region. It appears to have been a *terra incognita* until the nineteenth century. Even Raimondi hardly touched it.

One day Ricardo Charaja, a full-blooded Quichua from the town of Santa Rosa, who was my most dependable native assistant, located the remains of an old Inca road leading out of the Pampaccahuana Valley in the general direction of Machu Picchu. He pointed it out to Chief Topographer Bumstead. Rumors reached us of Inca ruins to be found in that direction. It was re-ported that "there was a large temple built on an island in the center of a lake, a very beautiful place, better than Machu Picchu."

It was with mingled feelings of keen curiosity and skepticism that Osgood Hardy and I undertook in April, 1915, to follow the newly discovered roadway as far as it would carry us. It began in an affluent of the Urubamba, not very far from Ollantaytambo at the junction of the Huayllabamba River with the Pampacca-huana, near a small ruin built of rough rocks laid in clay. Located on a promontory above the two streams, this ruin probably repre-sented a *tampu*, or resthouse, on the ancient road. It was probably used by the Inca nobles and the Virgins of the Sun.

We had engaged the services of an Indian guide who said he knew all about "the celebrated temple in the middle of a lake in the mountains" but he did not put in an appearance and we had to start without him. He caught up with us later, claiming that he thought we might not start because it was raining that morning! As a matter of fact, his provisions for the journey, consisting of a small quantity of parched corn and *habas* beans, had not been prepared in time.

Led by Ricardo Charaja, who greatly enjoyed his ability to act as a giude in a region far from his own home, we worked our way through a picturesque primeval forest and emerged in the upper part of a U-shaped valley, on whose grassy slopes we had no difficulty in following the remains of a paved highway constructed by the Incas. It led by easy gradients to a pass at the head of Huayllabamba Valley and thence descended by a series of sharp zigzags into the Huayruru Valley. Not an Indian hut was to be seen. In fact, the region seemed to be extraordinarily destitute even of animal life. In a wild, unfrequented valley like Huayruru, one is very likely to see a few deer and we hoped to run across an Andean bear; but nothing of the kind appeared and we made our way across the bottom of the valley as best we could, only to find the Inca road disappearing in a maze of great bowlders under the remains of a fairly recent landslide. On the other side of the valley we saw two Inca roads winding up the grassy slopes. We decided to take the one to the right, as that appeared more likely to lead in the direction of Macchu Picchu. The left fork probably goes to Palcay, the ruins of a small Inca country-house which I discovered by accident in 1912.

Halfway up the mountain side, some two thousand feet above the bottom of the valley we came to an interesting little Inca fortress, the name of which our guide, who had by this time joined us, gave as Runcu Raccay. It was apparently a fortified station on the old highway. Circular in shape, Runcu Raccay contains the remains of four or five edifices grouped about a little courtyard which was entered by a narrow passage. In the sides of the passage were bar-holds for the better securing of the gate. The stonework and the arrangement of the niches are typically late Inca. We pitched our camp near the ruins, our half-dozen Indian bearers from Ollantaytambo building themselves a temporary shelter as a protection against the cold rain which fell during the night.

Twenty-five years later Runcu Raccay was visited by Dr. Paul Fejos, and an attractive model of it is shown in his report to the Viking Fund. He did not find the bar-holds which we photographed in 1915, so they may have been destroyed.

From Runcu Raccay we followed the Inca road over a pass out of the Huayruru Valley and into that of one of the affluents of the Aobamba. In most places the road was still in such condition that our mules could follow it with safety, but occasionally the poor animals would get bad falls and had to be entirely unloaded and helped over slippery or precipitous rocks.

We had not gone far down into the new valley before we came to another fork in the road. The left branch led by a series of steps up a steep slope to a promontory, where we found the ruins of a compact Inca group, to which our guide gave the name of Cedrobamba. Since this word is half Spanish and half Quichua, meaning "cedar plain," it is obviously not the ancient name. No one seems to have lived in this valley for several centuries, so it is not surprising that the old name has been lost. The ruins of Cedrobamba are in the same style as the others located along the highway, and while too extensive to be merely a fortified resthouse like Runcu Raccay, Cedrobamba undoubtedly represents one of the important fortified outposts subsidiary to Machu Picchu. It commands an extensive view on three sides. The promontory is surrounded by steep precipices and is extremely difficult of access except over the paved roadway. It was probably supplied with water by a small ditch brought along the side of the mountain in the manner typical of Inca engineering.

We made a small clearing not far from the ruins and camped here for several days while the Inca roadway was being cleared and made passable for our mules. In several places rustic bridges had to be constructed and a considerable amount of jungle removed before the animals could pass over the ancient trail. The only place where we met serious difficulty was at the point where the road-way ran through a tunnel behind a huge, sloping ledge. The Incas had found it easier to tunnel behind the ledge than to cut the road-way in the face of the sheer cliff, but the tunnel was not wide enough for loaded mules. Of course the Incas had used llamas with small bodies and small loads. It was big enough for them.

While the road was being made passable for our animals, I went ahead with Ricardo and was delighted to find that as the road progressed it headed more and more in the direction of Machu Picchu. Pushing on in the hope of soon getting a glimpse of Machu Picchu Mountain, I discovered a group of ruins called Ccorihuayrachina, "the place where gold is winnowed or washed." Above the ruins a striking hilltop had been leveled off and sur-rounded by a retaining wall so as to make it useful as a signal station or possibly a primitive fortress. Beneath it we found a huge cave which showed signs of recent occupancy, probably by bears.

The Inca highway led into the ruins of Ccorihuayrachina by a long flight of stone stairs, from the top of which we secured a magnificent view of the Urubamba Valley in the vicinity of Machu Picchu Mountain. The most interesting feature of Ccorihuay-rachina is a row of five stone-paved fountains in what is now a swamp, near a huge, slightly carved bowlder. This may have been what the Indians referred to when they spoke of a temple in a lake, but it hardly came up to our expectations. The name Ccori-huayrachina "the place where gold is washed" may have been given to the locality by reason of the five fountains, where some imaginative Indian thought gold might have been washed. To me it seems likely that this was the residence of one of the most im-portant chiefs who owed allegiance to the rulers of Machu Picchu. It has recently been thoroughly explored by an expedition con-ducted by Dr. Paul Fejos and proves to be an important location.

From Ccorihuayrachina the trail led along the crest of the ridge, generally following an easy grade, often the normal con-

A portion of the Semicircular Temple showing the wonderfully graceful stone work of white granite ashlars, each one fitting so perfectly that this curved wall has stood for centuries held together only by friction.

Extraordinary stone work fitted into the granite ledge under the Semicircular Temple near to the entrance to a royal mausoleum that lay under the rock.

The interior of the Royal Mausoleum, a cave lined with granite ashlars. The stone bench on which my young Indian assistant is resting was probably intended for the mummy bundles of ancient Inca rulers, possibly Pachacuti members of the Pachacuti family.

Two of the memorial windows in the east wall of the Three Window Temple looking over to the East City and across the Urubamba valley to the mountains over which the sun rose. Pachacuti Yamqui Salcamayhua, descendant of a long line of Incas, whose great-grandparents were contemporaries of Titu Cusi, in an account of the antiquities of Peru says that the first Inca Manco Capac "ordered works to be executed at the place of his birth, consisting of a masonry wall with three windows, which were the emblems of the house of his fathers whence he descended." This is the only place I know of which fits that description.

One of the inner doors of the palace where I believe Titu Cusi and Tupac Amaru lived during the years prior to the advent of the Viceroy Francisco de Toledo in 1570. The very fine ashlars would correspond to paneling in a modern palace. The rough stones of the upper story were plastered and covered with thatch under the roof.

A closeup of the lower part of the problematical window whose holes may have been used to support the golden image of the Sun God which was captured by the Viceroy, Francisco de Toledo, when he took Tupac Amaru, the last of the Inca Emperors, a prisoner. Tupac Amaru had spent most of his life here at Machu Picchu which was then known as Vilcapampa.

The entrance to the King's Group, the finest collection of dwellings at Machu Picchu. The lintel is a monolith of white granite weighing about three tons. Through this door there passed, I believe, Manco and his sons at one time or another. I feel sure that Titu Cusi and Tupac Amaru lived here for many years.

A group of Campas Indians, formerly probably called Antis, living in the Pampaconas valley near Espiritu Pampa where we found the remains of Inca houses which may have been occupied by Tupac Amaru. It is the custom for men and boys to wear fillets. Married men also wear long gowns. The elevation, about 4000 feet, means that it is cold at night although very hot in the daytime since we are here less than 800 miles from the equator.

A burial cave at Choqquequirau showing a skull and some pottery. Arable land was so scarce and so carefully conserved behind well-built terraces, none of it was used for cemeteries. So far as we could discover, both at Machu Picchu and Choqquequirau, all burials were made in rocky regions or under caves where the mummy bundles, knees drawn up to chin and arms folded around the shins, could be partly protected from the weather.

*A corner of one of the houses in the Inca way-station of Runcu
Raccay on the Inca road from Ollantaytambo to Machu Picchu.
Our guide who had been helping to clear a place for the camp does
not look too pleased to serve as a model of an ancient soldier.*

*My mule train going through the snowy pass of Chucuito under
the slopes of Mt. Soiroccocha looking down into the Arma valley
through which the Inca soldiers of Manco went in order to reach
the Apurimac river. Crossing it on rafts they were then able to
attack Spanish merchants and travelers on the road from Lima to
Cuzco. No wonder the soldiers of Pizarro failed to reach Vitcos.
It took my pack train four days to go through the passes and deep
valleys that separated Puquiura and Vitcos from Pasaje where we
could cross the Apurimac. Soiroccocha is 18,220 ft. high. The
pass of Chucuito is 14,700 ft. or higher than Pikes Peak.*

The ruins of the Inca city of Qquente—"humming-bird"—in the Urubamba valley, which are of the same style and character as the ruins of Choqquequirau in the Apurimac valley. In this style of building the Incas did not take the trouble to fit the blocks closely together but laid them in clay in more or less irregular courses.

During a spell of remarkably clear weather, Osgood Hardy and I pitched our camp here at the foot of Mt. Salcantay, one of the highest peaks in the Andes and the crown of the Cordillera Vilcabamba. It offers a fine challenge to ambitious Alpinists for it has never been climbed. It is surrounded by numerous glaciers. The passes from valley to valley are usually covered with snow. It is well within the tropics, but its altitude is greater than that of Mt. McKinley.

My mule train on the old Inca road which we believe the Inca Titu Cusi followed with the Augustinian Fathers, Friar Marcos and Friar Diego, when he took them from Puquiura, near Vitcos, to the vicinity of Vilcapampa, his principal residence, the University of Idolatry. Father Calancha says they passed a spot called Ungacacha where they had to wade in bitterly cold water. Our guide called this lake Yanacocha. Its water is icy cold. It helped us to identify this ancient trail over which the Inca was carried in a litter while the monks had to walk.

The Inca road between Vitcos and Machu Picchu which we discovered in 1915 and which we believe to have been the road followed by Titu Cusi when he allowed the Augustinians, Friar Marcos and Friar Diego, to accompany him as far as the outskirts of Vilcapampa, his principal residence and the site of the University of Idolatry—Machu Picchu. The region is so high and bitterly cold that it is a barren waste which does not appear to have been cultivated.

The Urubamba valley road which we followed from Ollantay-tambo down into the granite canyon where we found Machu Picchu. The beautiful peak in the distance is Mount Veronica, which is a mile higher than Pikes Peak.

tours, and slowly took us toward the great promontory whose most conspicuous point is Machu Picchu Mountain. Here, within rifle shot of the city, the ancient trail disappears; but that did not worry us, for there was no denying the fact that we had reached the immediate neighborhood of Machu Picchu and done it by following the Inca road which undoubtedly connected the citadel with the Pampaccahuana Valley and the principal Inca towns of the region. In addition to locating the ancient highway, we had also been so fortunate as to discover a number of hitherto unknown ruins which seemed to represent stations at convenient intervals along the road. I had at last achieved my desire of penetrating the unexplored country southeast of Machu Picchu, a region which had tempted me for many years. We had learned a little more of that "something" which, as Kipling says, was "lost behind the ranges."

In order that we might have the satisfaction of actually reaching the citadel of Machu Picchu by the same route used by its former inhabitants, I asked Clarence Maynard, then the assistant topographer of the 1915 expedition, and during World War II a Major in the U. S. Engineers under General MacArthur, to go down the southwest bank of the Urubamba River to Choqquesuysuy and to the top of the saddle which connects Machu Picchu Mountain with the region we had just been across and from here atempt to find a practical route to the citadel.

Choqquesuysuy lies above the river at a bend where there is a particularly good view. Near a foaming waterfall some Inca chief built a temple whose walls, still standing, serve to tantalize the traveler on the river road. There is no bridge within two days' journey and the intervening rapids are impassable. Every time we had journeyed up and down the river I had longed to get across and see what these ruins contained. They are relatively so near to Machu Picchu that I felt sure they must have belonged to the same people. Accordingly, I was extremely glad when Mr. Maynard reported that he had succeeded in reaching Choqquesuysuy, which we learned later belonged to the late Inca period. Mr. Maynard found that a footpath connected Choqquesuysuy with the saddle at the top of the ridge below Machu Picchu peak.

A recent landslide had destroyed the lower part of the trail, but he repaired it with difficulty and got his animals safely across the treacherous slope. After a steep climb of about three thousand feet from the banks of the river he camped on a small pampa south of the saddle, and after several hours of hunting, he found signs of the ancient Inca roadway, now almost obliterated. By hard climbing, these fragments of paved road were traced to the saddle.

He found that there were three possible routes which might lead from the saddle to Machu Picchu. One was along the east side of the mountain; the second lay directly up the knife-like ridge and across the top of Machu Picchu peak; the third was along the precipitous west face of the mountain.

At the narrowest point in the saddle was a ruined guardhouse. On its far side the trail was again picked up and followed to a point where the side hill merged into a sheer rock wall. Every foot of the way had to be cut through a dense jungle. The footing was extremely treacherous. The mountain side exceedingly steep, and slippery with recent rains. Here and there fragments of the paved roadway were encountered, although in order to find them it was frequently necessary to cut over a considerable area. On such occasions the Indian workmen tried in every way to discourage further search, crying to one another, "There is no road." "No one can pass here." In the pouring rain they worked half-heartedly, making no serious efforts to assist in locating the old road. Finally, at a rock fall all signs of the trail disappeared; yet there was no indication that it had been carried away by a landslide. Eventually, one of the workmen uncovered a flight of stone steps covered with decayed vegetable matter, and leading to a cave, the entrance to which had been concealed by thick bushes.

Here again the Incas had avoided the necessity of cutting a path across the face of a sheer cliff, by carrying their road back of it through a natural tunnel. However, when Mr. Maynard attemped to follow this route he found the passage choked by large rocks, where the roof had caved in. Since he had no blasting powder, further progress along the old road seemed at a standstill. He decided that the only possible way of progressing was by swinging a short, rustic bridge across the face of the cliff, a plan which seemed rather dangerous and not too feasible. Accordingly, before undertaking it he decided to investigate the other two possible routes. Dividing the Indians into parties, trails were cut in various directions, in the hope of running across any other paved roads which might exist, but several attempts to reach the crest of the ridge were prevented by impassable precipices. Finally, a way was found around the precipices and traces of a road were discovered on the crest. This was followed toward Machu Picchu Mountain until it divided, one branch continuing toward the peak, the other descending the west face of the slope toward the great fissure which crosses the western precipices of the mountain. An attempt was made to follow each route.

The upper one soon disappeared in a maze of cliffs and fallen rocks; the lower one continued along the west side of the mountain for about a mile and finally ended at a landslide. This trail was very narrow and exceedingly steep, crossing rocky precipices and flights of stone steps bordered by a sheer drop of hundreds of feet. From here it led across a steep slope on which the road was held in place by well-constructed retaining walls. All of it was overgrown and every foot of the way had to be cut through a dense jungle. The stone paving was covered with century-long accumulations of vegetable mold. From the valley below we had often noticed the great fissure which ran horizontally across the face of the precipice and seemed as though it might have been used as part of the road between the city and the saddle.

Mr. Maynard made an effort to get past the great landslide which intervened between him and the fissure on the western precipice, but this proved to be impossible, the rotten rocks and the steepness of the slope making any climbing operations excessively dangerous. All three routes therefore had proved impracticable, and the one hope lay in the possibility of being able to bridge the cliff in the trail on the eastern slope, which was the one first investigated.

Sending one man back to camp for a rope, the rest were set to cutting poles which could be used to span the gap. Projecting from the face of the cliff about ten feet beyond the end of the trail, and a few feet above it, was a ledge of rock. Growing out of crevices at the end of the ledge and also at the end of the trail, were two small trees. They were rather unsafe foundations, but they formed the only means of further travel along this route. Poles were laid from tree to tree, and one of the Indians slid across, first having a rope tied tightly about his body, the other end being held by the men. Small sticks were lashed at right angles to the poles and where possible were wedged into cracks in the face of the wall. Brush and moss placed on this support completed the bridge, which was about two and one-half feet wide.

This was not a bridge over which one could carry a heavy load. In fact, I found it to be the kind of place where one only breathes easily after it has been safely negotiated. Beyond the cliff it was fairly easy to locate the Inca road, as it came out of the north end of the cave and penetrated the dense forest which clung to the steep slope. In places the roadway had been carried away by landslides, making progress extremely slow. Heavy rains also interfered with the work. The Indians, who had not constructed adequate shelter, suffered greatly at night and were very miserable and dejected, repeatedly threatening to quit entirely. It took great determination and courage on Mr. Maynard's part to keep his gang together and make them persevere in their efforts to reach the city.

Finally another point was reached where recent landslides and dangerous precipices made further progress absolutely impossible. It was therefore decided to move camp down into the bottom of the canyon to the bridge at San Miguel, climb from there to the city itself and attempt to work the trail back to the neighborhood of the dangerous landslide. This meant a descent of several thousand feet to the hamlet of Intihuatana. The trail, a modern one, over which mules had recently been driven, was too steep to permit of riding in many places. Unfortunately Mr. Maynard's feet had suffered from the rough climbing and the constant rain, so he was tempted to ride in some places where ordinarily he would have preferred to walk. At one point where the trail was bordered by a sheer drop of several hundred feet his mule slipped and fell to his knees. In attempting to rise, he lost his balance and started to go over the edge. Throwing himself out of the saddle, Mr. Maynard landed on his back in the trail. Whereupon the mule, relieved of his burden, by terrific effort scrambled back onto the road, on top of the unfortunate topographer, who in his journal laconically remarks: "Landed on my back on a rock. Throwing weight that way evidently righted the mule. He floundered around. His hoofs seemed to be all over me, but didn't step on me. Managed to roll out of way. Arrived at camp about eleven thirty."

The effort to connect the two trails was ultimately successful. By following the road south of the city up the stone stairways to the crest of the ridge, Mr. Maynard finally found that he had missed a stairway which led straight up the slope of the mountain and which avoided the region of landslides that had baffled his attempt to follow the road from the point where he had built the little bridge around the tunnel. Two of the Indians finally found the missing link in the trail and thus completed the opening of one of the old Inca roads which connected the city with the saddle back of Machu Picchu peak and thence with the rest of the district. A few days after the work was completed I was able to pick up the old road where I had been obliged to leave it some weeks before and enter the city by the same road as its builders used. I found that it was good enough for llamas and human burden-bearers. Wherever it followed the contour of a steep slope it was banked up and supported by a stone wall. Where it had to climb a steep grade, stone steps were built with care so that the bearers of burdens could be provided with secure footing. Finally, by a graceful curve, the road was brought to the top of the ridge and the city gate. Except on some of the steepest stairways, this old Inca road was about four feet wide, thus allowing the human freight carriers to pass without interfering with one another.

Thanks to Major Maynard, I had the satisfaction of going into "Vilcapampa the Old" over the very road used by the Virgins of the Sun when they fled here from Cuzco and the conquistadors.

Obviously, however, this was not the road from Vitcos to the "principal city," Vilcapampa Viejo, which was followed by the Friars when Titu Cusi took them on that terrible journey past and through the cold waters of "Ungacacha." That road had to be looked for elsewhere, northwest of Machu Picchu and on the side toward Puquiura and Rosaspata. We were fortunate in having a new map which had been prepared by our topographer, Albert Bumstead, as a result of our surveys made in the preceding years, which had opened a wide stretch of country between the Apurimac and the Urubamba Valleys that did not exist on any previous maps.

The route followed by the missionary priests presumably lay across a large, unexplored area, unknown to the local land-owners, and unsuspected by Peruvian geographers. We had heard rumors that there was a trail by which Indians sometimes came from the village of Puquiura to the plantation of Huadquiña, only a few miles from Machu Picchu, without going around through the Vilcabamba and Urubamba Valleys by the modern government roads which we had been using.

So I determined to make an effort to cross and recross this unexplored region and, if possible, find that road. We crossed the Urubamba near Ollantaytambo and went up a valley that led to a very high pass between the beautiful snow peaks of Salcantay and Soray.

Near Yanama we camped on a ridge by some small ruins near the remains of an Inca road. From here we made our way to Arma as best we could without guides, following old trails that sometimes led nowhere and that at other times led deep into dense jungles and across mountain torrents.

Near Arma we found a primeval forest located on the slopes of Mt. Soiroccocha about 16,000 feet above sea level—possibly the highest forest in the world. The fact that it seemed to be primeval and that there was no indication that it had ever been invaded by axe-men gave further testimony, if any were needed, that we were in a region extremely difficult of access. After making our way through a snowy pass we found ourselves in the Colpa Valley.

Here we found one or two mountain Indians and learned from them that we were not far from Rosaspata and the village of Puquiura where we hoped to find a guide who knew the route over the mountains. Inquiry among the natives of the Vilcabamba Valley finally resulted in our securing the services of an Indian who said he knew the trail to Huadquiña across the unexplored area, in the direction of Machu Picchu. As soon as he could get his family to prepare his travelling ration of parched corn and a few *coca* leaves, he started off in the right direction and took us up the Colpa Valley, which we had explored a few days before. Passing by an abandoned quartz-crushing plant we soon discovered a long stretch of Inca roadway that led in the direction of Choqquequirau by way of a pass called Choqquetacarpo. This Inca roadway was in a remarkably good state of preservation, although slides prevented us from using it for our mules. Near it, and not far from Choqquetacarpo, we found the ruins of an ancient rest house or tavern, consisting of a group of half a dozen circular houses.

From the Colpa Valley our guide now led us into a bleak region, a wild *puna* country, where there were many little lakes and numerous bogs. Had it not been for an unusually dry season and the remarkably fine weather of the preceeding months, we should never have been able to travel through it at all. In fact, it is undoubtedly on account of the large number and wide extent of the bogs which characterize this area between Pucyura and

Huadquiña that it had long remained unexplored by the Peruvians themselves.

At last the trail, which in many places followed an Inca highway, came to a dark green lake, larger than the rest, whose name I inquired of the guide. The answer gave me a thrill. As the guide shouted it back to me from the head of the caravan, I thought he said "Ungacacha"; in fact, it sounded more like that than Yanaccocha, or "Black Lake," its actual name, as I learned later.

Ever since I first came into this province looking for the capital of the last Incas, one of the places on my list was Calancha's "Ungacacha." Since 1911 I had been inquiring of Indians everywhere for a locality of that name, only to be met invariably with the reply that they knew of no such place.

It seems to me entirely probable that the "Ungacacha" referred to in Calancha's story of the sufferings of the Friars was Yanaccocha, and that the monk, who probably wrote it down sometime afterward from memory, and who very likely did not hear it any more clearly than I did when I inquired the name of the place, spelled it *Ungacacha*, instead of Yanaccocha. They look so different on paper that it is somewhat difficult to realize how closely the Indian pronunciation of one approaches the other.

The old Inca trail continued up the hillside in the direction of Machu Picchu and led toward the ruins of Yuracrumiyocc, which was the Inca store-house the foreman of Huadquiña had said was so magnificent, and which I had visited in 1911. At that time we could not quite understand its significance. Now we realized that it was a rest-house on the old Inca road between Manco's two capitals, Vilcapampa and Vitcos.

It appears that the builders of Machu Picchu had an elaborate system of highways throughout this little-known and almost unexplored country which lies between the Urubamba Valley and the Apurimac. This region was once densely populated, and Machu Picchu was its capital.

6.

The Origin of the City Now Called Machu Picchu

As a result of the discovery of the Inca road leading from Puquiura to the vicinity of Machu Picchu and the evidence in the burial caves that the Lost City was last occupied by women, besides the unmistakable testimony that here was a Temple of the Sun and a great Sanctuary, we may be sure that its name in the days of the Spanish Conquest was Vilcapampa and that young Tupac Amaru, last of the Inca Emperors, had lived here. It is pleasant to think that he had spent most of his life in this beautiful city of white granite, which "in the sublimity of its surroundings, the marvel of its site, the character and the mystery of its construction" surpassed anything his cruel conquerors ever saw or found. The secret was so well kept that the Chosen Women lived and died there in peace, unmolested by the Spanish conquerors. For three hundred years the city was unknown.

Our identification of what the city was in its last years tells us little or nothing of its origin. While many of the houses were doubtless built by Manco and Titu Cusi to accommodate the

243

Chosen Women and the attendants of the Sanctuary, the finer palaces and the temples were far too elaborate to have been constructed at that time. It was obviously a great Sanctuary long before they arrived. The finest buildings antedated the last years of the Inca Empire by centuries. The question naturally arises: Who built them and when?

According to the late Philip Ainsworth Means, the Inca Pachacutec who lived in the first half of the 15th century, from about 1400 to 1448, was a "very great man." This was also the opinion of that distinguished English authority Sir Clements Markham, who styles Pachacutec "the greatest man that the Aboriginal Race of America has produced." He had the advantage of inheriting a great empire which contained about 155,000 square miles of territory, approximately equal to our northeastern States from Virginia to Maine. It had been thoroughly organized and the great mass of the people were absolutely subject to the wishes of the hierarchy of tribal and imperial officials. In his kingdom were many skilful generals and wise counselors, so that he was able to carry on several difficult conquests, one of the earliest of which took him down the Urubamba Valley.

Prior to Pachacutec's time the Incas' frontier in that direction had been at Ollantaytambo, but he, doubtless having in mind those incursions of savages from the forest-country that had given rise to the Chanca Confederacy and to the formidable struggle with it, determined to push his power farther down the stream. Means says: "He did so by the usual Inca methods, combining guile and diplomacy with military aggression! The citadel of Machu Picchu rises in the heart of this region, and it is highly probable that the Inca Pachacutec gave orders for its construction, intending it to be thenceforward an eastern bulwark of his empire."

Although the empire inherited by this Inca was at that time large, Cuzco, his capital, was still only fifty miles from the jungle where war-like savages lived who were always ready to attack whoever ventured to penetrate the great forests of the upper Amazon. The construction of the Citadel of Machu Picchu at a point where its location could command the narrow valley through which the savages might attempt to make raids against the highly civilized Incas would have been a wise proceeding.

At the same time I cannot help feeling that a mountain fortress like the one first explored at Choqquequirau would have been entirely adequate for this purpose. The savage Indians had only crude weapons, blow-guns, bows and arrows. They did not need great walls and a mighty citadel to hold them at bay. It seems most unlikely to me that the beautiful granite temples of Machu Picchu were built as an outlying fortress against the tribes of the Amazon. If my theory is correct then what is the significance of this carefully constructed Sanctuary here in the most inaccessible part of the Andes.

As has already been told in the account of the battle of La Raya, Montesinos states that after the death in battle of the last of the great Amautas or kings who ruled Peru for more than sixty generations, his faithful followers retired to the mountains, going to Tampu-tocco, which was " a healthy place" where they hid the body of Pachacuti VI, their king, in a cave and where they were joined by refugees fleeing from the general chaos and disorder.

The Spaniards who asked about Tampu-tocco got the impression that it was at or near Paccari-tampu, a small place eight or ten miles south of Cuzco, in the vicinity of which there are the ruins of a small Inca town. Near it is a little hill consisting of several large rocks. The surface of one is carved into platforms and in one place into two sleeping pumas, a very unusual pattern, not really Inca. Beneath it are caves said to have been used by Spanish refugees who may have carved the pumas.

There is enough about the characteristics of Paccari-tampu to lend color to the story frequently told to the early Spaniards that this was Tampu-tocco. Yet the surrounding region is not hard to reach and is not at all inaccessible. There are no precipices. There are no natural defenses against an invading force large and strong enough to capture the neighboring valley of Cuzco. A few men might have hid in the caves of Paccari-tampu but it was no place where an independent kingdom might readily have been established by a disorganized handful of the followers and chief priests of Pachacuti VI. Furthermore there are no windows in the architecture which would justify the name of Tampu-tocco which means a *tambo* or place of temporary abode characterized by windows.

On the twenty-first of January, 1572, a legal inquiry was made by the Viceroy Francisco de Toledo. Fifteen Indians who were descended from those who used to lived near the important salt terraces around Cuzco, on being questioned, agreed that they had heard their fathers and grandfathers repeat the tradition that the First Inca, Manco Capac, came from Tampu-tocco when he arrived to take their lands away from their ancestors. They did *not* say that the first Inca came from Paccari-tampu, which, it seems to me, would have been a most natural thing for them to have said if it were true. In addition to this testimony, there is still the older testimony of some Indians born before the arrival of Pizarro, who, two years before, in 1570, were examined at a legal investigation made in Jauja. The oldest witness, ninety-five years of age, on being sworn, said that Manco Capac was lord of the town where he was born and had conquered Cuzco but that he had never heard what town it was that Manco came from. The Indian chief who followed him was ninety-four years old and also denied that he knew where Manco Capac was born. Another chief, aged ninety-two, testified that Manco Capac came out of a cave called Tocco and that he was lord of the town near the cave. Not one of the witnesses stated that Manco Capac came from Paccari-tampu, although it is difficult to imagine why they should not have done so if, as the Spaniards believed, this was the original Tampu-tocco.

At all events, there is an interesting cave at Paccari-tampu and the chroniclers, not one of whom knew of the important ruins at Machu Picchu, were willing enough to assume that this was the place where the first Inca was born and from which he came to conquer Cuzco. Yet it seems hardly possible that the old

Indians should have forgotten entirely where Tampu-tocco was. Their reticence in regard to it must be laid, it seems to me, to the fact of its having been successfully kept secret by reason of its location in a remote place whither the followers of Pachacuti VI fled with his body after the overthrow of the old regime, and in the same remote fastness of the Andes to which the young Inca Manco II fled from Cuzco in the days of Pizarro.

Certainly the requirements of Tampu-tocco described in Montesinos are met at Machu Picchu. The splendid natural defenses of the Grand Canyon of the Urubamba made it an ideal refuge for the descendants of the Amautas during the five or six hundred years of lawlessness and confusion which succeeded the barbarian invasions from the plains to the east and south. The scarcity of violent earthquakes, and also the healthfulness, both marked characteristics of Tampu-tocco, are met at Machu Picchu.

Pachacuti Yamqui Salcamayhua's story of the construction of a memorial wall with three windows at the place of Manco Capac's birth points clearly to Machu Picchu.

Although none of the other ancient chronicles gives the story of the first Inca ordering a memorial wall to be built at the place of his birth, they nearly all tell of his having come from a place called Tampu-tocco, "a country place remarkable for its windows." To be sure, the only place assigned by them as the location of Tampu-tocco is Paccari-tampu, which, as has been said, is about eight or ten miles southwest of Cuzco and has some ruins; but careful examination shows that there were no windows in the buildings of Paccari-tampu and nothing to justify its having such a name as Tampu-tocco. The climate of Paccari-tampu—it is part of the high plateau, elevation 12,000 feet—is too severe to invite or encourage the use of windows. The temperature in the shade or inside an unheated cabin is never far from freezing. On the other hand, to people accustomed to the climatic conditions of Cuzco, the climate of Machu Picchu seemed mild and consequently the use of windows was agreeable. Many of the houses at Machu Picchu have windows. In fact, since there are far more windows here than any other ruin it would be natural to refer to it as a country place remarkable for its windows. Obviously, from the very elaborate character of its structure, a highly venerated place, a veritable Holy City containing temples enough for the sun, the moon, the thunder and all the Inca Pantheon, no conquistador was allowed to see it or even hear about it when they were questioning the wisest men in Cuzco.

Accordingly, I am convinced that the name of the older part of Machu Picchu was Tampu-tocco, that here Pachacuti VI was buried, and that here was the capital of the little kingdom where, during the centuries—possibly eight or ten—between the Amautas and the Incas, there were kept alive the wisdom, skill, and best traditions of the ancient folk who had developed the civilization of Peru, using agricultural terraces as its base. It seems to me quite probable that Manco Capac, after he had established himself as Inca in Cuzco, should have built a fine temple to the honor of his ancestors. Ancestor worship was common among the Incas and nothing would have been more reasonable than the construction of the Temple of the Three Windows in their honor.

Furthermore, there is so little arable land capable of being developed within a radius of ten or fifteen miles of Machu Picchu that it would have been perfectly natural for the chiefs of this region to have sought to conquer the great stretches of arable land near Cuzco. When they once got control of Cuzco and the rich valleys in its vicinity, convenience, superstition, and regard for the great Amautas, from whom they traced their descent, would have led them to establish themselves once more at Cuzco. There was no longer any necessity for them to maintain Tampu-tocco. Consequently Machu Picchu may have been practically deserted for three hundred years while the Inca Empire flourished and grew until it covered a large part of South America. In the meantime Tampu-tocco—"out of sight, out of mind," a sacred place whose whereabouts was undoubtedly known to the priests and those who preserved the most sacred secrets of the Incas—was forgotten by the common people.

On the other hand it may have been kept in good condition as one of the great Temples of the Sun where the Chosen Women were educated for the service of the Incas.

If my theory of Machu Picchu as Tampu-tocco is correct, it may be that the principal sanctuary in Cuzco, now the Dominican Monastery but known to the conquistadors as the Temple of the Sun, was built during the reign of the Incas as an echo, on a large scale, of the Semicircular Temple at Machu Picchu. If this latter temple was constructed above the cave where tradition says Pachacuti VI, last of the Amautas, was buried, it would naturally have been the most revered spot at Machu Picchu. Certainly the stonework of its surroundings has rarely been equaled and never surpassed in beauty and strength. When the Incas left Tampu-tocco, therefore, and took up their residence in Cuzco, nothing would have been more likely than for them to have built their first temple in a manner resembling the finest temple at Tampu-tocco. Probably the semicircular character of the Machu Picchu temple was caused by accident rather than by design, and was due to the natural curve of the great rock beneath which lay the mausoleum of Pachacuti VI and his immediate family. This particular architectural feature in the Temple of the Sun in Cuzco was not required by the nature of the gravel bank on which it rests in common with all the rest of the city. Moreover, a wall with a flattened curve or "parabolic enclosure wall" is not characteristic of ancient Peruvian structures and occurs very rarely. It is extremely difficult to construct and requires the highest type of artistic stonecutting. What more likely, then, than that the builders of the Cuzco temple had the Semicircular Temple of Machu Picchu in mind? The occurrence in both structures of openings to which golden images of the sun could be attached, and their absence elsewhere, would also seem to lend color to this theory and helps to strengthen my belief that Machu Picchu was Tampu-tocco, and that the Inca rulers of Cuzco not only constructed at Machu Picchu a ceremonial wall with three windows to commemorate and honor the home of their ancestors but built in Cuzco a semicircular temple of the Sun resembling the beautiful one in their ancient sanctuary.

No one realizes better than the present writer, how fantastic this last suggestion will seem to those American archaeologists, who have been unwilling to follow my reasoning in regard to Tampu-tocco as the first name of the sanctuary on the slopes of Machu Picchu Mountain. To those who are willing to accept the story of the Spanish chroniclers that the original home of the Incas was the nearby village of Paccari-tampu, the origin of the city on the slopes of Machu Picchu Mountain is usually that put forth by the late Philip Ainsworth Means. Since the architecture of Machu Picchu contains examples of all kinds of structures found in the central Andes, it is barely possible that the city does not go farther back than the early 15th century, as Means contends. His theory undoubtedly meets the approval of those archaeologists who choose to shorten and limit the period of Inca civilization. Perhaps they are right in the length of time which saw anyone called an Inca occupying the cities of the Peruvian Highlands. But when one considers the number of centuries which were required to domesticate the llamas and alpacas as well as to discover, select and domesticate the scores of plants used for food and medicine, the very long time consumed in the evolution of their agriculture, engineering, masonry and metallurgy, and the advanced state of their textiles and pottery, it seems unwise to contend that Inca civilization was less ancient than that of the Mayas in Central America. It seems to me highly probable that the story of Machu Picchu covers many many centuries.

Undoubtedly in its last state the city was the carefully guarded treasure house where that precious worship of the sun, the moon, the thunder and the stars, so violently overthrown in Cuzco, was restored, where the last four Incas had their safest and most comfortable home and the Chosen Women whose lives had from early girlhood been devoted to all the duties of the Sanctuary found a refuge from the animosity and lust of the conquistadors.

Surely this remarkable lost city which has made such a strong appeal to us on account of its striking beauty and the indescribable grandeur of its surroundings appears to have had a most interesting history. Selected perhaps a thousand years ago as the safest place of refuge for the last remnants of the old regime, becoming the capital of a new kingdom, giving birth to the most remarkable family which South America has ever seen, partially abandoned when Cuzco once more flashed into glory as the capital of the Inca Empire, it was again sought out in time of trouble when another foreign invader arrived—this time from the north—with his burning desire to extinguish all vestiges of the ancient religion, and finally became the home and refuge of those Chosen Women whose institution formed one of the most interesting features of the most humane religion of aboriginal America. Here, concealed in a canyon of remarkable grandeur, protected by nature and by the hand of man, the "Virgins of the Sun," one by one passed away on this beautiful mountain top and left no descendants willing to reveal the importance or explain the significance of the ruins which crown the beetling precipices of Machu Picchu.

THE END

Bibliography

The most important source for the latest estimate of the culture and civilization of the Incas is the collection of monographs published in Volume 2 of the Smithsonian Institution's HANDBOOK OF SOUTH AMERICAN INDIANS, Washington, 1946. Of these the best for readers interested in the builders of Machu Picchu are the following:

"The Andean Highlands" by Wendell C. Bennett. Vol. 2, pp. 1-60.

"The Archeology of the Central Andes" by Wendell C. Bennett. Vol. 2, pp. 61-147.

"Inca Culture at the Time of the Spanish Conquest" by John Howland Rowe. Vol. 2, pp. 183-330.

"The Quechua in the Colonial World" by George Kubler. Vol. 2, pp. 331-409.

The best books for readers desiring to learn more of the History of the Incas and their predecessors are the works of Philip Ainsworth Means with their remarkably full notes and bibliographies. Of these the most useful are the following:

"Ancient Civilizations of the Andes" by Philip Ainsworth Means, New York, 1931.

"Fall of the Inca Empire and the Spanish Rule in Peru: 1530-1780" by Philip Ainsworth Means, New York, 1932.

"Memorias Antiguas Historiales del Peru" by Fernando Montesinos, translated and edited by P. A. Means; with an Introduction by Clements R. Markham. London, 1920.

"Relation of the Discovery and Conquest of the Kingdoms of Peru" by Pedro Pizarro, translated and
edited by P. A. Means, 2 vols. New York, 1921.

Those readers who may wish to learn more of the activities
of the Peruvian Expeditions of Yale University and the National
Geographic Society will find a fairly complete bibliography in
"Inca Land" by Hiram Bingham, Boston, 1922 (3rd ed. 1923)
pp. 347-351. Of the books and articles there listed, the more interesting and important are the following:

"The Collection of Osteological Material from Machu
Picchu" by George F. Eaton, New Haven, 1916.

"A Metallographic Description of Some Ancient Peruvian Bronzes from Machu Picchu" by C. H.
Mathewson, in the *American Journal of Science*, December 1915, pp. 525-602.

"Staircase Farms of the Ancients" by O. F. Cook, in
the *National Geographic Magazine*, May, 1916, pp.
474-534. This is the most important study that has
been published regarding the agriculture of the
Incas and their predecessors.

"The Andes of Southern Peru" by Isaiah Bowman,
New York, 1916.

"Vitcos, The Last Inca Capital" by Hiram Bingham,
in the *Proceedings of the American Antiquarian Society*, April, 1912, pp. 135-196.

"The Discovery of Machu Picchu" by Hiram Bingham,
in *Harper's Magazine*, April, 1913.

"In the Wonderland of Peru" by Hiram Bingham, in
the *National Geographic Magazine*, April, 1913, pp.
387-573.

See also "Across South America" by Hiram Bingham,
Boston, 1911. The complete account of the excava-
tions and material found at Machu Picchu is in
"Machu Picchu, a Citadel of the Incas" by Hiram
Bingham, New Haven, 1930.

The most important source material is listed in Means' books,
but of particular value are:

"Coronica Moralizada del Orden de San Augustin en el Peru" by Antonio de la Calancha, published in Barcelona in 1638.

"Relacion de la Conquista del Peru y Hechos del Inca Manco II" by Titu Cusi, edited by H. H. Urteaga and Carlos A. Romero, Lima, 1916

See also the numerous translations of the Chronicles made by Sir Clements R. Markham and published by the Hakluyt Society. All are listed in Means' "Fall of the Inca Empire."

Dr. Paul Fejos has made an important addition to our knowledge of the Inca ruins in the Cordillera Vilcabamba by his excellent report of the Wenner-Gren Expeditions, published by the Viking Fund in 1944. His many photographs, maps, and plans demonstrate how densely populated was the area tributary to Machu Picchu.

Index

Aclla-Huasi, 34
Aconcagua, 112
"Across South America," 112
Agriculture, 12-15, 18
  canihua, 14-15
  fertilizers, 12
  food plants, development of, 13-15
  quinoa, 15
  Irish potato, 14, 18
  maize, 14, 18
  medicinal herbs, discovery of, 13, 15
  sweet potato, 15
  terrace, 12-13
Almagro, 53
Alvistur, Don Tomas, 154
Amautas, 40
Amaybamba, 231
Amazon Basin, 11, 19, 20
Anaya, Atilano de, 68
Andenes, 129, 130
Andes, 9, 11, 13, 19, 20, 29, 33, 35, 36, 50, 51, 90, 97, 135
Anta, Plain of, 93
Anti Indians, 57, 65-66, 110, 149
Aobamba River, 153-156
Apurimac River, 51, 53, 98-99, 139, 141
Aqueducts, 11
Architecture, 5-9
  houses, 6-8
  temples and palaces, 5
Argentina, 4, 9, 19, 45
Arma, 241
Artega, Melchior, 120, 160, 161, 162, 163, 164, 165, 169, 171, 172, 175
Atachualpa, 45, 47, 52, 58
Ayacucho, 53
Aymara language, 19

Augustinian Friars, 49, 51, 53, 69, 70-80, 83, 127, 167, 178, 240
Augustian Monastery, 70
Aztec, defined, 4

Balboa, 231
Banbaconas, 139
Bandelier, Adolph, 112
Barbarian migrations, 40, 41, 42
Bar-holds, 7-8, 128
Bolas, 17, 27
Bolivia, 40
Bolivar, Simon, 89
Bowman, Isaiah, 113
Bronzes, 26-29
Buildings, 136
Bumstead, Albert H., 141, 240

Caceres, Lt., 96, 99, 102
Caciques, 47
Calancha, Father, 53, 59, 69, 70, 72, 74, 77, 110, 113, 114, 119, 129, 133, 134, 137
Campa Indians, 138
Carlos Inca, 79
Carrasco, Sergeant, 160, 161, 162, 163
Castelnau, 115
Ccollumayu Valley, 121-122
Ccolpa Mocco, 118
Ccorihuayrachina, 234
Cedrobamba, 233
Chamana River, 155
Champis, 28
Chanca Confederacy, 244
Charaja, Ricardo, 231
Charles V, of Spain, 53, 66, 67
Chauillay, 123
Chicha, 20, 36
Chile, 9, 11, 25, 45

257

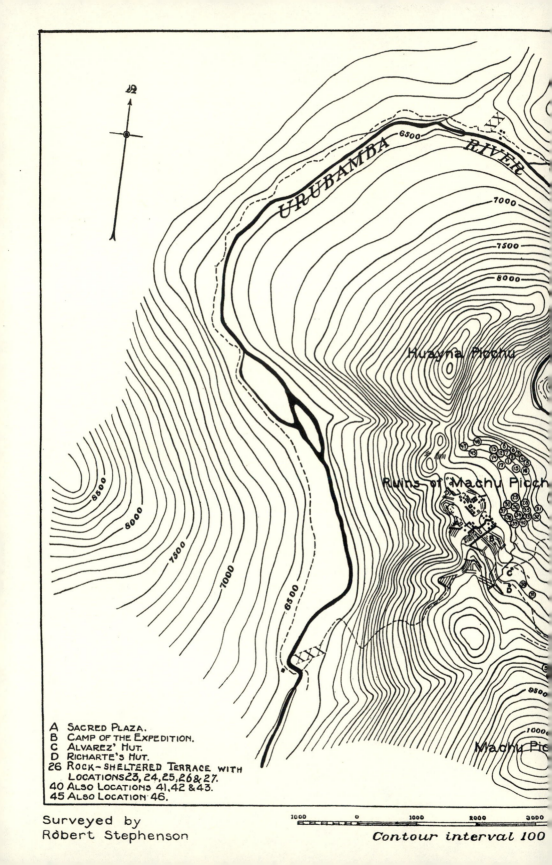

URUBAMBA RIVER

6500

7000

7500

8000

Huayna Picchu

Ruins of Machu Picchu

8500

8000

7500

7000

6500

9500

10000

Machu Pic

A   SACRED PLAZA.
B   CAMP OF THE EXPEDITION.
C   ALVAREZ' HUT.
D   RICHARTE'S HUT.
26 ROCK-SHELTERED TERRACE WITH
      LOCATIONS 23, 24, 25, 26 & 27.
40 ALSO LOCATIONS 41, 42 & 43.
45 ALSO LOCATION 46.

Surveyed by
Robert Stephenson

1000   0   1000   2000   3000

Contour interval 100

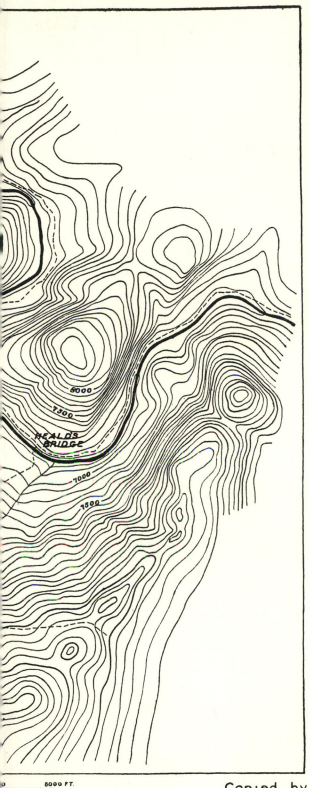

THE PERUVIAN
EXPEDITION OF 1912

UNDER THE AUSPICES OF

YALE UNIVERSITY
& THE NATIONAL
GEOGRAPHIC SOCIETY

HIRAM BINGHAM, DIRECTOR

MACHU PICCHU
& VICINITY

XX   Mandor Pampa
XXX San Miguel
      Bridge
      Trails

Copied by
A.B.C.Mott